Strategy: Key Thinkers

STRATEGY:
KEY THINKERS

A Critical Engagement

THOMAS M. KANE

polity

First published in 2013 by Polity Press

Polity Press
65 Bridge Street
Cambridge CB2 1UR, UK

Polity Press
350 Main Street
Malden, MA 02148, USA

ISBN-13: 978-0-7456-4353-3
ISBN-13: 978-0-7456-4354-0(pb)

A catalogue record for this book is available from the British Library.

Typeset in 10.5 on 12 pt Times New Roman
by Toppan Best-set Premedia Limited
Printed and bound in Great Britain by Clays Ltd, St Ives PLC

The publisher has used its best endeavours to ensure that the URLs for external websites referred to in this book are correct and active at the time of going to press. However, the publisher has no responsibility for the websites and can make no guarantee that a site will remain live or that the content is or will remain appropriate.

Every effort has been made to trace all copyright holders, but if any have been inadvertently overlooked the publisher will be pleased to include any necessary credits in any subsequent reprint or edition.

For further information on Polity, visit our website: www.politybooks.com

To Cindy Brophy, her husband Patric and their children.
True Christian neighbours

CONTENTS

ACKNOWLEDGEMENTS

One of the most rewarding things about publishing a book is having the opportunity to say thank you. As I have worked on *Strategy: Key Thinkers*, a variety of people in a variety of roles have offered me invaluable understanding and help. I draw special attention to Heather Currey, Scott Edmunds, Jay Jansen, David Oliver, Shawn McBurnie, Kate Whyte, Debra Wilkinson and Professor Rudiger Wurzel, all of whom have supported me at critical moments, and each of whom, in one capacity or another, has listened to my story. I would also mention my editors Dr Louise Knight, Pascal Porcheron and David Winters at Polity, both for their professional skill and for their collegial spirit.

I also thank my colleagues Dr Matthew Ford and Dr David Lonsdale for their advice on scholarly matters.

INTRODUCTION: BRINGING STRATEGY TO LIFE

The reasons why strategy matters are stark. We live in a world in which others are willing to kill us. Moreover, all of us cherish goals which have the potential to involve us in conflict. These goals may be as visceral as the drive to live and protect our families or they may be as intellectual as the mandates of a religion or political ideology, but few of us would choose to leave such aspirations hostage to the forbearance of our rivals, and most of us would be willing, under certain circumstances, to use force ourselves as a tool for advancing them. If we are to realize our hopes for any period of time, this will to fight for them is a logical necessity. Moralists throughout time have recognized it as conditionally honourable and just.

Securing one's goals through force is easier said than done. This is obvious for those who are weak, but true even for those who appear strong. Goliath has fallen so many times in the course of human history that political thinkers from Machiavelli to the contemporary international relations scholar Kenneth Waltz have taken it as axiomatic that those who rise are doomed to decline. Waltz adds that attempts to defy this principle will only bring on one's collapse all the sooner (Waltz 2000: 36–8). If this proposition is true, even our moments of success are but precursors to failure, and all of our hopes are ultimately futile.

Nevertheless, with the will to fight for our goals comes the hope that our ingenuity will permit us to succeed in them, if not absolutely and eternally, at least satisfactorily and renewably. Without this hope, David would not have bothered.[1] David, one may also recall, exchanged

---

[1] Machiavelli encouraged this hope as well. Chapter 3 discusses his arguments further.

his sling for Goliath's mighty sword and went on to found a kingdom. Strategy is the skill which permits David to discern the uses of sling and sword alike, and to combine them for such purposes. This book aims to help readers understand this faculty, so that they might use and develop it.

The first step towards understanding anything is to clarify the concept which one wishes to grasp. The highly esteemed scholar Colin Gray has defined strategy as a bridge between military power and political goals (Gray 1999a: 17, 2010: *passim*). Edward Mead Earle might add that, even in the midst of war, an effective strategy must also connect one's goals with one's economic means, one's form of government, one's diplomatic relations, one's broader culture and an open-ended variety of similar considerations (Earle 1943: viii) Rather than thinking of strategy as a bridge, we may wish to picture it as a busy airport terminal. Earle adds that strategy involves long-term efforts to secure future aspirations, as well as short-term attempts to achieve immediate ones, perhaps stretching such metaphors to absurdity.

This book will amalgamate Gray's and Earle's thoughts by defining strategy as people's efforts to take control of their political destiny. Since Goliath's physical strength does not seem sufficient for those purposes, this book will treat strategy as primarily a mental activity. Although strategic thinkers must pay attention to material factors such as the size of armies and the effects of weapons, they are primarily interested in the challenges of using military instruments effectively, not in the instruments themselves. This statement requires a caveat – the fact that strategy is an intellectual endeavour may not mean that it is a coldly rational one. Carl von Clausewitz, perhaps the best-known strategic thinker of all time, reminded readers that the genius of a great general was not the genius of a great physicist, and that success in war depends on intangibles of will, charisma, experience and intuitive judgement, at least as often as it depends on logical analysis. With those points in mind, this book will focus on strategy as it pertains to states and other organized political communities, and on strategy in situations which involve a meaningful likelihood of violence. Accordingly, this book is primarily concerned with military strategy, although it does not limit itself narrowly to that.

Once one has defined the word strategy, one must ask how it works and how to practise it. There may be bodies of knowledge in which one can catalogue answers to such questions and trace the ways in which researchers have improved upon them over time. Strategy does not work like that. Although a physician can apply specific and widely recognized treatments to specific and widely recognized conditions with confidence that today's established methods are more reliable than earlier or poorly tested ones, a strategist would be foolish to take this approach.

Not only does strategy involve a far broader range of issues than medicine, the fact that strategists must pit their abilities against thinking opponents makes the techniques which are known to have worked in the past particularly *un*likely to succeed in the future. The pitfalls of attempting to fight the last war are proverbial. If one's enemies are competent, they will have studied previously successful methods as well and will be prepared to counter them. One student of this subject, Edward Luttwak, suggests that this paradox is the defining feature of strategy (Luttwak 1987: 3–5). For these reasons and others, every wise strategic decision must involve an exceptionally large element of improvisation, even if the strategist ultimately concludes that, under his or her particular circumstances, the familiar approach actually is the most promising one.

Strategists require factual information about their goals and their means for achieving them. Such material is the anatomy and pharmacology of their art. Nevertheless, to perform the crucial improvisation, strategists benefit from guidance of a different kind. Over time, a variety of authors have distinguished themselves for their offerings in this regard. We know their works through their ability to clarify the issues which concern us, through the testimony of successful strategists who have acknowledged their value and perhaps through the intuitive response we experience when we encounter insight.

Insight comes from the mind, which means, for most practical purposes, that it comes from the minds of particular humans. For this reason, our understanding of strategy is largely based upon the writings of individual thinkers. Moreover, strategic insights appear to be timeless, at least in considerable part. Therefore, classic works by long-dead authors often seem more useful than competing offerings from those writing today.

Indeed, Gray described his 2010 opus on the nature of strategy as a mere exercise in 'rearrang[ing] the deck chairs' on a metaphorical ship built by writers dating back to the fifth century BC[2] (Gray 2010: ix). Gray justified his efforts by noting that deck chairs do, from time to time, need to be rearranged. One should note that Gray's reverence for ancient works is controversial (Gray 2010: 6). Certainly, those who wish to benefit from older works of strategic thought must be alert to the possibility that times may have changed. Nevertheless, there is little

---

[2]One hopes that this ship is not the *Titanic*.

doubt that the classic works remain essential to understanding strategic issues today, and no doubt whatsoever that they remain essential to understanding the origins of contemporary strategic thought.

Gray identifies the most valuable strategic classics as Carl von Clausewitz's *On War*, Sun Tzu's *The Art of War* and Thucydides' *History of the Peloponnesian War*, in that order of importance (Gray 2010: 6). Later, Gray notes Niccolò Machiavelli, Antoine-Henri Jomini, Basil H. Liddell Hart, J. C. Wylie, Edward Luttwak, Bernard Brodie and Thomas Schelling as strategic thinkers whose works also demand at least some degree of attention (Gray 2010: 6). This author, as readers of later chapters will see, draws on roughly the same canon, with inevitable additions and changes in emphasis. All such lists are subjective and potentially arbitrary, but this author hopes that he has uncovered enough useful ideas within his chosen works to convince readers that he has made valid selections.

Where Gray reconfigured insights taken from older classics, this book attempts to illuminate the insights themselves. This author's project, like Gray's, owes heavy tribute to the earlier authors. Nevertheless, this author's project, again like Gray's, rests upon a foundation of fresh analysis. Although scholars have had centuries to study the classic works of strategic thought, no one has definitively established what those well-studied texts actually mean.

Authoritative interpretations of the strategic classics often contradict each other. Thus, historian Azar Gat can accuse Machiavelli of dull adherence to obsolete concepts while political thinker Leo Strauss encourages readers to see Machiavelli as perhaps the most radical innovator of all time (Gat 1989: 2; Strauss 1958: 290–9). The twentieth-century strategic thinker Michael Handel can portray the ancient Chinese thinker Sun Tzu as a rationalist, whereas the contemporary religious scholar Thomas Cleary, commenting in his role as translator of Asian military classics can characterize the same Chinese thinker as a mystic[3] (Handel 1996: 174; Zhuge and Liu 1989: 14). As Colonel Philip Meilinger has noted, the variety of different ways in which scholars and practising strategists have interpreted – or, perhaps, misinterpreted – Clausewitz's *On War* approaches the point of parody (Meilinger 2007: 124–5).

This author joins those debates by performing a close reading of selected strategic classics and using it as the basis for a critical

---

[3] I might also mention 2012 Hull graduate Andrew Lockey, whose final-year dissertation builds on Cleary's ideas in what this author and the Board of Examiners viewed to be a promising and potentially original way.

re-evaluation of the ideas within them. In so doing, he attempts to introduce those works in a way that newcomers to the field will find useful, bring out the value of those works for twenty-first-century strategists and contribute, at opportune points, to outstanding theoretical debates. His first objective, in other words, is educational, while the second two are those of original scholarly research. Given the controversies over the meaning of the strategic classics, it is impossible to succeed at the former without also succeeding at the latter.

Although numerous other works offer contemporary readings of the strategic classics, this one is distinctive in its scope and approach. Where much of the literature on this subject focuses on individual thinkers (e.g. Quentin Skinner's *Machiavelli*), limited historical periods (e.g. Azar Gat's *The Origins of Military Thought from the Enlightenment to Clausewitz*) or narrowly selected concepts (e.g. Barry Watts's *Clausewitzian Friction and Future War*), this book attempts to bring out the dominant themes from the most critical works of all eras. This inclusive approach permits the author to treat his subjects as comprehensively as possible, and to trace the evolution of key ideas through the writings of the classical authors.

Edward Mead Earle compiled essays on a wide range of influential strategic thinkers in *Makers of Modern Strategy: Military Thought from Machiavelli to Hitler*. To this extent, his work resembled *Strategy: Key Thinkers*. *Makers*, however, was an anthology in which different authors wrote different chapters. This limited the book's ability to follow themes from one strategic classic to another. Moreover, the original edition of *Makers* appeared in 1943. Although there have been revised editions, the deck chairs on Gray's ship have been rearranged considerably since then.

Michael Handel offers a more recent attempt to compare and contrast multiple strategic classics from a variety of historical periods in his *Masters of War: Classical Strategic Thought*. Beatrice Heuser presents another up-to-date work in this genre with *The Strategy Makers: Thoughts on War and Society from Machiavelli to Clausewitz*. Heuser took up similar themes in *The Evolution of Strategy: Thinking War from Antiquity to the Present*. *Strategy: Key Thinkers*, however, differs from all three of these books in its analytical approach, and thus also in its contribution.

Handel has attempted to correct for the difficulties in applying works from other cultures and historical periods to the present by deliberately reading the works of his subjects in a rigidly literal fashion (Handel 1996: 17). Heuser, by contrast, attributes supreme importance to cultural and historical influences. Thus, Handel finds the works of

Sun Tzu in particular to be riddled with obvious contradictions and oversimplifications, while Heuser concludes that the most basic concepts of strategic thought lack fixed meaning (Handel 1996: 80; Heuser 2010b: 503). Where Gray would have it that strategic truths are eternal, Heuser finds that they pop up and vanish amidst different historical periods 'like colours in a woven carpet' (Heuser 2010b: 503).

Where Handel and Heuser focus on concepts, this book emphasizes the classic thinkers' broader arguments, and the reasoning behind them. Although the author takes note of cultural and historical context, he also works on the premise that important aspects of the human condition are universal or nearly so, and that the classic works of strategic thought address these aspects. This has led him to perform a different sort of analysis from either Handel or Heuser. Readers will depart with a different perspective on the meaning of the strategic classics.

Each approach has its own value. Handel's literalism helps us to isolate ideas, which, in turn, helps us assess and apply them. Heuser's approach helps us to understand what those ideas meant to their original authors. As we come to appreciate how much the basic ideas in our field have fluctuated in the past, we develop a valuable awareness of the uncertainties buried within our own assumptions.

This book, for its part, aims at helping readers engage with the classic authors' thought processes, and perhaps even to emulate them. The greatest strategic thinkers seem to have intended that readers should use their texts in this way. Clausewitz famously compared the role of a strategic theorist to that of a swimming teacher, who shows pupils how to practise strokes on land before they eventually perform similar movements in the water (Clausewitz 1976: 120). The students do not parse out their instructor's teachings and analyse them from a position of detachment; they try them for themselves, and discover how they feel. As later chapters will detail, Sun Tzu, Thucydides and others seem to have encouraged this approach as well. This active engagement may, indeed, be what rescues strategy from the formlessness which Heuser so vividly describes.

In this spirit, *Strategy: Key Thinkers* works through the ideas of the classic writers on strategy as follows. The first two chapters explore Sun Tzu and Thucydides. One of the advantages of addressing a variety of classics between a single set of covers is that it allows one to bring out points of comparison and contrast among the various works. Although Thucydides wrote a different sort of book from Sun Tzu and lived in a different part of the world, he turns out to be concerned with many of the same themes. Both, for instance, are concerned with the tremendous costs of war, both are acutely aware of its frequently surprising vicissitudes and both – in different ways – advise readers on the intellectual challenge of acting wisely in the face of its capriciousness.

Similar themes appear in the works of the influential Roman writer Vegetius. As chapter 3 explains, his ideas inform those of the even more influential Renaissance author Niccolò Machiavelli. Machiavelli heralded a revolution in both military practice and strategic thought based upon the disingenuously simple proposition that disciplined infantry forces managed with single-minded ruthlessness can trample over some of the uncertainties which strategists of all eras find so troubling. Chapter 4 introduces Carl von Clausewitz as a cartographer who set out to map the strategic world which Machiavelli immodestly claimed to have discovered. In the process, of course, Clausewitz wrote a far deeper work of his own.

Thucydides suggested that there might be fundamental differences between strategies based upon land warfare and strategies based upon the various uses of ships. In the early twentieth century, other inventions such as aircraft and nuclear weapons suggested yet other alternative approaches to strategy – while complicating even land warfare to the point at which nineteenth-century practices became unsustainable. Chapters 5, 6 and 7 take up these issues, and the thinkers who responded to them. Twentieth-century history also drew attention to the ways in which terrorists, guerrillas, political subversives and other so-called irregular forces can challenge the state-organized armed forces which many strategic thinkers at least superficially treat as the norm. Chapter 8 deals with the theorists of this phenomenon. The ninth chapter looks back at the ideas discussed throughout this work and suggests implications for western democracies in the second decade of the twenty-first century.

Further reading

Gray, Colin S. (1999) *Modern Strategy*. Oxford: Oxford University Press.

Gray, Colin S. (2010) *The Strategy Bridge: Theory for Practice*. Oxford: Oxford University Press.

Kagan, Donald (1995) *On the Origins of War*. London: Pimlico.

Murray, Williamson, Knox, MacGregor and Bernstein, Alvin (1994) (eds) *The Making of Strategy: Rulers, States and War*. Cambridge: Cambridge University Press.

Stevens, Alan and Baker, Nicola (2006) *Making Sense of War: Strategy for the 21st Century*. Cambridge: Cambridge University Press.

1 HEARING THE THUNDER

The Chinese military thinker Sun Tzu's book *The Art of War*, written in approximately 500 BC, remains one of the world's most widely admired works on strategy. If experience can produce insight, it is easy to see where someone living in ancient China might have found the inspiration to write a work of enduring value on this topic. For over twelve centuries beginning with the rise of the Chou Dynasty in 1111 BC, Chinese rulers contended with such legendary western commanders as Alexander the Great for the grim honour of introducing the world's most advanced military methods and using them to wage the world's largest wars. Sun Tzu lived at the dawn of this period, and his writings are an urgent reflection on the demands of a militarily sophisticated age.

This chapter summarizes Sun Tzu's reflections on strategy. The first major section discusses Sun Tzu's way of discussing this topic. Sun Tzu viewed armed conflict as a practical tool for achieving state goals, and he claimed to have identified principles that determine which side in any war will achieve victory. The first step towards developing an effective strategy, he argued, is to assess the capabilities of the opposing sides in terms of these principles.

A second major section explains how Sun Tzu advised political leaders and military commanders to use the knowledge they gain by making such assessments. *The Art of War* suggested that it is wiser to defeat one's enemies through superior strategy – in other words, by out-thinking them – than through brute force. A third major section details Sun Tzu's ideas about the ways in which one might come up with a superior strategy and the steps one might take to make it work.

Sun Tzu concludes that all these methods depend on deception. This heightened his interest in espionage and related operations.

Sun Tzu ended his own book with a chapter on spies. The fourth, and final, major section in this chapter suggests that this is, indeed, a fitting climax to Sun Tzu's argument. This final section also notes that twentieth-century writers have suggested that *The Art of War* is unrealistic. Although we can never know how Sun Tzu would have answered such criticism, the ancient Chinese writer's chapter on espionage suggests his likely response.

Strategy: the first step

Chinese rulers in earlier centuries had treated war as a gentlemanly sport, in which demonstrating one's personal chivalry was as important as defeating the enemy in battle. Traditional Chinese thinkers described war as a quasi-religious ceremony, in which one maintained the harmony of the universe by performing customary acts in traditionally approved fashion. Sun Tzu declared such attitudes to be obsolete. The opening sentences of *The Art of War* describe warfare, not as a game or a ritual, but as a critical state enterprise in which one cannot afford to fail.

Those sentences go on to suggest that the way to improve one's chances of success is to gather factual information and analyse it rationally (Tao 1987: 94). The fact that Sun Tzu describes war as a matter of importance to the state, and not to anyone or anything else, is noteworthy. Again, he is rejecting outdated attitudes. Warriors, Sun Tzu is warning, must work together to achieve state goals. They must not attempt individual acts of bravado purely out of desire for glory. In a different passage, he emphasizes the point that even rulers must resist the temptation to make military decisions for personal reasons (Tao 1987: 125).

Moreover, when Sun Tzu ties war to statecraft, he suggests far-reaching ideas about what strategy involves. At a minimum, he is warning strategists that they need to understand more than weapons and battlefield manoeuvres. To fulfil their purpose, they must take the state's political circumstances into account. Strategy would be complex under any circumstances, and this makes it much more so.

The Prussian military thinker Carl von Clausewitz discussed the relationship between politics and strategy at length. Chapter 4 below discusses his writings on this subject. Sun Tzu merely declares that the relationship exists. Nevertheless, Sun Tzu frequently returns to political issues as he discusses the problems of strategy. For instance, *The Art of War* comments extensively on the proper relationship between the ruler of the state and military officers leading the state's troops on campaigns.

Many other ancient Chinese thinkers explored connections between the problems of governing a country and the problems of waging war. This shows that educated people in ancient China recognized both the complexity and the importance of these links. One may assume that Sun Tzu also understood that defining war as a matter of importance to the state would force him to address a wide range of issues that he could have avoided by focusing exclusively on fighting. Apparently, he considered these broader issues to be crucial.

Having told readers to study war, Sun Tzu goes on to specify the topics he thinks they ought to investigate. Sun Tzu focuses on the practical question of what the opposing sides will be able to do. There are, he says, five basic factors that determine victory and defeat (Tao 1987: 94). These are politics, weather, terrain, the personal qualities of the commanders and 'doctrine', which he defines as the way in which the opposing armies are organized (Tao 1987: 94). Sun Tzu's concept of doctrine also includes the measures both sides have taken to provide their forces with supplies.

Developing this theme further, Sun Tzu suggests questions that strategists might ask themselves in order to assess the five factors effectively. Some address the physical capabilities of the opposing sides. Question 5 asks which side has more powerful forces (Tao 1987: 95). Others are more open-ended. The third question asks which side is best positioned to exploit environmental factors such as the landscape (Tao 1987: 95). Others require political and psychological judgement. The first question asks which side's ruler is wiser and more competent (Tao 1987: 95). None, however, refer to the supernatural, nor do any refer to either side's observance of tradition.

Ancient Chinese rulers and generals normally consulted fortune-tellers before making strategic decisions. Not only did they presumably hope that such oracles could provide them with valuable guidance, their culture presented this ritual as a necessary part of leadership. To ignore the ritual – or, worse, to tamper with it – would be a violation of proper conduct, and might, in the eyes of the superstitious, invite bad luck. The general and strategic thinker Wu Ch'i (c. 440 BC to c. 361 BC), advised rulers to observe such rites in order to win trust and support from the people (Sawyer 1993: 207). Wu Ch'i discreetly failed to mention whether or not he believed that fortune-tellers could actually predict the future.

Sun Tzu, by contrast, urged strategists to dismiss all superstitious customs. Useful strategic knowledge, he claimed, cannot come from attempts to communicate with the spirit world, nor from divine revelations, nor from comparisons with past events, nor from astrology (Tao 1987: 126). The fact that Sun Tzu classified historical analogies as a form of superstition in this list underscores his determination to free strategists from tradition. According to Chinese legends, the mythical emperors of distant antiquity had been paragons of wisdom and proper behaviour. Moralists from the Confucian school of thought urged contemporary rulers to imitate the virtuous ancients.

In Sun Tzu's more pragmatic view of war, useful intelligence can only come from people with direct knowledge of enemy activities (Tao 1987: 126). Not only does he recommend espionage, he advises readers to practise it ruthlessly. In one passage, for instance, he advises strategists to contain breaches of security by killing everyone who knows about a particular plot (Tao 1987: 127). In another, he recommends giving one's own agents false information and deliberately betraying them to the enemy (Tao 1987: 127). Confucians would have been unlikely to approve.

The second step: using one's knowledge

For those who follow Sun Tzu's teachings, the knowledge one gains by studying the five fundamental factors becomes the foundation for one's strategy. One compares one's own capabilities to those of one's opponents in order to determine what one must do to achieve one's goals. Sun Tzu declares that the commander who makes this comparative assessment most effectively will win every battle (Tao 1987: 96). Elsewhere, Sun Tzu re-states the point in his famous saying 'know the enemy and know yourself; in a hundred battles, you will never be defeated' (Tao 1987: 100).

Those lucky enough to discover that they are stronger than their opponents might assume that they can simply smash their enemies with brute force. Sun Tzu warns that this is never the best approach, even for those who have the resources to succeed with it. To begin with, war is costly and disruptive for all of society. Here, the fact that Sun Tzu views warfare as a tool of government becomes important. *The Art of War* goes into detail about various ways in which the mere activity of military campaigning impoverishes the community (Tao 1987: 126).

First, Sun Tzu notes that warfare requires large amounts of money. In making this point, he observes that its direct cost to the state treasury is only part of its expense. People throughout the country will bear all manner of financial losses due to the war effort, and this will sap their collective means as well as hurting individuals. Having discussed war's cost in 'gold', Sun Tzu goes on to address its price in terms of human and social capital. Labourers needed for agriculture will be occupied transporting military supplies, and, even when they return to the fields, they will be 'exhausted'. Moreover, there will be 'continuous commotion' throughout the land. Sun Tzu leaves readers to imagine the mischief this upheaval may trigger.

Sun Tzu goes on to observe that armies may fight in this ruinous manner for years without either side managing to overcome the other. A commander who neglects an opportunity to hurry this process, Sun Tzu tells us, does not know his job (Tao 1987: 126). Long campaigns are equally hard on troops and their gear. *The Art of War* reminds readers that soldiers lose their effectiveness as they tire (Tao 1987: 120). Sun Tzu estimates that the cost of replacing worn-out equipment amounts to 60 per cent of the total expense of waging war (Tao 1987: 120).

Moreover, Sun Tzu suggests, other risks of war increase as time passes, particularly as one moves one's forces from place to place, engages the enemy in combat and undertakes other demanding activities. Sun Tzu does not define these other risks as precisely as he sums up war's economic costs. Nevertheless, he alludes to them repeatedly throughout his work. For instance, Sun Tzu warns strategists to avoid attacking cities if possible (Tao 1987: 97). When Sun Tzu explains his reasons for giving this advice, he turns out to be concerned about more than the obvious dangers of storming city walls. In order to assault a city, Sun Tzu notes, one must spend months preparing siege equipment. During that time, lower-ranked commanders may lose patience and do something rash. Although Sun Tzu ends the example at this point, one can see that the besieging army's problems have only begun.

The longer and more intensively one engages in military operations, *The Art of War* warns, the more deeply one will become enmeshed in cascades of unpredictable disasters. One will no longer know either one's enemies or oneself. One's ability to practise strategy will suffer accordingly. Meanwhile, the enemy is likely to take advantage of one's confusion. This led Sun Tzu to reflect that, although there are certainly examples to remind us that it is dangerous to rush military operations, he cannot think of a single case in which 'a clever operation . . . was prolonged' (Tao 1987: 97). There are 'evils inherent in employing troops', and Sun Tzu warns us that we can never understand the art of using military force effectively until we appreciate that point (Tao 1987: 97).

No matter how great one's resources, one must always seek to use them as swiftly, efficiently and decisively as possible. One must seek, wherever possible, to manoeuvre one's enemies into assuming a greater share of war's inherent evils than oneself. Thus, coming up with a short-term plan to attack the enemy or repulse the enemy's attack is only the most obvious part of making strategy. *The Art of War* advises strategists to 'create a situation' that will make one's plans feasible (Tao 1987: 95). What does this mean in practice? Sun Tzu scatters partial answers to this question throughout the early chapters of his work, usually expressing them in poetic language. The victorious side in a battle, *The Art of War* tells us, 'is as one yi [a measurement of weight] balanced against a grain' (Tao 1987: 102). In a properly coordinated attack, Sun Tzu writes, troops strike the enemy 'as a grindstone against eggs' (Tao 1987: 103).

Such imagery does not tell strategists exactly how to 'create situations', but it does suggest principles that may guide them in their efforts. As one reads further through *The Art of War*, one finds that Sun Tzu recapitulates those principles multiple times, explaining his ideas in increasingly specific terms as he goes on. For instance, Sun Tzu pays particular attention to the principle of timing one's actions properly, conserving one's resources when possible, but acting without hesitation when one can achieve some advantage by doing so. Early chapters of *The Art of War* discuss this theme in a purely impressionistic way. In one passage, Sun Tzu reflects on the way a hawk times its dive to intercept its prey with enough momentum to snap bones (Tao 1987: 103). Later, Sun Tzu describes military situations in which the concept may apply, noting that troops which have time to settle in their chosen positions will be rested, whereas those who must charge against them will arrive fatigued (Tao 1987: 105).

Later still, Sun Tzu gives even more concrete examples of ways one might put the principle of effective timing into practice. If one manages to catch one's enemies as they are crossing a river, one can strike at a moment when half of the opposing force has crossed, so that the enemy troops on one side will have difficulty helping their comrades on the other (Tao 1987: 113). If one manages to set fire to the enemy's camp, one should attack the moment enemy troops abandon their positions to fight the fire, but not before (Tao 1987: 124). Sun Tzu notes that this moment may come before the flames actually reach anything important, and reminds generals that, having set a fire, they must take care not to position their own troops downwind from it (Tao 1987: 124).

Readers could easily mistake Sun Tzu's specific examples for step-by-step instructions about how to carry out certain operations. Sun Tzu undoubtedly believed that the methods he described in his examples would work under the right conditions, and that they are worth mastering so that one can use them if those conditions arise. Nevertheless, he warned readers that there can be no recipe books for strategy. When he claimed those who follow his advice are certain to triumph, he was referring to his counsel about concepts, not his instructions about the details of particular stratagems.

Sun Tzu reminded readers of this point early in his work. The essence of successful strategy, he noted, is to strike in a way the enemy has failed to anticipate. Since the enemy's expectations depend upon the context of the engagement, there is no way to reduce this approach to a formula (Tao 1987: 95–6). This statement suggests that Sun Tzu offered his guidelines for setting fires and ambushing enemy forces as they cross rivers to illustrate his more abstract concepts, not as dogma. The techniques described in the illustrations will be appropriate in some situations but not in others. The ideas behind them, in Sun Tzu's view, will always be valid.

The fact that one must plan every operation afresh, one may note in passing, makes accurate information yet more important to Sun Tzu's way of making strategy. Since one cannot deduce how the enemy has failed to prepare or where one might stage an unexpected manoeuvre through mental effort alone, one must extract such 'keys to victory' from up-to-date reports about the particular circumstances in which one is fighting. Thus, despite the fact that Sun Tzu devotes entire chapters to 'Terrain' and 'The Nine Varieties of Ground', he precedes all this material with a caveat in an earlier chapter warning that one cannot hope to use terrain effectively without consulting guides who know it well (Tao 1987: 109).

Situations within situations

Effective timing is only one of the methods by which Sun Tzu hoped to 'create situations'. The hawk, to revive Sun Tzu's metaphor, may have to circle for hours before suitable prey appears. In war, those who merely wait for opportunities may have to wait forever. Sun Tzu acknowledged that this may, at times, be the painful reality. Even expert strategists, he notes in the opening lines of his chapter on

'Dispositions', cannot miraculously transform strong enemies into weak ones. Accordingly, Sun Tzu notes, the simple fact that one knows how to achieve victory does not mean that one can do it in practice (Tao 1987: 101).

Sun Tzu goes on, however, to explore a more optimistic thought. Even when there is no way to create the situation one desires, it may still be possible to create a situation in which it will become possible to create such a situation. This is particularly true for those who have the foresight to begin the process well in advance. Thus, the most ingenious strategists may not appear particularly talented. Observers are not normally impressed when others accomplish things which appear easy, and a skilful commander chooses to fight at times and in places where he has taken measures to ensure that he will have the advantage (Tao 1987: 101).

Such a commander's groundwork – both figurative and literal – makes his final victory look as easy as hearing thunderclaps. One may also note that such a commander's defeated opponents are likely to blame their failure on the excuse that they could not possibly have won under the circumstances. The reason why Sun Tzu titled this chapter 'Dispositions' turns out to be that he is advising readers to do their best to 'position' themselves in ways that allow them to sidestep the frustrating state of affairs he described at the beginning of the chapter. This careful positioning – and not mere opportunism – is what allows a skilled general to strike with lethal momentum (Tao 1987: 102).

This idea leaves strategists with the challenge of figuring out what a suitable disposition might be. Readers are entitled to complain that this is easier said than done. Nevertheless, Sun Tzu goes on to explain why he believes that it is possible. Even the most limited situations, he suggests, can develop in an enormous variety of ways, depending on how different factors combine. There are, he notes, only five musical notes, but there are an effectively infinite variety of songs (Tao 1987: 103). As a strategist, one strives to act in ways that combine with existing circumstances to improve one's future options.

One way of doing this, Sun Tzu suggests, is to take advantage of the fact that different types of forces can do different types of things. Therefore, just as one can combine the five musical notes into any number of tunes, one can combine actions by different types of forces to produce any number of tactical effects. This concept of combined arms warfare is commonplace throughout military history. Hannibal, Alexander the Great and Napoleon Bonaparte are but three who have achieved renown for their success at choreographing manoeuvres involving infantry, cavalry and, in the last case, artillery. Armoured vehicles took over the traditional roles of cavalry in the twentieth century, and air power added a fourth component to the mix.

The Art of War discusses combined arms warfare in abstract terms. Instead of talking about halberdiers, cavalry, archers, charioteers, armed river boats, elite units of picked troops or other types of military units that would have been familiar in Chou Dynasty China, Sun Tzu talks about combining actions by ordinary forces and extraordinary forces. One uses ordinary forces to occupy one's enemies and extraordinary forces to defeat them (Tao 1987: 103). Later Chinese strategic writers from the third century AD to the twentieth have concluded that he left the exact nature of the two types of forces vague on purpose (Tao 1987: 35). Troops who play an ordinary role in some situations may play an extraordinary role in others.

When one is fighting in cleared farmland, for instance, one might think of infantry as an ordinary force. One might use infantry to hold one's enemies in place while cavalry takes advantage of its extraordinary speed to encircle the enemy flanks and win a decisive victory. In jungle warfare, however, the two types of forces might reverse roles. The terrain might restrict cavalry (or armoured vehicles) to predictable operations along roads while permitting lightly armed foot soldiers to encircle the enemy by going through the forest. Japanese infantry devastated Allied forces using such flanking manoeuvres during Japan's Second World War offensives in Burma and Malaya.

Sun Tzu himself hints that he intends commanders to decide which forces are ordinary and which are extraordinary on a case-by-case basis. He concludes his discussion of the two types of forces by comparing troops to stones and tree trunks. On a level field, both are static. On a slope, however, stripped logs and round rocks will roll downhill, gaining speed as they go. A commander's job is to gather round boulders on a mountain top and ensure that they cascade down upon the foe (Tao 1987: 104).

Sun Tzu believes that a commander's skill at matching forces to situations is more important than the number of troops she or he has under his or her command. Although Sun Tzu clearly appreciates the importance of numerical superiority, he emphasizes that there is a difference between the size of an army in theory and the number of troops that actually fight in any particular battle. Only the second number matters. A large army which has dispersed its forces is no stronger in any actual battle than a smaller army which has remained concentrated (Tao 1987: 106).

All these ideas about ways of deploying forces depend upon having troops that will do what the strategist requires of them. This leads to another principle that runs throughout Sun Tzu's work – the principle of cultivating one's own military capabilities. Considerable portions of *The Art of War* advise commanders about how to supply, organize and lead troops in ways that make them as strong, versatile and reliable as possible. These are clearly among the surest measures any strategist can take to create circumstances that will maximize his or her chance of winning future battles.

Various sections of *The Art of War* apply the principle of cultivating one's strategic capabilities to all the different levels of a military and political organization. Responsibility for improving strategic potential extends from the commanders of the smallest military units to the ruler of the state. Sun Tzu also emphasizes that attempts to develop one's military capabilities will only succeed if one persists with them. Other ancient Chinese writers, notably the third century BC political theorist Han Fei Tzu, castigated rulers for changing their policies to reflect changes in political fashion, and in response to manipulation by their courtiers. Sun Tzu does not dwell on the topic of court intrigue, but he seems to be concerned with similar problems.

In an effectively administered military organization, *The Art of War* tells us, leading the entire army is little different from commanding a small band (Tao 1987: 103). Although Sun Tzu does not elaborate, this statement reveals important points about his attitude towards organizing, supporting and leading armed forces. The fact that Sun Tzu feels the need to make this statement suggests that he is aware that, under most circumstances, management of a large force would be far more complex than management of a few men. Indeed, most military commanders throughout history have had to devote more effort to routine management than to planning master strokes of the sort Sun Tzu admires.

'Amateurs talk strategy', Omar Bradley noted over two millennia later. 'Professionals talk logistics' (Pierce 1996: 74). Sun Tzu appears to recognize the truth in such observations. Nevertheless, Sun Tzu might add that the reason why professionals 'talk logistics' is that logistics are what make it possible for them to practise strategy.

One also notes that Sun Tzu focuses on making large forces responsive to their supreme commander. *The Art of War* largely ignores the possible advantages of enabling lower-ranked members of those forces to act independently. One reason may be that Chinese strategic thinkers of Sun Tzu's era were – with good reason – acutely concerned about the risk that individual warriors might do rash or cowardly things in battle. Sun Tzu was probably more interested in controlling personal initiative than in fostering it.

Nevertheless, Sun Tzu's emphasis on central control distinguishes Sun Tzu from twentieth- and twenty-first-century writers on strategy, many of whom see properly channelled independence in the lower ranks as the key to achieving war-winning breakthroughs of the very sort *The Art of War* advises commanders to seek. This emphasis also distinguishes Sun Tzu from other military thinkers in ancient China. A strategist of the second century BC named Han Hsin summed up the reasons why his superior Liu Pang was able to defeat his opponents and found the Han Dynasty by saying that, although Liu Pang was himself a poor general, he was an excellent commander of generals (Kane 2007: 157). Sun Tzu offers little direct advice for those who wish to improve their skills as commanders of generals.

Just as Sun Tzu provides specific examples of ways in which commanders might – when appropriate – apply his principles on the battlefield, he provides examples of specific techniques they might use to establish control over their forces. *The Art of War* alludes to the fact that it is important to organize large groups of soldiers into a manageable system of units (Tao 1987: 103). Sun Tzu goes into some detail about the importance of providing forces with suitable equipment to make such administrative systems function in combat. *The Art of War* cites a lost work titled *The Book of Military Administration* as a guide to the various uses of flags, banners and musical instruments for signalling (Tao 1987: 109).

At this point, Sun Tzu pauses to explain the theory behind *The Book of Military Administration*'s recommendations. The fact that devices such as drums and banners allow troops to locate each other and send simple messages amidst the confusion of battle serves the broader purpose of helping commanders maintain psychological control over their subordinates, along with the even broader purpose of ensuring that troops work as a team to play their part in the strategist's plan. Clear signalling enables large numbers of troops to receive directions simultaneously. Assuming that the majority obey orders, it becomes difficult – or, at least, conspicuous – for individuals to do otherwise (Tao 1987: 109).

In these passages, Sun Tzu devotes as much space to the problem of restraining would-be heroes as he devotes to the problem of deterring shirkers. He is not content to rely on the personal courage of individuals to motivate troops in battle. In his view, commanders can – and must – instil military virtues throughout their forces by practising effective leadership. An effective commander, Sun Tzu tells us, drags troops to victory as if racing down a path, physically dragging a reluctant companion along with him (Tao 1987: 121). One way of doing this is to put one's forces in situations where troops must fight effectively to survive. Sun Tzu recommends this technique to promote teamwork as well as tenacity and ferocity. Even men who hate each other, he notes, will work together when their survival depends upon it (Tao 1987: 121).

Sun Tzu then adds that those who wish to make their troops capable of such performance must carry out a comprehensive programme of conditioning them for it. Simply throwing unprepared soldiers into a desperate situation will not be enough. (In fact, it is likely to prove disastrous.) Commanders who want their troops to perform consistently, *The Art of War* notes, must practise effective 'administration' (Tao 1987: 121). Sun Tzu does not explain what he means by 'administration' in this instance, and readers might have found it useful if he had. One would imagine that preparing troops to cooperate in the ways *The Art of War* describes would involve, among other things, a rigorous and well thought-out programme of training. Sun Tzu says surprisingly little about training anywhere in his work, and he misses an obvious opportunity to discuss the topic here.

Sun Tzu does, however, discuss other measures commanders must take in order to improve their troops' performance. Commanders must, for instance, pay attention to soldiers' physical condition (Tao 1987: 120). Even the most dedicated warriors fight more effectively when they have had adequate food and sleep (Tao 1987: 120). Leaders must also establish – and maintain – the correct sort of personal relationships with their troops.

Few will be surprised to learn that Sun Tzu advises commanders to put a higher priority on discipline than on popularity (Tao 1987: 115). *The Art of War* adds, however, that harsh measures are only effective once a commander has earned respect through other means (Tao 1987: 115). Sun Tzu also implies that it is a mistake to humiliate one's subordinates (Tao 1987: 115). Throughout this section, *The Art of War* stresses the importance of consistency, and of continually reinforcing command relationships through training exercises (Tao 1987: 115).

Just as Sun Tzu advises strategists to match their tactics to the circumstances of particular campaigns, he advises commanders to match their leadership techniques to the psychological state of their subordinates (Tao 1987: 121). To perform these functions effectively, *The Art of War* suggests, commanders must present the proper demeanour. A leader, Sun Tzu suggests, should be both authoritative and enigmatic, not only to give subordinates the impression that s/he has an effective plan, but to avoid behaviour which might help enemies figure out what his or her strategy happens to be (Tao 1987: 121).

In addition to discussing organizational and psychological preparations for war, Sun Tzu pays painstaking attention to the fact that military organizations depend upon material supplies. Not only do they require food, he notes, they require other resources ranging from glue for repairing broken equipment to cash stipends for use in entertaining foreign envoys (Tao 1987: 97). *The Art of War* reminds readers that one cannot dispatch armed forces on a campaign until one has provided them with at least a rudimentary stockpile of such materials (Tao 1987: 97). Moreover, armed forces require increasing quantities of new supplies for as long as they continue to operate (Tao 1987: 98). Thus, Sun Tzu advises commanders to use captured food and equipment whenever possible (Tao 1987: 97–8). Although Sun Tzu emphasizes the fact that this reduces the burden on one's state's economy, one may also note that captured material may be more rapidly available in the area of operations, and that seizing it denies it to the enemy.

Although Sun Tzu writes a great deal about equipment, he says surprisingly little about what would appear to be an army's most important hardware – its weapons. One might have imagined that he would have discussed the merits of different types of armaments. One might have imagined that he would have discussed the proportion of one's forces one should equip with bows, halberds, armoured chariots and the like. One might have imagined that he would have discussed the possibility of gaining an advantage over the enemy by adopting superior weapons technology.

Sun Tzu was undoubtedly familiar with such issues. If he was indeed the same person as the general Sun Wu, he may have spent part of his own military career promoting innovations in weapons technology. As Box 1.1 notes, Sun Wu, a native of the ethnically Chinese state of Ch'i, distinguished himself as an advisor to the ruler of the allegedly 'barbarian' state of Wu. Chinese military advisors continually urged Wu's rulers to equip their troops with such supposedly advanced armaments as bows and war chariots (Kane 2007: 50). The Wu people appear to have found chariots unsuitable for the marshy regions they wished to campaign in, but they adopted archery with some success (Kane 2007: 50).

Moreover, the state of Wu introduced the rest of China to its own military inventions. Wu was located on the Yangtze River, and its armed forces used river boats to raid their enemies' shores. The other Yangtze River states copied this technique, going on to develop larger warships (Kane 2007: 50). Although Sun Tzu presumably wrote his thirteen chapters on strategy before his personal involvement with Wu began, it seems unlikely that someone who was otherwise so well

Box 1.1 Who was Sun Tzu?

According to Chinese tradition, Sun Tzu was the son of a distinguished commander in the state of Ch'i (Qi), a kingdom famous for the excellence of its armed forces (Tao 1987: 11–12). The date of his birth is uncertain, but was presumably around the year 500 BC, which is towards the end of an era in Chinese history known as the Spring and Autumn period. Not only was Sun Tzu's home country noted for its military, it was a centre of trade, culturally developed and active in the increasingly vicious political struggles of Spring and Autumn China. This allowed the young Sun to observe the realities of statecraft at close range, even as he obtained a fine academic education.

At some point during his youth in Ch'i, Sun Tzu wrote his thirteen-chapter *The Art of War*. The manuscript appears to have circulated widely and attracted favourable attention. Later, Sun Tzu put his ideas into practice. When the government of Ch'i collapsed, Sun fled to the southerly kingdom of Wu. There, he requested a position as a military advisor to the king.

The ruler of Wu admired Sun Tzu's writings and granted the strategist an audience (Szuma 1979: 28–9). At this meeting, Sun Tzu offered to demonstrate his abilities by training the king's concubines to serve as soldiers. The king gave him permission to try. When the women refused to take Sun Tzu's instructions seriously, the strategist ordered two of them beheaded. When the king tried to intervene, Sun Tzu reminded him that a commander in the field has the right to disregard orders from the sovereign, and proceeded with the executions. The surviving concubines performed their weapons drills flawlessly from then on.

The Han Dynasty historian Ssu-ma Ch'ien (Sima Qian), writing in approximately 104 BC, described the rest of Sun Tzu's career with a list of his military victories (Szuma 1979: 29).

Over the centuries, numerous Chinese military thinkers have annotated *The Art of War*. Some did so openly, but others may have modified the text anonymously, making it impossible for present-day readers to determine who actually wrote what. Indeed, some historians have questioned whether the Sun Tzu described in Ssu-ma Ch'ien's account ever existed at all. Nevertheless, even sceptics commonly accept that whoever originally wrote *The Art of War* lived in the sixth century BC (Kane 2007: 53). Ssu-ma Ch'ien's version of events remains plausible, and a considerable number of experts support it.

informed about military affairs would have overlooked these developments. Moreover, if he had seemed ignorant of these issues, one doubts that that the king of Wu would have offered him a position.

Therefore, the fact that Sun Tzu does not write more about weapons in *The Art of War* appears unlikely to be a mere oversight. One can only speculate about what Sun Tzu's reasons for excluding this topic might have been. Perhaps he was sceptical about weapons technology for the same reason that he was sceptical about relying on mere superiority of numbers. Sun Tzu may have wished to stress the fact that practically no weapon is, by itself, a panacea. Weapons are useful only if one's strategy puts one's troops in a position to use those weapons effectively. Sun Tzu may have been trying to encourage commanders to focus on the strategic problem of positioning their troops, rather than on the weapons the troops carry. Nevertheless, his omission is puzzling.

Box 1.2   Reading Sun Tzu

For at least two thousand years, even Sun Tzu's admirers have acknowledged that it is easier to quote from *The Art of War* than to apply its ideas effectively. Ssu-ma Ch'ien writes of a second century BC battle in which the general Han Hsin overcame considerable handicaps to defeat a dangerous opponent. Afterwards, the victorious general's subordinates marvelled at his accomplishment. The subordinates recalled that Han Hsin had ordered them to take a position in front of a river, thus sacrificing the advantages of defending from behind a body of water, cutting off their own lines of communication and directly violating one of Sun Tzu's teachings.

The subordinates – who, one notes, had been disciplined enough to obey these commands – asked Han Hsin where he had got such an idea, and how he had known that it would work. Han Hsin responded that those who understood *The Art of War* more thoroughly would realize that he had acted in the spirit of Sun Tzu's writings. Although Sun Tzu had noted the fact that it is generally preferable to keep water obstacles to one's front, he had also noted the advantages of putting troops in positions where they had to achieve victory to survive. Since, Han Hsin continued, many of his soldiers were unreliable, the latter piece of advice was clearly the one which applied in his case (Szuma 1979: 273).

Han Hsin, in other words, felt no obligation to follow all Sun Tzu's instructions to the letter. On the contrary, he selected the lines he found most promising and interpreted them to fit his own analysis of his circumstances. As the main text notes, Sun Tzu himself explicitly supports

Han Hsin's approach. This might lead one to ask what *The Art of War* actually teaches, if it can mean such different things to different people. Does Sun Tzu say anything definite at all?

Sun Tzu clearly intended to. Although *The Art of War* encourages readers to come up with their own methods for applying strategic principles, it also asserts that there are right and wrong ways of doing so. Unsurprisingly, Sun Tzu declares that his own approaches are the correct ones. The strategist adds that rulers should dismiss any commanders who fail to follow his advice (Tao 1987: 95). Readers may still complain that Sun Tzu has not told us how to heed his counsel in real-life situations.

In order to resolve this ambiguity, it may be useful to note that Sun Tzu appears to base many of his ideas on a branch of metaphysics known as Taoism (Daoism). The Taoist author Lao Tzu's influential work *Tao te Ching* states that there are objective truths, but that it is impossible to encapsulate them in words (Lao 1972: 1). Nevertheless, although it is impossible to explain such truths, it remains possible – and worthwhile – to try to appreciate them.

The *Tao te Ching* offers a great deal of advice to those who would appreciate the Tao. In much the same fashion that Sun Tzu emphasizes the importance of intelligence, Lao Tzu emphasizes all forms of observation (Lao 1972: 15). The sages of ancient times, Lao Tzu writes, were ever alert (Szuma 1979: 28–9). In a similar vein, these masters refrained from committing themselves to irreversible action. Thus, they preserved as many options as possible (Lao 1972: 1).

Just as Sun Tzu's advice may strike readers as ambiguous, Lao Tzu noted that the ancient sages appeared enigmatic, like a pool clouded by silt (Lao 1972: 1). Mud, however, settles and, when it does, the murky waters become clear. By remaining attentive and flexible, one prepares oneself to seize the occasion when critical facts become available and when the practical implications of abstract principles becomes possible to discern (Lao 1972: 15). If Sun Tzu took a Taoist view of such matters, the main difference between the brilliant general Han Hsin and his mediocre subordinates may be that the subordinate officers assumed they already knew what *The Art of War* meant, but Han Hsin remained ready to discover it.

Earlier sections have noted the significance of Sun Tzu's decision to present war as an offshoot of politics. Yet another reason why this is important is that, by recognizing the connection between politics and strategy, *The Art of War* suggests further ways for strategists to shape circumstances to their advantage. One can, Sun Tzu notes, upset the enemy's alliances through diplomatic means (Tao 1987: 99). Indeed, Sun Tzu sees this as the second-best way to pursue one's war aims, inferior only to out-thinking one's opponents themselves (Tao 1987: 99).

Just as one can use diplomacy to improve one's situation on future battlefields, one can use military strength to improve one's negotiating position. Later chapters of *The Art of War* acknowledge that politics is a treacherous business (Tao 1987: 122). Nevertheless, those who enjoy a fearsome reputation and the ability to maintain it typically find it easier to enforce their agreements with other states (Tao 1987: 122). Meanwhile, their opponents typically find it difficult to locate allies who are willing to stand against the strong state (Tao 1987: 122).

Deception, espionage and reckoning with the enemy

In short, *The Art of War* suggests a wealth of ideas about ways to 'create situations' in which it will become possible to win a politically meaningful victory. Nevertheless, Sun Tzu warns, all those who hope to use any of these ideas successfully must reckon with the fact that the enemy will try to stop them. To make matters worse, the enemy will begin with the advantage. Note that Sun Tzu does not merely allow for the possibility that the enemy may initially be in a superior position – he assumes that this will always be the case.

The very reason why one must act to create a new situation is that one's current circumstances are, in some way, problematic. Changing those circumstances will require effort, and, until one has completed the process, the enemy will be free to exploit one's difficulties. Thus, in Sun Tzu's view, attempts to gain advantages are innately dangerous (Tao 1987: 108). Sun Tzu illustrates this point by discussing what may happen to a commander who tries to march his troops to a new location in which they will enjoy more favourable terrain.

If the commander orders his troops to bring all of their gear and supplies, they will be too heavily laden to reach the new position in time. If, however, the commander orders them to abandon their impediments and carry out cross-country movements without sleep, they will reach the battlefield exhausted and poorly equipped (Tao 1987: 108). If they must then fight the enemy, Sun Tzu warns that the commanders themselves are likely to be captured (Tao 1987: 108). One may normally assume that, if the commanders are captured, their troops have been defeated as well.

There is no safe way to move an army, and no way to improve one's position without moving. Similar principles apply to practically anything else one might do to gain an advantage. The only way to 'create situations' without suffering disaster in the process is to prevent one's enemies from taking the opportunities one gives them. One must keep one's enemies from realizing that the opportunities exist, or, failing that, manipulate one's enemies into wasting them. This is why Sun Tzu repeatedly reminds his readers that all warfare is based on deception.

To mislead one's enemies, one must conceal one's true motives and capabilities. In Sun Tzu's view, the highest achievement in deploying one's forces is to hide them in positions which, even if known, would give no clue as to one's intentions (Tao 1987: 106). As a principle, one should preserve as many options as possible for as long as possible, 'pretend[ing] to be as shy as a maiden' until one's foes provide you with an opportunity to act (Tao 1987: 123). At that moment, Sun Tzu adds, one must move without hesitation.

Sun Tzu adds that one must police one's campsites to minimize the amount of information one leaves behind for enemy scouts (Tao 1987: 121). One must, in his view, take every opportunity to move forces by stealth (Tao 1987: 121). One must, he writes, develop an enigmatic personality, and one must keep even one's own officers ignorant of one's plans (Tao 1987: 121). One must not repeat one's techniques, even when they have succeeded in the past (Tao 1987: 107). One may, under appropriate circumstances, take advantage of the enemy's own attempts to gather intelligence by deliberately feeding opposing spies false information (Tao 1987: 127).

The Art of War also suggests more active approaches to prevent enemy strategists from taking full advantage of the opportunities they might otherwise exploit. One method is to strike first, so that one's opponents must respond to your attacks instead of launching operations of their own. Sun Tzu asks himself how he might deflect an imminent attack by a dangerous opponent, and reflects that he might try to divert his enemies by moving against something they 'cheris[h]' (Tao 1987: 120). Just as one can beat enemies into passivity with the proverbial stick, one can also distract them with the proverbial carrot. Sun Tzu notes that, while one may need to attack one's rivals in order to subjugate them in a comprehensive way, one may often render them ineffectual for indefinite periods by continually spurring them to change their policies in pursuit of apparent opportunities (Tao 1987: 111–12).

Not only does this passage suggest further ways of undermining the enemy's ability to practise strategy, it illuminates a variety of more subtle themes in Sun Tzu's strategic thought. Those who recall Sun

Tzu's discussions about the risks and difficulties of moving troops from one position to another will realize that he undoubtedly sees enticing the enemy into dithering as a significant accomplishment with far-reaching implications. The fact that Sun Tzu suggests these approaches not merely as campaign tactics but as methods for achieving political influence over neighbouring dukes reminds us that he sees military strategy as being intimately connected to broader political activity. Moreover, Sun Tzu's distinction between policies aimed at subduing one's neighbours and policies aimed at keeping them occupied invites one to reflect on the various reasons why one might prefer one of those approaches rather than the other.

Sun Tzu also famously advises commanders to exploit opposing generals' personal weaknesses. *The Art of War* pays particular attention to the vices of overconfidence, cowardice, short-temperedness, excessive sensitivity to questions of honour and soft-heartedness (Tao 1987: 112). Sun Tzu concludes that these five character flaws inevitably lead to ruin, and that they demand careful study (Tao 1987: 112).

Here, Sun Tzu seems to be discreetly warning readers to discipline themselves against developing vices that their enemies can exploit. This is noteworthy since Sun Tzu's twentieth-century critics have accused him of overlooking the fact that whatever techniques he recommends to his readers will also work for his readers' enemies. The critics, notably Michael Handel, conclude that this undermines Sun Tzu's entire approach to strategy. In Handel's view, the fact that both sides can use the same methods means that neither side can ever obtain a significant advantage, and that the very idea of creating a situation in which one can defeat one's opponents at minimal cost is merely an impossible ideal (Kane 2007: 17).

Despite Handel's criticism, Sun Tzu appears aware that both sides will attempt to deceive each other. Sun Tzu does not, however, give up on the idea of creating advantageous situations. His view appears to be that, since both sides will use the same methods, one must try to be better at them. One must recognize the central importance of deceiving the enemy and seeing through the enemy's deceptions. One must, for instance, be aware of common ruses, along with ways of detecting them. Sun Tzu lists a number of such tricks in the ninth chapter of his work (Tao 1987: 114).

Sun Tzu also stresses the importance of suborning members of the enemy's own deception and intelligence-gathering services (Tao 1987: 127). Properly placed double agents can warn you about the opposing side's tricks while helping you perpetrate covert activities of your own (Tao 1987: 127). Sun Tzu adds that it is wise to use spies to watch your other spies (Tao 1987: 127). Presumably, he hopes that this will reduce the risk that the double agents who claim to be betraying the opposing side to you will turn out to be triple agents who have remained loyal to your enemies all along (Tao 1987: 127).

Conclusion

Sun Tzu places his chapter on espionage at the very end of *The Art of War*. The final parts of a book commonly combine the points from earlier sections into a unified argument. Sun Tzu does not make it clear whether this was what he had in mind when he put his material on espionage last, but the topic does, indeed, seem to connect several key ideas in his work. The raw material of strategy, he tells us, is knowledge. Although there are innumerable ways to use that knowledge in warfare, all of them depend on deceiving the enemy.

Espionage, if effective, provides commanders both with sources of information and with instruments for conducting deceptions. Other strategic thinkers – notably Carl von Clausewitz – might counter that espionage often does *not* prove effective. One may also observe that, if one defines espionage narrowly in terms of human secret agents carrying out clandestine missions, there are numerous alternative methods for obtaining information and deceiving the enemy. Sun Tzu himself discussed many of them. In one section, to pick an obvious example, he advises commanders about things to look for when the enemy army has come close enough so that they can see it for themselves (Tao 1987: 114).

Nevertheless, despite these qualifications, espionage and the many comparable activities often grouped together under the term 'intelligence' hold out the promise that there may be more effective ways to achieve strategic goals than simply plunging into combat. Those who work to enhance their strategic effectiveness may still fail, but those who do not even attempt this task cannot possibly succeed, and Sun Tzu urges his readers to try. Moreover, rulers and military commanders commonly neglect both strategy in general and espionage in particular for reasons that range from superstition, prejudice and outdated notions of honour to the short-sighted reluctance to pay for them. Sun Tzu uses his chapter on espionage to condemn such negligence as both ruinous and morally irresponsible. Thus, he returns to the argument he advanced in the first lines of his book, where he called on readers to accept that war is a 'matter of vital importance to the state' and urged them to approach it rationally.

Other Chinese thinkers took this rationalism even farther. In approximately 350 BC, a courtier named Shang Yang urged the ruler of a kingdom known as Ch'in to review all of his policies to ensure that they maximized the wealth and power of the state (Kane 2007: 62). Neither sentiment nor tradition was to stand in the way of logic and pragmatism. When, for instance, Shang Yang determined that people's loyalty to their relatives might compromise their obedience to the regime, he introduced policies to undermine trust within families, indifferent to the suffering this caused and equally indifferent to the fact that the Chinese have customarily revered the family as the centrepiece of civilization and the most sacred of all institutions.

Shang Yang's teachings helped shape the school of thought known as Legalism. Over the following two centuries, Ch'in's rulers applied Legalist methods to conquer their rivals and found the largest empire the Chinese world had ever known. Only fifteen years later, the Ch'in Empire disintegrated, leaving an assortment of rebel armies to fight over its remains. The Han rulers who eventually restored order throughout the Chinese world quietly retained some of the more useful Legalist techniques, but they abolished the Legalists' more notorious policies and they savaged the Legalists in their rhetoric. Meanwhile, the scholars of the period rejected Legalism as a philosophical movement.

Sun Tzu, by contrast, has remained consistently influential for more than twenty-one centuries. One reason may be that he was intellectually more modest. Although he urged readers to solve military and political problems through a rational process of observation and analysis, he remained aware that these problems arise in the context of broader human concerns which military power cannot fully address. Moreover, Sun Tzu remained aware of the fact that war will always be more chaotic, more complex and more horrible than even the most gifted thinker can fully comprehend.

Thus, Sun Tzu warns sovereigns never to wage war lightly – even, presumably, if a rational appraisal of the circumstances indicates that the odds are overwhelmingly in their favour. Later generations of Chinese writers highlighted this as one of Sun Tzu's most valuable contributions (Kane 2007: 123). Shang Yang ridiculed such scruples as fuzzy-minded naivety, and he would have been entitled to note that Sun Tzu and his admirers failed to prove their assertions through any rigorous process of logical argument. Nevertheless, Shang Yang's own legacy suggests that Sun Tzu's position is rationally valid in the more fundamental sense of being true.

Further reading

Baskin, Wade (ed.) (1972) *Classics in Chinese Philosophy*. New York: Philosophical Library.

Kane, Thomas (2007) *Ancient China on Postmodern War: Enduring Ideas from the Chinese Strategic Tradition*. London: Routledge.

Lao Tsu (Lao Tzu/Laozi) (1972) *Tao Te Ching*, trans. Gia-Fu Feng and Jane English. New York: Vintage Books.

Sawyer, Ralph (trans.) (1993) *The Seven Military Classics of Ancient China*. Oxford: Westview Press.

Sawyer, Ralph (trans.) (1996) *One Hundred Unorthodox Strategies: Battle and Tactics of Chinese Warfare*. Boulder, CO: Westview Press.

Sun Tzu (1963) *The Art of War*, trans. Samuel B. Griffith. Oxford: Oxford University Press.

Tao Hanzhang (1987) *Sun Tzu's Art of War: The Modern Chinese Interpretation*, trans. Yuan Shibing. New York: Sterling.

2 HONOUR, INTEREST AND FEAR

Long wars, Sun Tzu cautioned, consume those who take part in them. When conflicts drag on, he continued, no strategist, however brilliant, can prevent eventual disaster (Tao 1987: 97). This warning was equally valid 5,000 miles to his west where, less than a century after Sun Tzu presumably wrote his book, the city-states of ancient Greece waged a pair of wars involving practically the entire world as the Greeks knew it and lasting almost thirty years. Thucydides, a general who took part in this struggle, believed that it was more significant than any earlier event in history (Thucydides 1997: 3). Accordingly, he recorded the events of this conflict, claiming, in the process, to have captured lessons for all time (Thucydides 1997: 14).

Thucydides shares Sun Tzu's concern with using armed force and other strategic instruments to achieve meaningful political goals. In considering this general issue, the Athenian addresses many of the same sub-topics, from the importance of economics to the importance of knowing one's enemies to the sheer complexity of war. Thucydides also raises points that might conceivably have appeared in Sun Tzu's work, but did not. The Athenian discusses naval warfare, for instance, along with the peculiar problems of making strategy under different types of governments. Thus, he introduces new themes into our understanding of strategy. This chapter explores those themes.

Since Thucydides presented his work as a history, reading it is a different experience from reading most works of strategic theory. Therefore, this chapter begins with a paragraph outlining the period which Thucydides wrote about. A third section discusses methods of finding strategic principles within Thucydides' work. The rest of the chapter will analyse three case studies from Thucydides' much longer history in detail, in order to illuminate crucial themes within his work.

Background

Thucydides came from the city-state of Athens, which had become the richest and perhaps the most militarily powerful polity in the Greek world. Athens was a democracy, and its people took the same pride in their political system that patriots in modern democracies claim to take in theirs. Nevertheless, Athens had an almost equally powerful rival. This was the warrior state of Sparta, which had fought alongside the Athenians in earlier wars with Persian invaders, but then clashed with Athens on ever-increasing numbers of issues over the following decades. Thucydides' work, *The History of the Peloponnesian War*, describes how Athens attempted to manage this conflict and then, when war broke out, to win it. Athens lost both the war and its democratic way of life, not because Sparta had superior forces, but because the Athenians wasted potential advantages, continued the war when they might have had peace and eventually exhausted themselves in an ambitious attempt to conquer Sicily.

Reading Thucydides

Where most strategic thinkers discuss universal principles, Thucydides discusses one specific war. Where many strategic thinkers tell readers what to do, Thucydides tells readers only what happened. The Athenian expresses the hope that his history will help readers interpret the future, but he normally leaves them to determine its precise meaning for themselves (Thucydides 1997: 14). Even when he seems to explain issues, his points can be subtle.

In one passage, for instance, Thucydides tells readers that the Spartans fought the Athenians because they were afraid that Athens was becoming a threat to them. Thucydides goes on to describe the Spartan leaders' debate about whether or not to fight. In this debate, the Spartans who successfully argued in favour of war based their case on a different set of reasons (Welch 2003: 305–6). The seventeenth-century political thinker Thomas Hobbes, who admired *The History of the Peloponnesian War*, pondered this inconsistency (Welch 2003: 305–6). Hobbes concluded that we must ignore the superficial details about what the Spartans actually said and accept Thucydides' deeper interpretation.

A sceptic might wonder how we know that Thucydides was right. Others might wonder whether we (or Hobbes) have understood Thucydides correctly (Welch 2003: 305–6). Alternatively, one might wonder whether Thucydides intended readers to notice the apparent contradiction and reflect more deeply on the combination of factors that might have motivated the Spartans. Readers encounter similar apparent contradictions and similar questions of interpretation in the works of other key thinkers on strategy, notably Machiavelli.

On other occasions, Thucydides offers readers more direction. In the first book of his history, for instance, he explains why he views the Peloponnesian War as the greatest 'movement' in world history – greater, even, than the legendary war against Troy or the more recent wars against Persia. In the process, he proposes general principles one can use to assess the impact of wars and other acts of strategy. Thucydides claims, for instance, that the war between Athens and Sparta was more significant than the wars of legendary times, not only because the states that took part in it controlled more people and territory, but because they possessed the economic, administrative and technological ability to expand over practically unlimited regions unless other states prevented them (Thucydides 1997: 4). Lines such as these help us understand how Thucydides might have interpreted other situations. If Thucydides were alive in the twenty-first century, for instance, he would probably be more concerned about power struggles among nations than about threats from terrorist groups.

The Peloponnesian War took place at the same time that Greek thinkers such as the physician Hippocrates were developing their concepts of the scientific method (Kagan 1965: 100–3). Knowing this gives readers further clues about how to use Thucydides' work to improve their understanding of strategy. Hippocrates studied diseases through a two-step process in which he observed their symptoms and then looked for patterns in his observations. *The History of the Peloponnesian War* uses almost exactly the same procedure to analyse the plague that spread through Athens in 430 BC. Thucydides seems to follow a similar approach when he describes purely strategic events. Therefore, one may assume both that he considered all the details in his history to be important, and that he believed that one could figure out what made them important by studying the ways in which they fit together to produce their final outcomes.

Thucydides provides exceptional amounts of detail when he describes speeches and debates. Since he appears to be using the

Hippocratic method, this suggests further points about understanding his work. First, he thinks that talk mattered. Thucydides apparently assumed that the speakers deliberately influenced meaningful strategic decisions. Many twentieth- and twenty-first-century scholars would disagree. The military historian Martin van Creveld, for instance, denies that rational planning and debate actually influence war (Van Creveld 1977: 236). (Van Creveld understands that military and political leaders think their plans and arguments make a difference, but he believes that those leaders are deluding themselves.)

Second, the likelihood that Thucydides took a Hippocratic approach suggests that he was interested not just in the things particular individuals said but in larger patterns. Thucydides was almost certainly sensitive to relationships among the speakers, to speakers' motivations for saying the sorts of things they said, to the ways in which listeners reacted and to the consequences of the speakers' statements. Other Greek thinkers of his period, notably Plato, presented their ideas by writing dialogues in which different characters made different arguments and readers had to make up their own minds which characters were right at any particular moment. Thucydides appears to have reported historical speeches for similar purposes.

Many authors overlook this point. International relations theorists, for instance, often claim that Thucydides was an early supporter of the school of thought called Realism. Such theorists often base these claims on a well-known line from Thucydides' work, which runs 'the strong do what they have the power to do and the weak accept what they have to accept.' Indeed, one sees this proposition presented as an established fact in university-level textbooks (Goldstein 1996: 56). Thucydides did not, however, say that he agreed with this position. To understand the line, one needs to consider it in context.

This line comes from an episode in which an Athenian army had landed on the hostile island of Melos. Athens was far stronger than Melos, but the Athenians hoped to avoid a costly battle. Therefore, they sent a group of envoys to convince the Melians to submit without a fight. The envoys began by saying that they did not want to waste time debating abstract moral principles. Instead, they suggested that both sides simply accept that 'the strong do what they have the power to do' and get on with the business of negotiating terms for Melos's surrender.

The Melians refused to give in, indicating, at a minimum, that the Athenians' blunt statement failed as a negotiating technique. The fact that Athens later defeated Melos and put the entire male population to death suggests that the Athenians themselves behaved the way realist theorists often claim that people behave, but the fact that Athens eventually lost the Peloponnesian War suggests that such realism may be insufficient as a guide to long-term strategy. Thucydides himself probably wanted readers to consider all of these points and more. Although he apparently saw some truth in the statement about the strong and the weak, he also apparently wanted readers to recognize the shortcomings in that way of thinking.

Three strategic debates

Thucydides offers readers a great deal of information and little guidance about how to work their way through it. Those who wish to learn from his writings must make up their own minds which of his themes to pursue. What remains of this chapter will introduce Thucydides' ideas by exploring three key episodes from his history. The first of these episodes is the one in which the Spartans decided to go to war with Athens. The second is the one in which the Athenian statesman Pericles developed a strategy for his people to use in response.

A third takes place seventeen years later, after Athens and Sparta had signed a truce and the Peloponnesian War seemed to be at least temporarily over. At that point, a different war between Sicilian city-states presented the Athenians with an opportunity to conquer the entire island of Sicily. The Athenians debated the question of whether or not to seize this opportunity. In each of these episodes, this chapter will discuss in some detail the way Thucydides described the process by which the various states made critical strategic decisions. The chapter will then summarize the aftermath of those decisions more briefly.

Focusing on these episodes is a useful way to begin studying Thucydides for two reasons. First, these episodes mark turning points in the history of the Peloponnesian War. By exploring them, one gains a basic understanding of the events that inspired Thucydides' work. Second, these episodes featured debates in which historical figures discussed basic issues in strategic thought. Among other things, these historical figures discussed what they hoped to accomplish by going to war, how they thought that military force would help them to accomplish it and what problems they expected to encounter in the process. Thucydides goes on to show that the reality of war practically always proves more complex than even the wisest strategists anticipated.

Simple principles

Sparta's decision to fight Athens was, in many ways, the point at which the Peloponnesian War began. Nevertheless, Thucydides does not begin his history with this event. Thucydides appears to believe – and probably rightly – that anyone who wants to understand Sparta's decision needs to know about the events and arguments that led up to it. The Peloponnesian War, like so many wars, grew out of a series of less-remembered conflicts among small states.

One of those states, Corcyra, appealed to Athens for protection from its opponent Corinth. In 433 BC, the Athenians voted to support the Corcyraeans. Although Corinth had once been strong, it could no longer defeat such a formidable opponent as Athens. The Corinthians did, however, have an alliance with Sparta, the one power that could.

The Corinthians, along with several of Sparta's other allied states, petitioned Sparta to declare war on Athens. Initially, Sparta's leaders were reluctant to do so. In July of 432, however, Sparta's governing assembly agreed to let representatives from Corinth and their other allied states present their case. Sparta's allies proposed several key ideas about the reasons why states should consider war and the factors that might influence them.

First, Corinth's supporters attempted to 'inflame' the Spartans by accusing the Athenians of violating various treaties and of inciting revolts against their allied states (Thucydides 1997: 34–5). After Sparta's smaller allies had made these appeals, the Corinthian ambassadors offered a more intellectual argument. The Corinthians accused Sparta's leaders of being naive about international politics. 'Time after time', they claimed, they had warned the Spartans about Athens's aggressive moves to subjugate the Greek world, and time after time, the Spartans had found reasons to disregard the warnings.

Now, the Corinthians claimed, Sparta could no longer afford to procrastinate. If it did not curb the growth of Athens, the Athenians would become unstoppable. Thus, the allies advanced two distinct ways of looking at the function of war. Sparta's lesser allies had emphasized the moral and emotional dimensions of war, urging the Spartans to take up arms to right a wrong. Corinth portrayed war as a tool for preventing potential rivals from putting themselves in a position from which they might threaten you.

One notes that the Corinthians were not merely talking about defending one's homeland against invasion – they were urging the

Spartans to prevent such an invasion before it could begin by countering Athens's moves in remote places. Professional strategic thinkers may be pleased to observe that the Corinthian approach guarantees them a steady supply of work. The Corinthians assume that successful strategy requires long-term planning and continual awareness of how other states' long-term plans might unfold. Corinth's ambassadors also called for expert assessment of all strategically relevant events, even those, such as the dispute over Corcyra, which might superficially seem obscure.

Corinth's ambassadors went on to suggest that different societies make strategy in different ways. They have different needs, different capabilities, different weaknesses and different ways of conducting affairs. A wise strategist takes such differences into account when interpreting other states' behaviour, and when making policies for dealing with those states. Moreover, a wise strategist must think critically about his or her own society's approach, so as to avoid falling into attractive but dangerous patterns of behaviour.

Sparta, the Corinthian ambassadors claimed, had permitted Athens to grow strong at least partially because of its people's conservative attitudes. Spartans traditionally resisted new ideas, avoided foreign adventures and fought, when necessary, on the defensive. Indeed, the Corinthians stated, the Spartans had elevated their preferred policy of mutual non-interference to the level of a moral principle (Thucydides 1997: 37).

A more objective observer might have noted that the Spartans adopted this attitude for practical reasons, as well as traditional and psychological ones. Sparta's territory had not always belonged to the Spartan people. The Spartans had conquered it and enslaved the original population. At the time of the Peloponnesian War, the slave population, known as the helots, greatly outnumbered the ruling Spartans. Whenever Sparta's leaders contemplated sending troops abroad, they had to consider the possibility that the helots would take advantage of the foreign distraction to revolt.

Nevertheless, the Corinthians warned, Sparta's time-worn approach would prove fatal against Athens. The Athenians, Corinth's ambassadors claimed, 'are addicted to innovation' (Thucydides 1997: 36). Where Spartans were willing to accept an austere lifestyle in order to preserve stability, the Corinthians alleged, Athenians remained eager for new adventures even when they already possessed more than they could use (Thucydides 1997: 37). If Spartans based their foreign policy on the ethic of live and let live, the Corinthians concluded, Athenians did the opposite (Thucydides 1997: 37).

Corinth's ambassadors acknowledged that the Athenians often paid a price for their boldness. The Athenians, they noted, frequently gambled on poor odds and suffered the inevitable consequences (Thucydides 1997: 37). Nevertheless, the Corinthians added, the Athenians were also quick to recover from setbacks. The Athenians also applied their minds to the task of developing improved ways to accomplish their goals (Thucydides 1997: 37).

In this respect, the Corinthians' claimed, the Athenian approach was objectively superior. 'It is the law as in art, so in politics, that improvements ever prevail . . .' (Thucydides 1997: 37). Against such an opponent, the Corinthians argued, Spartan conservatism had become morally and practically obsolete. If Sparta wished to preserve stability, they warned, it would have to go beyond merely resisting direct acts of aggression. It would have to take the initiative and use its own power 'justly' (Thucydides 1997: 37).

At that time, a group of Athenian citizens happened to be in Sparta. Thucydides leaves their reasons for being there ambiguous (Thucydides 1997: 38). Historian Donald Kagan argues that they were, in fact, authorized representatives of the Athenian government and that their unspecified 'business' was merely a pretext to excuse their presence at the time when Corinth and its supporters were making their case (Kagan 1994: 54). Whatever the Athenians' original mission, they asked to address the assembly as well, and the Spartans agreed to hear them.

The Athenians discussed recent history at length, claiming that their city had achieved supremacy honourably and used its power responsibly. Nevertheless, they added that little of this mattered. Like the Corinthians, the Athenians offered the Spartans advice about strategy. Where the Corinthian concept of strategy had emphasized differences among states, the Athenian concept emphasized similarities.

All states, the Athenians said, follow the principle that the strong rule and the weak submit (Thucydides 1997: 41). All respond to the 'pressure' of 'fear, honour and interest' (Thucydides 1997: 41). Moreover, although one must admire those who attempt to treat weaker states fairly, it is natural for those states to resent domination. If Sparta had been in Athens's position, they suggested, it would have behaved in much the same way as Athens did, and if Sparta was to oust Athens as the dominant power, it would provoke the same resistance that Athens was encountering.

Thus, the Athenians claimed, the Spartans had no need to view the Athenians as unusually threatening, nor did they have any grounds for believing that they could change the Greek world for the better by overthrowing Athens as the dominant power. Like the Corinthians, the Athenians urged the Spartans to think dispassionately about the strategic questions before them. The Corinthians, however, had portrayed the nature of strategy in a way that made it seem as if Sparta was facing a crisis in which only drastic action could prevent catastrophe. The Athenians suggested that the events Sparta was facing were routine, and that drastic action was unlikely to justify the risk: '[C]onsider the vast influence of accident in war, before you are engaged in it' (Thucydides 1997: 42). Better, they concluded, to settle matters through negotiation and well-considered planning, rather than to plunge into combat and permit the struggle to take on a brutal, unpredictable life of its own.

In addition to its Assembly and several other branches of government, Sparta had two kings. One of those kings, Archidamus, urged his countrymen to take a moderate course, preparing for war in case fighting should become unavoidable but pursuing Athens's offer of a peaceful settlement. The Assembly, however, voted to declare war without further negotiations, and the rest of the Spartan government confirmed that decision later in the summer. Even as the Corinthians feared, Sparta's leaders put off fighting for over a year, but their allied state Thebes independently attacked Athens's allied state of Plataea the following summer, provoking a crisis which forced Sparta to send an army against Athens.

Both the Corinthians and the Athenians summed up simple principles for strategists to consider when contemplating war. Readers of *The Peloponnesian War* often assume that Thucydides himself was arguing in favour of these principles. Thucydides does, as noted above, claim that the Spartans declared war because they feared the growth of Athenian power. This may not prove that he personally accepted the Corinthian argument but it indicates that he believed that the Spartans did. Moreover, if imitation is the sincerest form of flattery, one may note that Thucydides habitually explains strategic decisions in terms of 'fear, honour and interest', suggesting that he agrees with the Athenian speakers about those issues.

Complex realities

Although Thucydides seems to see value in concisely stated principles, he also emphasizes that such principles can never be more than a starting point for strategy. Every strategic decision is different, and a mind-boggling range of issues may affect each one, depending on the circumstances of particular cases. Throughout his work, Thucydides alternates between describing speeches in which people sum up strategic issues in simple terms and describing the complications that arise when those people attempt to put their simple ideas into practice. One sees examples of this contrast in the sections where Thucydides discusses Athens's entry into the war.

The Corinthians may (or may not) have been right to argue that Athens was gradually making itself more dangerous to the other Greek city-states. They were wrong to imply that the Athenians were recklessly seeking conquests in 433. Many Athenian citizens had, in fact, been reluctant to join forces with Corcyra. Although Athens gained a strategic advantage by combining its navy with the Corcyraean fleet, the Athenians only agreed to the alliance after the Corcyraeans stressed the point that, if Athens abandoned them to defeat at the hands of Corinth, the Corinthians would gain control of Corcyra's ships instead (Kagan 1995: 42–5). This would endanger Athens in any future war with Corinth or its ally Sparta.

Despite having such powerful motives of interest and fear, the Athenians dispatched only ten of their 200 warships to Corcyra (Kagan 1995: 46). Moreover, the Athenians ordered the commanders of those ships only to fight if Corinthian forces actually assaulted the Corcyraeans. Kagan interprets this as evidence that the Athenians were trying to balance a policy of deterring Corinth from attacking Corcyra with a policy of avoiding any dramatic action that might provoke a larger war (Kagan 1995: 46–7). Whatever the Athenians' intention, they were clearly responding to strategic dilemmas that none of the speakers before the Spartan assembly had fully accounted for with a mix of policies that none of the speakers before the Spartan assembly had fully described.

If Kagan is right about these issues, the Athenian policy failed. Corinth refused to back down in the face of Athens's show of force. The Spartans gave the Athenians little credit for their self-restraint. Sparta and its allies attacked Athens's home territory of Attica, forcing the Athenians to defend their land in an all-out war.

The Spartan-led army greatly outnumbered Athens's land forces. If the Athenian army had followed the ancient Greek tradition of marching out to fight its opponents on an open field, it would have faced almost certain destruction. Nevertheless, even as the Corinthian ambassadors had warned the Spartans, the Athenians appreciated the value of creativity in war. An Athenian general and popular leader named Pericles proposed an innovative strategy for repulsing Sparta's attack.

Pericles clearly stated his overall goal. In his view, Athens had to avoid giving Sparta any indication that it would submit to intimidation. If the Athenians offered the concessions to avoid war, he warned, the Spartans would merely return with greater demands (Thucydides 1997: 72–3). Accordingly, in his view, the Athenians had to demonstrate that they were willing and able to defend their independence against all challenges.

This goal did not require Athens to destroy Sparta's army. Therefore, Pericles advised his fellow citizens not to engage the Spartan army in battle at all. The city walls of Athens were virtually impregnable, given the siege technology of the time. Moreover, the Athenians had extended the walls to protect the road that led to their main port, the smaller – and also walled – city of Piraeus. If the Athenians chose to remain behind their walls, the Spartans could not force them to come out.

Given these facts, Pericles argued, Athens was stronger than Sparta. Like the Corinthian ambassadors before the Spartan assembly, he stressed the point that different states have different capabilities and behave in different ways. Sparta, he noted, was a society of farmers. Although its people worked hard in peace and served willingly in war, they had no wealth to support a long campaign. They fought wars by overwhelming their enemies with their land forces, but, if that failed, they lacked the resources to attempt alternative approaches, or even to continue with their traditional methods for an extended time. Moreover, Sparta's government was poorly organized for adapting to unfamiliar circumstances and unlikely to remain committed to a long war.

The Athenians, on the other hand, were merchants and seafarers. Their way of life had allowed them to accumulate money, and their ships allowed them to trade throughout the world. Therefore, they did not need to farm, nor did they need to defend any territory beyond their well-fortified cities. As long as the cities of Athens and Piraeus remained safe, the Athenians could afford to let the Spartans overrun their other lands. Athens could support itself through trade and wait for its enemies to exhaust themselves.

Once the Spartans realized that waging war against Athens was costly and futile, Pericles predicted, they would withdraw. That experience, he hoped, would teach the Spartans that they could neither intimidate the Athenians nor conquer them. Given the Spartans' aversion to risk and expense, they would be particularly unlikely to try again. One notes that Pericles presented this process as something that would happen of its own accord. Although he suggested that Athens might pressure Sparta to abandon the war faster by using its fleet to raid its enemies' coasts, he urged his countrymen not to 'combine schemes of fresh conquest with the conduct of the war', adding that he was 'more afraid of our own blunders than of the enemy's devices' (Thucydides 1997: 75–6).

Just as Pericles sought a way to neutralize Sparta's numerical superiority in ground forces, the Spartans – demonstrating more imagination than either Pericles or the Corinthians appear to have given them credit for – attempted to undermine Athens's strategy by turning the Athenians against one another. Most Athenians felt loyal to their ancestral villages, even though they acknowledged the city of Athens as their capital. As Archidamus led the Spartan army into Athenian territory, he allowed his troops to pillage some of those villages and not others, hoping that if he could not goad his enemies into emerging from their fortifications to defend their towns, he could at least provoke resentment and suspicion between those who had lost their homes and those who, as yet, had not.

Archidamus' strategy almost succeeded. Athenian citizens, outraged by the spectacle of enemies devastating their lands within sight of their city walls, gathered in a mob to demand action. Pericles prevented them from staging a suicidal counter-attack only by refusing to convene an assembly that would have allowed them to vote on the issue. Fate then struck the Athenians an even more devastating blow. A plague broke out within the city walls (Thucydides 1997: 103).

For a time, Athens descended into anarchy. People openly committed crimes and debaucheries of all kinds, assuming that they would die of the illness before they suffered any other consequences (Thucydides 1997: 104). The plague eventually subsided and the Athenians restored order in their streets. Nevertheless, after two years of such sufferings, few survivors wished to turn back to fighting Sparta. Indeed, the Athenian citizens voted to offer the Spartans their surrender.

Pericles remained convinced that yielding to Sparta, even on negotiated terms, would ultimately destroy Athens's independence. The statesman addressed his fellow citizens and convinced them to continue the war. Shortly afterwards, Pericles died. As previously noted, Thucydides normally refrains from openly stating his own beliefs. At this point in his history, he makes an exception.

Athens was at its greatest, Thucydides writes, during the years when Pericles was in office (Thucydides 1997: 110). Thucydides attributes this to the fact that Pericles was a man who could 'lead [the multitude] instead of being led by them'. Thus, Pericles was able to pursue a policy of prudent moderation in state affairs, preventing the Athenian public from giving in either to manias or to despair. Pericles also kept less public-spirited citizens from hijacking state policy for their own ends. Later Athenian leaders, Thucydides comments, permitted excess, emotion and egoism to prevail (Thucydides 1997: 111).

At first, the Athenians may have welcomed many of the changes. Pericles' moderate policies may have avoided risk and tempered the people's passions, but they were insufficient as a military strategy. After two years, the Spartans had not given up on the war. Moreover, although they had not found a way to breach Athens's walls, they had already come up with one innovative plan, and might develop newer and more threatening ones at any time. A future plague, or some other twist of fortune, might weaken Athens enough to permit the Spartans to destroy it.

To prevent such a catastrophe, the Athenians had to strike blows as well as receive them. Athens had to undercut Sparta's surprising will and ability to carry on the fight. Pericles himself had pointed out that Athens's navy gave it a tool for doing so. Hit-and-run raids, however, did not inflict enough damage to interfere with Sparta's war effort. Despite Pericles' misgivings, Athens had no choice but to counter-attack on a grand scale. Whatever the virtues of Pericles' original approach, his successors had to adapt it to their circumstances.

Athens and Sparta fought for eight more years. Athens eventually prevailed, partially because its generals disregarded Pericles' warning against 'fresh conquests'. In 425, the Athenians seized a strip of Spartan territory known as Pylos. Afterwards, rather than withdrawing to safety as Pericles' original strategy might have suggested, they occupied it and built a fortress there. They then used this fortress as a base to incite rebellion among Sparta's helot population. The following year, the Athenians seized the island of Cythera. This gave them a second base on the other side of Sparta's coast.

As the Athenians won victories, they took increasing numbers of Spartan soldiers prisoner. Sparta could not afford to lose these forces, especially at a time when it faced a helot revolt in its own territory, and the Spartan government became increasingly eager to get the prisoners back. Athens's combined successes forced some of Sparta's allies out of the war and tempted others to change sides, undercutting the warrior state's previous advantage in numbers of troops (Thucydides 1997: 268). The campaigns in that period had not, however, been one-sided – Sparta had also struck at crucial parts of the Athenian Empire, inflicting such casualties that, in Thucydides' judgement, the Athenians lost whatever confidence their victories might have inspired (Thucydides

1997: 268). (The Spartan general Brasidas' campaign against Thrace, described in Box 2.1 on Thucydides' career, was the centrepiece of this Spartan counter-attack.) Both sides now wanted peace, both feared the outcome of further battles and, accordingly, both sides signed a peace treaty in 421.

Box 2.1 Thucydides' Career

Scholars have little certain knowledge of Thucydides' life. The historian was born in approximately 460 BC and died shortly after Athens's final defeat in 404.

Much of what we know about his career comes from his own history, in which he mentions himself in passing. Thucydides and his troops were stationed on the island of Thasos, off the coast of a region known as Thrace.

Despite the fact that this region is across the Aegean Sea from the Athenian home territory of Attica, the cities of Thrace were among Athens's most valuable allies. Thrace provided the timber Athens needed to build its ships. The Thracians also contributed a substantial portion of the funds Athens needed to purchase grain and other necessities. Moreover, the river Strymon flowed through western Thrace from north to south, standing in the way of any Spartan land army that might wish to attack other Athenian allies farther east. The Thracian cities of Eion, on the coast and Amphipolis, farther inland, controlled key crossings over the river.

Although the Thracians had pledged to support Athens, many resented Athenian influence and would have welcomed a Spartan victory. This may be one of the reasons why the Athenians sent Thucydides there. Thucydides tells us that he personally owned gold mines in the region, and that he had 'great influence' with its inhabitants (Thucydides 1997: 244). His family and business contacts might have given him an advantage in detecting and overcoming Thracian plots to betray the Athenians to Sparta.

In the winter of 424, a Spartan general named Brasidas invaded Thrace. Despite Thucydides' connections, Brasidas managed to contact a clique of Amphipolitan citizens who were willing to help him. Amphipolis relied on a bend in the river for its outer defences. Brasidas attacked the bridges crossing the river, taking advantage of a snowstorm to conceal his troops as they approached. Meanwhile, his supporters in the city attacked the bridge garrison from behind.

Brasidas captured the bridges and overran the outer districts of the city. At that, panic spread throughout Amphipolis. Since Amphipolitan traitors had helped Brasidas, no one knew whom to trust. Thucydides speculates that, if Brasidas had attacked Amphipolis' fortified inner section immediately, he could have stormed the entire city that very night. Brasidas then could have marched south and attacked Eion, which would probably have fallen as well. Thucydides estimates that the entire process would have taken little over a day.

Instead, Brasidas halted his advance and gave his troops permission to loot. Thucydides suggests that he was waiting for his supporters within the city to stage a larger uprising. If so, he was disappointed, because the uprising did not come. This delay gave Athens's supporters in Amphipolis time to man the inner walls with reliable troops and send a message to Thucydides.

Thucydides writes that his forces on Thasos were 'half a day's sail' from Amphipolis (Thucydides 1997: 244). Naturally, he set out at once to lift the siege and to reinforce Eion. Brasidas realized that he had to act swiftly. Therefore, he offered the inhabitants of Amphipolis the right to remain in their homes and enjoy all their customary political rights – or, if they preferred, to leave unmolested – if only they would surrender the city to him. By the standards of ancient Greek warfare, this was an extremely generous offer and the Amphipolitans accepted it.

Therefore, by the time Thucydides' forces reached the mainland, Amphipolis had fallen. Brasidas promptly assaulted Eion from multiple directions, using boats to strike the point at which the city defences encountered the river while the rest of his forces attacked overland. Thucydides' forces beat off the attack. The historian appears to take some pride in the speed with which he managed to land his troops and organize a successful defence.

Although Thucydides had saved Eion, Thrace was now in danger. The generous surrender terms that Brasidas offered the Amphipolitans turned out to have broad value as propaganda. Citizens of other cities sent messengers to Brasidas, promising to open their gates to him in return for similar treatment. These developments provoked an uproar in Athens.

The Athenians held Thucydides at least partially responsible for the disaster. Accordingly, they stripped him of his command. Thucydides then left Athens permanently, possibly to avoid trial, or possibly because the Athenian assembly sentenced him to banishment. This period of exile may have helped him refine his history, both because it gave him time to revise his work at leisure and because it allowed him to gather information from Sparta's supporters. One may speculate about how his own experiences may have influenced his view of such matters as politics in the Athenian democracy.

Sicily

The Athenians forced the Spartans to make peace by drawing on their traditional boldness and willingness to innovate. Thus, *The History of the Peloponnesian War* implies that this spirit of initiative is vital to the art of strategy. To quote the motto of Britain's Special Air Service, fortune favours the brave. Nevertheless, Thucydides seldom suggests a principle without also exploring situations in which that principle fails to account for the complexities of practice. Boldness served Athens well in 425 and 426, but, even as Pericles feared, the Athenians ultimately went too far.

Even as the war which began over Corcyra ended, new wars among other minor states broke out. On the island of Sicily, the city of Egesta attacked a neighbouring people called the Selinuntines. The Selinuntines had an alliance with Syracuse, the dominant city-state on the island. Syracuse honoured this alliance by attacking Egesta, prompting the Egestaeans, who had an alliance with Athens, to send to the Athenians for aid.

This presented Athens with the opportunity to seize all of Sicily on the pretext of supporting their ally. Sicily was rich, and many younger Athenians perceived a campaign to conquer it as a glorious adventure. Moreover, Syracuse was allied to Sparta. The Egestaeans warned the Athenians that it would be wise for them to subjugate Syracuse while they had the opportunity, rather than waiting and taking the risk that a stronger Syracuse might join forces with their enemies once again in some future conflict.

Despite the fact that Athens had a great deal to gain by conquering Sicily, doing so was bound to be difficult. Sicily was across the Ionian Sea from Athens, on the fringes of the Greek world. Moreover, it was a large island with a large population. In Thucydides' judgement, an Athenian campaign to subdue Sicily was fated to be almost as difficult as Athens's war with Sparta itself (Thucydides 1997: 313).

Thucydides states that most Athenians failed to understand how challenging a war to conquer Sicily would be. Although the Athenians sent scouts to visit Sicily and evaluate the situation there, this effort did little to improve their understanding, since the Egestaeans beguiled the scouts into presenting a report slanted to make the prospect of invading Sicily seem as alluring as possible. Thucydides characterizes this report as being 'as attractive as it was untrue' (Thucydides 1997: 317). The Athenians accordingly voted to send a fleet of 60 ships to aid Egesta and 'order all other matters in Sicily as they should deem best for the interests of Athens' (Thucydides 1997: 317).

Five days later, the Athenian general Nicias, a hero of the war against Sparta, called on his fellow citizens to reconsider. Nicias, perhaps unlike many other Athenians, understood that invading Sicily would involve extraordinary risk and expense. Such a project would have been questionable under any circumstances. Moreover, Nicias warned, Sparta remained as hostile and powerful as ever. The Spartans could break the peace treaty at any moment. Under those circumstances, Nicias argued, the idea of starting a new war with a new set of enemies was foolhardy.

Supporters of invading Sicily then responded to Nicias' argument. The most prominent advocate of war was the dashing Olympic champion Alcibiades, famous both for his ambitions and for his lavish lifestyle. Alcibiades transparently hoped to gain money (of which he was chronically short) and fame by leading an invasion force. Where others might have attempted to divert attention from their extravagance and personal motivations, Alcibiades claimed these traits as virtues. To those who objected that he put his own interests before the common good, he responded that, by showing the world how magnificently an Athenian could live, he was helping the entire city develop a valuable reputation for wealth and power.

Alcibiades then encouraged the Athenians to hope that conquering Sicily could be easy. Nicias may have been right to warn of possible difficulties, but those difficulties were not inevitable. A well-informed and imaginative strategist could surmount them. Alcibiades listed numerous opportunities that such a strategist might exploit, ranging from the Sicilians' tendency to fight among themselves to the fact that many of the barbarian tribes that inhabited the western Mediterranean hated Syracuse and would probably be willing to join forces with the Athenians for an attack on that city. Athens's navy would allow it to land troops where it found opportunities – and to withdraw them from wherever it encountered setbacks – thus allowing the Athenians to maximize their gains and minimize their risks.

One notes that Alcibiades enticed the Athenians with many of the same ideas that other strategists discussed at other points in *The History of the Peloponnesian War*. Like the Corinthians before the Spartan Assembly, he stressed the nearly limitless potential of innovation. Like Archidamus, he sought opportunities to manipulate political situations to undermine enemy states from within. Like Pericles, he appreciated the strategic advantages of sea power.

Although Alcibiades and Pericles might have agreed about means, they differed over goals. Pericles had sought to preserve Athenian independence through a firm but judiciously applied policy of self-defence. Alcibiades urged the Athenians to expand their empire as aggressively as they could, for 'if we cease to rule others, we are in danger of being ruled ourselves' (Thucydides 1997: 323). Not only did Alcibiades think in the way that Athens's enemies accused the stereotypical Athenian of thinking, he proudly admitted to it (Thucydides 1997: 324).

The Athenians responded to Alcibiades' speech with wild enthusiasm. Since Nicias did not believe that he could convince his fellow citizens that invading Sicily was a bad idea, he tried a different tactic. Nicias pretended to have accepted the decision to send a fleet to Sicily. He then suggested that the Athenians discuss the practicalities of doing so.

Nicias described the challenges that an invasion force would encounter, and the resources it would need to overcome them. Sixty ships, he warned, might not be enough. To maximize its chances of victory and minimize its chances of failure, Athens should attack with overwhelming strength, both in ships and in ground forces. According to Thucydides, the cautious general hoped that the Athenian people would grow discouraged when they realized how much sacrifice attacking Sicily would require (Thucydides 1997: 326).

Nicias may have hoped to quell the Athenians' appetite for war, but his words had the opposite effect. The idea of mounting an enormous campaign further excited the war's potential supporters while reassuring many who had previously doubted the wisdom of invading Sicily. The Athenians elected Nicias, Alcibiades and a third general named Lamachus to share responsibility for commanding the expedition.

Whatever Alcibiades' flaws, his plan for conquering Sicily might have worked. The Athenians, however, proved unable to execute his plan, largely due to failings within their democratic political system. The first of their mistakes concerned a scandal and a political intrigue. One morning, as the three generals prepared their forces, the people of Athens awoke to discover that unknown vandals had defaced the sacred statues of the god Hermes that stood throughout the city. Alcibiades' political opponents suggested that he had taken part in the crime.

Alcibiades volunteered to stand trial immediately, so that the Athenians could remove him from his position as general if they found him guilty, and so that he could command his forces with a clear reputation if they found him innocent. His enemies, however, realized that he would convince the Athenians to acquit him if he had the opportunity to speak in his own defence. Therefore, they postponed the trial, hoping that it would be easier to convict him of more serious charges later.

The three generals and their invasion fleet set sail. When the vast Athenian armada arrived off the coast of Sicily, however, Nicias' strategy of attacking with overwhelming force produced unintended results. The size of the fleet made it clear that the Athenians had come for no other reason than to conquer new territory for their empire. Many of the peoples who had previously supported them became wary that, if they permitted the Athenian conquest to succeed, Athens would soon impose control over them as well.

The Athenians had counted on being able to buy supplies and repair their ships in friendly ports. Instead, those ports refused to allow them to land. In order to obtain provisions, they had to divide their fleet, take detours from their original route and plot against states that they had formerly relied on as allies. Meanwhile, in Athens itself, Alcibiades' opponents contrived to charge the flamboyant general not only with mutilating the sacred statues but with plotting to overthrow the democracy. Accordingly, the Athenians sent a ship to bring Alcibiades back to face trial and almost certain execution.

Alcibiades fled, and eventually defected to Athens's enemies. That left Nicias as the senior commander of the Athenian expedition. Although Nicias felt more certain than ever that invading Sicily had been a mistake, he feared the public reaction if he returned to Athens without even attempting to do what the Athenians had sent him west to do. Therefore, he remained with his forces in Sicily but conducted the campaign as cautiously as possible – thus missing one opportunity after another.

Syracuse, which had been vulnerable in the early phases of the campaign, corrected its weaknesses and convinced Sparta to enter the war on its side. After two years of fighting, the Spartans and Syracusans destroyed Athens's fleet and massacred the Athenian army. That left Athens at war with Sparta once again, and this time it had crippled itself by raising the most powerful land and naval forces it could muster and sending those forces across the sea to their doom. Athens fought on for another year, but its cause had become hopeless. In the face of imminent defeat, a clique of powerful Athenian citizens staged a coup, ending the Athenian democracy.

Thucydides ends his history abruptly, with these crises unresolved. Other authors, notably Xenophon, discuss the turbulent years that followed. In those years, the Athenian people regained and lost their democratic system of government multiple times. Meanwhile, the Spartans defeated what remained of Athens's land and sea forces and forced the Athenians to accept dependent status within a Sparta-dominated Greece. Athens ultimately survived as a state, but only by submitting to its enemy.

Conclusion

As Thucydides describes Athens's long journey to self-inflicted defeat, he continually raises points about strategy. Indeed, he raises more issues than any particular reader is likely to be able to absorb at any particular time. To complicate the reader's task further, he revisits many issues repeatedly, and his lessons often seem to contradict one another. Athens could not have defeated Sparta if it had not boldly conquered Pylos and Cythera, but it would not have exposed itself to destruction if it had not boldly set out to conquer Sicily. *The History of the Peloponnesian War* is far richer in ideas than the ancient Chinese manuals on strategy, but even specialists in classical studies find it difficult to be sure what those ideas mean.

Readers are entitled to feel frustrated. These sorts of difficulties prompted scholar David Welch to write an article titled 'Why International Relations Theorists Should Stop Reading Thucydides' (Welch 2003: *passim*). Thucydides' defence might well be that he wrote about things that actually happened. His work is complex because strategy is complex.

As Welch himself ultimately concludes, the difficulty of interpreting Thucydides seems to reflect a gap between making strategy in the real world and explaining strategy in terms that satisfy academic theorists (Welch 2003: 318). Sun Tzu wrote as a theorist when he suggested that he had identified five basic factors that would allow anyone who mastered them to win wars (Tao 1987: 95). Thucydides offers no such rules for strategists to follow.

Thucydides does, however, suggest a reason why Athens survived siege and plague at the beginning of the war only to collapse at a point when it seemed to have become powerful. The historian attributes Athens's fortunes to the personal qualities of its leaders. Pericles did not preserve Athens's freedom by applying the 'right' strategic principles – indeed, as earlier sections have noted, Pericles' strategy was flawed. Nevertheless, Pericles' judgement, integrity and broad vision of what Athens needed to accomplish in order to remain independent allowed him to lead effectively. Readers are entitled to hope that, by reflecting on the situations Thucydides described, they can learn to think at least a little more like Pericles.

Further reading

Kagan, Donald (1969) *The Outbreak of the Peloponnesian War*. Ithaca, NY: Cornell University Press.

Kagan, Donald (1974) *The Archidamian War*. Ithaca, NY: Cornell University Press.

Kagan, Donald (1981) *The Peace of Nicias and the Sicilian Expedition*. Ithaca, NY: Cornell University Press.

Pangle, Thomas L. and Ahrensdorf, Peter J. (1999) *Justice Among Nations: On the Moral Basis of Power and Peace*. Lawrence, KS: University Press of Kansas, ch. 1.

Thucydides (1997) *The History of the Peloponnesian War*, trans. Richard Crawley. Ware: Wordsworth Classics.

3 CONQUERING FORTUNE

Chapter 1 noted that the downfall of the Ch'in Empire inspired Chinese strategists to ponder the limits of military power. The downfall of the Roman Empire inspired European strategists to ponder the humiliations of military weakness. These explorations of Rome's military decline suggested far-reaching ideas about society itself. The Romans themselves commonly assumed that they had achieved glory through their collective virtues, and that they had later lost it due to their shared corruption (Rapoport 1968: 413). In this spirit, those who have sought strategic lessons from the Roman experience have often ended up commenting not merely upon war in the narrow sense but upon all the attitudes and institutions of the people who wage it.

Two commentators on Rome's rise and Rome's fall stand out for their influence on current understandings of strategy. These are the fourth-century Roman author Flavius Vegetius Renatus, whose *De re militari* helped to preserve Rome's strategic tradition into the gunpowder age, and the fifteenth-century Florentine author Niccolò Machiavelli, who reprised the writings of several Romans – including Vegetius – in his treatises on the exercise of power. No less a strategic thinker than Carl von Clausewitz declared that the Florentine's works are essential to anyone with an interest in politics and war: 'No reading is more necessary than that of Machiavelli' (Aron 1985: 58).

This chapter explores these authors' contributions, focusing on their ideas about how communities acquire strategic capabilities. Both writers advise strategists on how to wage war and engage in other forms of conflict. Both also explore the links which connect social strength to administrative effectiveness to military and political power. The first section summarizes important themes from *De re militari*, discussing the reasons why strategists in later centuries have continued to find this work valuable. A second section discusses the ways in which Machiavelli expands similar ideas into a more comprehensive guide to establishing a powerful state and wielding its power effectively. Machiavelli's advice appears clear and persuasive. Nevertheless, the Florentine's teachings have deep implications, and strategists are wise to consider those implications carefully before attempting to become Machiavellians.

Box 3.1   Who were the Authors?

Vegetius reveals certain details about his life in his writings, and scholars are reasonably confident that they have deduced others, but his precise identity remains a mystery. He was almost certainly a Christian who held a high position within the Roman government, and he probably intended *De re militari* for Emperor Theodosius I, who reigned from 379 to 395 AD (Dorjahn and Born 1934: 150; Shrader 1981: 168). Researchers have determined that Vegetius lacked military experience of his own, and probably served Theodosius as a finance minister (Dorjahn and Born 1934: 150; Shrader 1981: 168). Vegetius' lack of such experience may help explain why he was so quick to describe his personal knowledge of warfare as mediocre, and his role within the bureaucracy may help explain how he developed such an acute appreciation of the administrative dimension of strategy.

Machiavelli was not a soldier either, but few could accuse him of lacking first-hand knowledge of war or politics. Although his family came from the lesser nobility, his parents were poor. '[A]t an early age', he once remarked in a letter to a friend, '[I] learned how to scrimp rather than to thrive' (Viroli 2005: 12). Such a background could easily have excluded him from political life as well, since his aristocratic heritage won him no support from the democratically minded and his poverty brought him no respect among the upper class, but in 1498, at the age of 29, he scraped his way into a job within the Florentine bureaucracy. He initially served as a member of the second chancery, an administrative body which existed mainly to process government correspondence (Skinner 1981: 6).

Florence was, at that time, a republic, and its governing elite admired the intellectual movement known as humanism. This movement emphasized the Roman classics, and Quentin Skinner suggests that Machiavelli secured his position through his brilliance as a humanist scholar (Skinner 1981: 3). The young Machiavelli's background and abilities also happened to suit the political interests of certain newly influential Florentine politicians, and this may help to explain how he managed to establish himself as a secretary to the committee known as the Ten of War, which handled both military and diplomatic affairs (Skinner 1981: 6). Machiavelli went on to travel throughout Europe as a diplomat, to plan strategy in Florence's wars against Pisa and to direct the reorganization of the Florentine armed forces (Wood 1965: xii–xv).

Then, in 1512, troops of the Holy Roman Empire attacked Florence, overwhelmed its new army, abolished its republican government and reinstalled the Medici family as its rulers. Machiavelli lost his position in the government. In the winter of 1513, opponents of the Medici organized a conspiracy against the new rulers. Their plot failed, and although Machiavelli had not, in fact, been involved in it, he came under suspicion. The Medici had him questioned under torture, and, although his interrogators found no grounds to execute him, the new regime condemned him to imprisonment.

After his release, Machiavelli asked the Medici to let him serve in their government as he had once served under the Florentine Republic. As part of his campaign to win the new sovereigns' favour, Machiavelli presented Lorenzo de' Medici with the manuscript he entitled *The Prince*. The Medici, however, ignored Machiavelli's appeals, leaving him outcast and in poverty. This was the period in which he wrote *The Art of War* and *Discourses on Livy*, addressing them not to high officials, but to his friends.

Machiavelli spent over ten years as a political nonentity. In 1526, with help from Pope Clement VII, he finally secured a commission as secretary to the committee charged with renovating Florence's walls (Wood 1965: xvi). Within months, as fate would have it, another imperial army sacked Rome and defeated the Pope. The Medici family, which had relied on the Vatican to support its increasingly unpopular rule, fled Florence, and the city council reinstated the republic (Skinner 1981: 86–7). Once again, Machiavelli found himself on the losing side, and, once again, the new rulers dismissed him from government. Machiavelli became ill and died on 21 June 1527, less than a month after suffering this blow (Wood 1965: xvi).

Vegetius: uniting the whole

The opening lines of Vegetius' work suggest that *De re militari* will be a technical manual. Like many twenty-first-century handbooks of this nature, the work begins with what contemporary legal writers call a 'roadmap' – a paragraph listing the topics to be covered in later sections (Vegetius, 1993: 1). After this utilitarian start, Vegetius digresses to explain his reasons for composing such a work. Here, he portrays himself as a scholar who has chosen to write down his knowledge as a gift for the emperor (Vegetius 1993: 1–2).

In these lines, Vegetius seems to cultivate the idea that he is merely reviving the quaint custom of presenting rulers with learned treatises, without any particularly urgent occasion for doing so. Only at the end of his preface does he hint at more practical concerns. There, he expresses his hope that the emperor will be able to read *De re militari* and find useful material for managing the affairs of the state. Vegetius adds that the demands of statecraft are always urgent (Vegetius 1993: 1–2).

Vegetius then returns to the technical material he promised in his first lines. He bases his descriptions of military techniques on practices the Roman army followed during the periods when it was at its strongest, citing numerous earlier authors as sources (Vegetius 1993: 33). His first book begins by addressing such basic matters as where to find suitable young men for the army. Readers learn that peoples from hot regions possess greater intelligence, but lack the steadfast character needed for hand-to-hand combat (Vegetius 1993: 3). Although those from cold climates typically have more warlike personalities, they are also too stupid to be of much use, so it is best to choose soldiers from temperate regions (Vegetius 1993: 3).

De re militari goes on to explain induction procedures in detail, noting, for instance, the preferred height for a cavalryman (five feet, ten inches), the professions which produce good soldiers (trained blacksmiths are valuable but former pastry cooks should be shunned) and the exercises troops should perform in their training (Vegetius 1993: 6–8). Later chapters cover in equal depth techniques for organizing forces, directing campaigns, engaging in sieges and waging naval warfare. As Vegetius discusses the methods for performing various tasks, he also explains why he considers these activities important. In the process, he outlines a broader philosophy of the strategic art.

Like Sun Tzu, Vegetius urges strategists to apply all the powers of the human mind to achieve results as efficiently as possible. 'He who wishes a successful outcome, let him fight with strategy, not at random' (Vegetius 1993: 62). The Chinese author would have also applauded the Roman's emphasis on indirect means. 'It is preferable to subdue an enemy by famine, raids and terror, than in battle where fortune tends to have more influence than bravery' (Vegetius 1993: 108).

Vegetius places such faith in skill that he would voluntarily sacrifice the apparent advantages of numerical superiority (Vegetius 1993: 63). Oversized armies, he notes, are slower, more vulnerable to logistical shortfalls, potentially more casualty-prone, potentially more fragile psychologically and generally more vulnerable to accidents. For a commander who hopes to follow the example of Rome in its days of glory, smaller forces are actually more useful. In soldiers, Vegetius values discipline and martial expertise over physical strength (Vegetius 1993: 2–3). Although he certainly wants his troops to possess courage, he is even more concerned with deploying them in advantageous terrain (Vegetius 1993: 109).

Not only does Vegetius share many of Sun Tzu's aspirations, he frequently recommends similar means for achieving them. Like the Chinese author, he urges commanders to keep their forces versatile through painstaking attention to such matters as logistics, organization and communication. *De re militari* all but duplicates *The Art of War*'s widely quoted paean to intelligence: 'It is difficult to beat someone who can form a true estimate of his own and the enemy's forces' (Vegetius 1993: 109).

Nevertheless, *De re militari* warns, there are limits to the powers of ingenuity. Vegetius freely admits that the Greeks outdid the Romans in intellect and the arts (Vegetius 1993: 3). The Romans conquered the Greeks, not through brilliance but, in Vegetius' view, through discipline, selection of recruits, their physical training regime and 'acquaintance in field practice with all possible eventualities' (Vegetius 1993: 3). Vegetius believes that there are abstract principles of strategy, and that thoughtful leaders can apply them to win victories, but he is more concerned with institutionalizing a high standard of strategic practice throughout every level of his own side's armed forces than with conceiving a grand scheme to outwit the enemy commander.

This helps to explain why Vegetius provides so much detail about Roman military procedures. For him, procedure and strategy are inseparable. When he takes up the topic of campaign planning, he depicts commanders selecting from a short menu of possible actions. These commanders may commit their entire forces to pitched battle, or they may hold back and engage in skirmishes. The art of strategy, *De re militari* suggests, begins with determining which of these two approaches is most likely to prove effective under the prevailing circumstances (Vegetius 1993: 80–7).

Once commanders have determined which course to follow, their troops carry out the decision by performing well-rehearsed drills. Vegetius does not seem to think that this will limit troops' ability to adapt to the unexpected. On the contrary, he appears to think that it will help armed forces maintain the maximum possible degree of flexibility. The standard Roman battle formation, for instance, stipulated that the first troops to engage the enemy should advance six feet ahead of the soldiers behind them, so that every individual would remain free to rush forward, step back or take a running jump as he saw fit (Vegetius 1993: 89). Troops who had not learned to deploy in this carefully prescribed pattern could easily find themselves hemmed in by their own comrades at exactly the moment when they most needed freedom to act.

Standard methods provide commanders with a repertoire of actions. Cunning, knowledge, judgement and analytical skill come into play as commanders put these actions into execution. Thus, *De re militari* fuses historically successful recipes for carrying out various procedures with aphorisms for implementing these procedures shrewdly. Vegetius concludes his study of field strategy and tactics with a chapter listing 'general rules of war' (Vegetius 1993: 108–11).

These 'rules' are, indeed, general. One, for instance, observes that 'opportunity in war is usually of greater value than bravery' (Vegetius 1993: 109). Another notes that 'no plans are better than those you carry out without the enemy's knowledge in advance' (Vegetius 1993: 108). Such advice appears to stand on its own, but the fact that Vegetius introduces his general rules at the end of a much longer section which provided instructions for performing specific functions in standardized ways suggests that he sees the abstract maxims and the concrete prescriptions as intertwined.

Vegetius also has another reason for dwelling on the details of historically successful military procedures. As he does so, he directs readers' attention to the fact that fourth-century Rome had lost the ability to use the techniques which had served it so well in the past. Once, the Roman cavalry had required all its troopers to be at least five feet ten inches in height, but sufficient numbers of tall recruits were no longer available (Vegetius 1993: 6). Once, a Roman commander had been able to rely upon units trained, equipped and organized to carry out the standard procedures which *De re militari* advocates, but Rome's legions had been 'broken by neglect' (Vegetius 1993: 32).

To compensate for the decay of Rome's own military organizations, Roman commanders increasingly relied upon auxiliary forces supplied by the various states and tribes which offered submission to Rome. Since the different peoples of the Roman Empire had different military systems, auxiliary troops came to Rome's army with differing expectations of military service, differing types of weapons, differing ideas about tactics, differing standards of discipline and differing levels of morale. Moreover, they had no experience of working together and no shared bonds of comradeship. A general attempting to command an army pieced together from such materials cannot practise strategy as *De re militari* describes it.

Vegetius suggests reasons why Rome permitted its army to deteriorate. In his discussion of military training, he suggests that the Romans became apathetic about their armed forces due to a lengthy period of peace (Vegetius 1993: 9). In his discussion of recruitment, he hints at harsher social criticism, noting that the hardy soldiers of early Rome were not yet corrupted by easy living (Vegetius 1993: 4). Not only does Vegetius allege that fourth-century Rome's culture of self-indulgence sapped the Roman people's will to endure the dangers and privations of war, he observes that this same culture stimulated economic demand for workers in a wide range of civilian occupations (Vegetius 1993: 6). Therefore, the very young men whose skills, health and intelligence would have made them most valuable to the armed forces found increasing opportunities to pursue well-paid non-military careers (Vegetius 1993: 6). Recruiters had to make do with those who were left over.

When Vegetius turns to the subject of military organization, he is audacious enough to accuse unspecified officials of misusing their authority. Rome's legions declined, he tells us, because 'corruption usurped the rewards of valour and soldiers were promoted through influence when they used to be promoted for actual work' (Vegetius 1993: 32). Having blamed the collapse of the legions on mismanagement, Vegetius later assures readers that leaders who return to the effective methods of earlier times can restore Rome's forces to their ancient prowess (Vegetius 1993: 84). Indeed, Vegetius tells us, this hope underlies everything he has written (Vegetius 1993: 84).

Although Vegetius expresses passion about these social and political issues, he handles them discreetly. He addresses them only when they arise in the course of discussions concerning narrowly military affairs. When he summarizes his work in his introduction, he does not mention them at all. Although he proposes reforms, he emphasizes steps which commanders could take to train and motivate troops more effectively (Vegetius 1993: 85). Nowhere does he demand more sweeping changes to Rome's government or its policies.

One can only speculate about the reasons why Vegetius exercised such restraint. Perhaps he feared that a more inflammatory work would offend powerful people. Perhaps he hoped that a quiet approach would be more persuasive. Perhaps he saw some good in fourth-century Roman society, and hoped only to revitalize Rome's military while avoiding radical political change. The final possibility is genuine – there is strong evidence that Vegetius was a Christian, and that he lived under a Christian emperor (Dorjahn and Born 1934: 148). If so, he would probably have welcomed many of the changes in Roman life, and, although he wished to revive certain practices from Rome's earlier periods, he might have been wary about a wholesale return to the pagan past.

Vegetius could have made harsher arguments if he had chosen. Rome and its people were suffering bitterly for squandering their military capabilities. The twentieth-century historian Philippe Contamine summarizes what certain fourth-century commentators observed on this matter:

> 'Above all it must be recognized that wild nations are pressing upon the Roman Empire and howling about it everywhere, and treacherous bar-barians, covered by natural positions, are assailing every frontier.' In these terms the anonymous author of the treatise *De rebus bellicis* described the condition of Romania around the years 366–75. A genera-tion later, according to St. Jerome, the situation had deteriorated further: 'I cannot enumerate without horror all the calamities of our age. For the last twenty years and more Roman blood has been shed daily . . . [The saint goes on to list approximately a dozen regions of the Empire which have, in his words] lain prey to Goths, Sarmatians, Quadi, Alans, Huns, Vandals and Marcomans who have ravaged, destroyed and pillaged them. (Contamine 1984: 3)

Moreover, Rome's armed forces suffered from worse abuses than an unfair system for granting promotions. Indeed, much of the Roman military was fictitious (Rapoport 1968: 427). Administrators at various levels listed imaginary troops in their records to please superiors and justify higher budgets. Meanwhile, flesh-and-blood soldiers were often unavailable for military campaigns because they were performing the functions of the civilian government, or simply because their com-manders had hired them out as labourers (Rapoport 1968: 426–7). Although historians can only estimate the full extent of these practices, they were apparently widespread enough to cripple Rome's forces in several wars (Rapoport 1968: 427).

This petty corruption grew out of Rome's more fundamental failure to maintain a working system of government. To gain an idea of how Roman politics operated in Vegetius' time, one might observe that the average ruler's risk of being assassinated stood at approximately 50 per cent (Rapoport 1968: 422). That figure was rising. Many of the men who achieved power in the cut-throat environment of the imperial court were crassly self-interested or openly deranged, but even those who might have preferred to rule for the good of the Roman people had to devote most of their energies to intrigue.

Emperors had to regard successful military commanders as rivals. Many Romans suspected – with good reason – that their rulers deliberately neglected the armed forces in order to weaken potential contenders for the throne (Rapoport 1968: 426). Since wars gave commanders opportunities to win booty and fame, emperors also had an incentive to pursue passive policies abroad (Rapoport 1968: 426). This helps to explain why St Jerome's 'Goths, Sarmatians, Quadi, Alans, Huns, Vandals and Marcomans' remained able to plunder Rome's provinces so freely. This also helps to explain why the provinces gradually assumed increasing responsibility for looking after their own interests, and why the empire itself ultimately dissolved.

As previously noted, the Romans themselves were widely aware that they had brought about many of their own misfortunes. Twentieth- and twenty-first-century scholars have occasionally downplayed this issue, but medieval and early modern thinkers continued to find it deeply significant (Rapoport 1968: 411). This may help to explain why *De re militari* inspired fresh reflections on strategy throughout the Middle Ages and beyond. Although Vegetius restrained his comments on the deeper relationships between strategy and society, his readers were sensitive to this theme in his work, and they were ready to take up his points.

Vegetius himself would almost certainly have stressed that his readers throughout the centuries have profited from his guidance on military technique as well as his reflections on political theory. The tenth- and eleventh-century counts of Anjou admired *De re militari* and appear to have used it as a blueprint for organizing their own fearsomely effective army (Shrader 1981: 169). A twelfth-century historian describes an incident in which another nobleman, Geoffrey IV the Handsome, searched through Vegetius' book to find a workable method for breaching the walls of an enemy city (Shrader 1981: 169). Vegetius' most illustrious followers, as viewed from a twenty-first-century perspective, have been those who have recognized that the tactical, organizational and sociopolitical ideas to be found within *De re militari* are parts of a unified whole.

Towards the end of the fifteenth century, developments ranging from the invention of the cannon to the rise of a powerful monarchy in France ruined once-powerful states, shattered once-stable political relationships and prompted urgent debate on strategic issues. For many, this debate began with such basic questions as who should control the armed forces and who should serve in them. Discussions of such matters led to more technical considerations of how best to train, organize and equip one's troops, and how to use them in war. The strategic thinkers of this period found that *De re militari* provided them with a guide to the combination of issues which interested them most. These thinkers pioneered the modern approach to waging war, and, as historian Charles Shrader has noted, the ideas they revived from Vegetius have proven more revolutionary than the 'new weapons and tactics' which they 'introduced at the same time' (Shrader 1981: 171).

Vegetius also confronts his readers with a more challenging truth. Rome lost its disciplined forces due to changes in its government and society. Those who would recreate the legions from a community in which they do not presently exist must also remake that community's way of life. This idea animates the works of the man Shrader introduces as Vegetius' partner in shaping modern strategy, Niccolò Machiavelli (Shrader 1981: 171).

Machiavelli: greater than Columbus?

According to Machiavelli, the essence of statecraft is the effective use of force. In his most famous work, he advised his prince to 'take up [no] other thing for his study, but war and its organisation and discipline . . .' (Machiavelli 1950: 53). Even in this brief exhortation, one notes, Machiavelli reveals his affinity with Vegetius. Where others might have urged war leaders to cultivate their courage, cleverness, leadership ability or a wide range of other martial qualities, Machiavelli urged them to study organization and discipline. The fact that medieval commanders tended to neglect the administrative dimension of warfare makes the Florentine's decision to emphasize it particularly noteworthy.

Machiavelli went on to write a book specifically about military topics, entitled *The Art of War*. Here, his debt to Vegetius became obvious. Machiavelli's *Art of War* covers the same topics as *De re militari*, and in the same order (Machiavelli 1965: xx). The Florentine repeats the Roman's advice on such crucial topics as recruiting, training, field command and siege techniques, sometimes copying the earlier author word for word (Machiavelli, 1965: xxi–xxii). Vegetius was not Machiavelli's only source of inspiration – considerable portions of *The Art of War* come from the works of Frontinus, Polybius,

Livy and others (Machiavelli 1965: xx). Nevertheless, Machiavelli was clearly picking up where Vegetius left off, and he knew what he was doing.

Moreover, Machiavelli had his own vision of where Vegetius' ideas might lead. Even when the Florentine seems to be repeating things which the Roman already said, he presents those ideas in a new manner. The way in which Machiavelli expresses his points often recalls arguments which he developed further in other works. Where Vegetius observed the symbiosis between a society and its military establishment, Machiavelli suggests a theory which purports to explain nothing less than how that relationship works and how one might re-engineer it to serve some larger – if uncertain – purpose. Although the full meaning of the Florentine's thought may remain forever elusive, Machiavelli is notoriously direct about how he intends readers to put his ideas into practice.

As one compares *De re militari* to *The Art of War*, Machiavelli's new agenda literally becomes apparent from the very first page. When Vegetius wrote his introduction, he obscured his sociopolitical ideas. Machiavelli dedicates *The Art of War* to his friend Lorenzo di Filippo Strozzi and begins by noting that many of their contemporaries assume that warfare and civil life are separate and incompatible (Machiavelli 1965: 3). This attitude, Machiavelli goes on to say, merely proves that 'our discipline is now depraved to such a degree that it is totally different from what it was in ancient times' (Machiavelli 1965: 4).

The ancients, Machiavelli continues, based their society on the idea that civil life and military affairs were intimately connected at every point (Machiavelli 1965: 4). This, Machiavelli emphasizes, is the correct view. No good thing could survive, the Florentine argues, if people did not defend it with armed force (Machiavelli 1965: 4). Here, he repeats what he wrote in a more famous book dedicated to a more famous Lorenzo – *The Prince*. 'The chief foundations of all states, whether new, old or mixed, are good laws and good arms. And as there cannot be good laws where there are not good arms, and where there are good arms there must be good laws, I will not now discuss the laws, but will speak of the arms' (Machiavelli 1950: 44).

Readers of the last sentence could assume that Machiavelli intends to remain neutral in ongoing political debates. Such readers would be mistaken. The sentence in which the Florentine promises to speak only of 'good arms' comes from a chapter in which he urges rulers to abandon the widespread practice of relying on foreign mercenaries and instead conscript their subjects to form militia armies. Book One of Machiavelli's *Art of War* takes up the same issue.

Box 3.2   Reading Vegetius and Machiavelli

Machiavelli's reputation for being a devious character extends to his writing. Practically everyone who is familiar with his works agrees that they can be misleading to the unwary, and scholars actively debate the best methods for interpreting them. Vegetius seems more straightforward – indeed, historians have specifically commented upon his frankness (Shrader 1981: 168). Nevertheless, the two authors have many points in common, both in the ways in which they approach the study of strategy and in the ways in which they express their ideas. The similarities between the authors become particularly apparent when one examines the ways in which they use history.

Vegetius presents himself largely as a historian. He does not claim to be an expert on warfare, nor does he claim that his ideas are his own. Rather, he claims to have collected and organized material which earlier writers had already compiled (Vegetius 1993: 2). The Roman may, in fact, have had more confidence in his own thoughts than such disclaimers imply. Ancient writers often expressed modest doubts about their own abilities (Vegetius 1993: 2, n. 1). The fact that Vegetius was writing for the emperor about a subject in which rulers commonly pride themselves on their own mastery made him particularly conscious of the fact that it would have been unwise for him to seem impertinent.

Nevertheless, Vegetius actually does derive most of his details on military procedures from earlier works. This is natural since he argues that ancient techniques were generally superior, and that the best way to improve the armed forces of his own day would be to recover them. As the main text notes, Vegetius acknowledges that there are certain cases in which more recent practices are actually superior. In those cases, the Roman refers readers to those who have more experience with the up-to-date techniques. Vegetius contributes to our understanding of strategy, not by discovering previously unknown information but by combing earlier sources for relevant points and organizing them into a compelling new account.

Machiavelli suggests that he has taken a similar approach. Certainly, he draws much of his material from classic works, and certainly, he recommends reintroducing a wide variety of ancient practices. In the preface to his *Discourses on Livy*, he laments the fact that the rulers of his own time read history for pleasure without even considering the possibility that they might learn from it (Machiavelli 1950: 104). The Florentine continues that he has written his study of Livy to correct this tendency (Machiavelli 1950: 105).

Such passages led the contemporary military thinker Azar Gat to conclude that Machiavelli assumed 'man and society' to remain eternally the same (Gat 1989: 2). According to Gat, Machiavelli believed that '[h]istory could thus teach us lessons which were valid in every period' (Gat 1989: 2). Gat cites numerous other scholars to support this interpretation of Machiavelli's works. To Gat, this renders Machiavelli's strategic ideas useless. '[I]t was in the military sphere – rapidly and decisively influenced by technological change – that this outlook on history and theory faced an almost immediate breakdown' (Gat 1989: 2).

Machiavelli himself, however, offers more subtly crafted arguments about the uses of history. The preface to *Discourses on Livy* certainly suggests that readers should take inspiration from earlier times. *The Prince*, however, sneers at those who fail to consider the possibility of change (Machiavelli 1950: 90). Machiavelli does not advise princes to mimic historical practices – he advises them to find approaches which will make new institutions seem as stable and worthy of respect as those which are ancient (Machiavelli 1950: 89). Indeed, he adds, 'men are much more taken by present than by past things' and rulers who succeed in their innovations will enjoy greater influence than those who merely cling to the legacy of glorious ancestors (Machiavelli 1950: 89).

The Florentine seems to follow similar principles when he writes. Certainly, he takes much of his material from classic manuscripts. Certainly, he illustrates complex ideas with historical examples. Certainly, he uses stories out of history to stir readers' emotions, and certainly he defends potentially controversial ideas by citing precedents. Nevertheless, when he finds revered texts and past events inconvenient, he rewrites them. This chapter details the way in which he modified *De re militari*, and he reworked his other sources with equal verve.

Machiavelli wrote poems and plays as well as treatises on statecraft. Therefore, it may not be surprising that his works on war and politics share many characteristics of high-quality fiction. His writings have multiple layers of meaning, from the literal and obvious to the metaphorical and elusive. He uses language creatively, often seeming to suggest points which he does not explicitly express. He peppers his works with allusions to books, events, folklore and other sources of ideas with which he thinks his readers ought to be familiar, and many of these references are subtle.

Indeed, in the introduction to *Discourses on Livy*, Machiavelli warns that those who wish to understand his ideas will have to look beneath the surface. 'I hope to carry [my writings] sufficiently far, so that but a little may remain for others to carry it to its destined end' (Machiavelli 1950: 105). Elsewhere, he invites readers to accept the *Discourses* 'as one accepts whatever comes from friends, looking to the intention of him who gives, rather than to the thing offered', and, although this may be a self-effacing appeal for others to forgive inadequacies in his work, it may very well also be a hint that his true friends will be able to catch his points without requiring him to spell them out in embarrassing detail (Machiavelli 1950: 101–2). Machiavelli adds that he is sure he has selected his friends well.

Here, Machiavelli seems to live up to his treacherous image. Therefore, it seems noteworthy that the straightforward Vegetius offers his readers comparable advice. As the main text notes, the Roman addresses *De re militari* to the emperor. Although he is quick to acknowledge that his reader is already well versed in military affairs, he expresses the hope that his work will permit the sovereign to 'recognise in your spontaneous dispositions for the safety of the state the principles which the builders of the Roman Empire long ago observed' (Vegetius 1993: 2).

Vegetius is, of course, engaging in flattery. Other writers of his time began essays directed towards powerful people with similar phrases (Vegetius 1993: 2, n. 1). Nevertheless, since strategy itself depends so heavily on human judgement in complex and inherently unpredictable situations, a book which spurs readers to 'recognize' principles which they had already begun to apprehend through 'spontaneous' intuition may well be more valuable than a book which simply provides instructions. The fact that Vegetius and Machiavelli require their readers to work may in fact be a substantial part of what gives their writings enduring value.

Militias were controversial, both because civilians were reluctant to be forced into service and because, as Machiavelli himself notes, the militia system will only work if the ruler governs in such a fashion that conscripts will fight when called upon and demobilize when the war is over (Machiavelli 1965: 21). A government which wishes to rely upon such an army must secure support from the governed, and those who rule can never fully welcome this prospect. Moreover, forming the institutions necessary to induct, equip, train and deploy the new military organizations requires extensive legislation in the literal sense of the word. Machiavelli, who had successfully campaigned to establish a militia in Florence and had personally gone on to organize it, was undoubtedly aware of these points.

Indeed, practically everything Machiavelli wrote concerns the laws in one way or another. The Florentine refrains only from insisting that these laws be morally good. Machiavelli recognized both good and evil as meaningful concepts, and he apparently thought it was possible to judge between them, but he saw no reason to limit one's options by committing oneself to either one. On the contrary, he advised, one should maintain a flexible approach, exhibiting goodness as long as a reputation for benevolence remains 'useful' and freely performing wickedness when evil methods prove 'needful' (Machiavelli 1950: 65).

With this advice, Machiavelli gives usefulness and needfulness priority above all the other qualities one might hope for in the practice of government. This makes his ideas arresting for anyone with an interest in strategic thought. Strategy, by practically any functional definition, has to do with using resources to achieve goals in an environment which frequently imposes severe constraints upon one's actions. In other words, strategy is about the useful and the needful. Machiavelli has transformed all of politics – which Aristotle helpfully defined as nothing less than the entire human quest to live and live well – into strategy.

Nevertheless, Machiavelli's advice raises a question. If one is supposed to do whatever proves useful or needful, what is it that one's actions should be useful and needful for? For most of us, perhaps, the easiest answer would be 'oneself'. Machiavelli, however, is counselling something more than ordinary selfishness.

Many fifteenth-century princes, for instance, found that mercenaries served their purposes well. Those princes would also have feared that providing their subjects with weapons and military training might actually threaten their personal interests. Machiavelli preferred republican political systems to rule by princes in any event – but republican governments presumably make policy on behalf of their citizens, and selfish citizens might doubt that it is in their interests to accept the Florentine's teachings on economic matters, which hold that states should deliberately keep their people poor. (And why, one might ask, should Machiavelli care whether a state is a republic or a princedom, if the only thing that really matters is pragmatic self-interest?)

Machiavelli's ultimate purposes must remain forever in doubt. Where one influential scholar invites us to view the Florentine as a 'philosopher of liberty', another flirts with the 'old-fashioned and simple opinion according to which Machiavelli was a teacher of evil' (Skinner 1981: 48–77; Strauss 1958: 9). Debates on these issues will undoubtedly continue to produce insights into the Florentine's ideas and, indeed, into the nature of political life, but they are unlikely to produce a definitive overall conclusion. Machiavelli does, however, reveal some of his underlying intentions, and one of his goals holds particular significance for strategists. Like most strategic thinkers, he is riveted by the challenge of coping with the combination of chance, complexity and intervention by external factors which he describes as fortune.

Indeed, Machiavelli notes, fortune has so much influence on events that strategy itself can seem futile (Machiavelli 1950: 91). The most optimistic response the Florentine can muster is that, although fortune governs half our actions, the rest remain under our control (Machiavelli 1950: 91). Thus, a Machiavellian approach to strategy consists largely of capitalizing upon whatever options one currently happens to have in order to build up as much control over one's future circumstances as possible. Ultimately, Machiavelli emphasizes, one can only rely on the things which 'depend on yourself alone, and your own ability' (Machiavelli 1950: 90).

Machiavelli illustrates the process by which strategists may assert control over their own affairs by comparing fortune to a flood-prone river (Machiavelli 1950: 91). Although it is impossible to stop the deluges once they have begun, one may take advantage of drier periods to raise levees and dig drainage ditches, so that future floods will do less harm (Machiavelli 1950: 91). Fortune is quick, Machiavelli adds, to overwhelm points which have no 'dykes or barriers' to stop her (Machiavelli 1950: 91).

The struggle against fortune, Machiavelli stresses, is a personal one. Not only does Machiavelli's approach to strategy demand the analytical skill to figure out how to maximize one's control over one's situation, it demands passion. 'I certainly think that it is better to be impetuous than cautious', Machiavelli writes: 'for fortune is a woman, and it is necessary, if you wish to master her, to conquer her by force; and it can be seen that she lets herself be overcome by the bold rather than by those who proceed coldly' (Machiavelli 1950: 94).

Here, Machiavelli implies more than he actually writes. In his original text, the word translated here as 'fortune' is *fortuna*. Fortuna is not simply a woman; she is a Roman goddess. Although her formal worship had given way to Christianity, she remained a well-recognized figure in fifteenth-century popular tradition, and even continued to play a role in theology (Skinner 1981: 23–9). Machiavelli could have expected readers to view her as symbolically significant, if not literally divine.

Moreover, the Florentine uses the word Fortuna interchangeably with the word God. He opens his chapter on fortune's role by referring to events controlled by 'fortune and by God' (Machiavelli 1950: 91). This may suggest that he sees the two as equals of a sort, and it may also suggest that he sees them as one. In later sentences, Machiavelli abandons the monotheistic term and refers to Fortuna alone, apparently finding that to be enough (Machiavelli 1950: 91). What Machiavelli says of the Roman goddess, he seems equally willing to say of Allah, Jehovah or Jesus Christ.

When the Florentine addresses the subject of religion directly, he advises readers to use it to manipulate others, but to discard its teachings whenever they become an obstacle. Not only does the Florentine's strategy supersede politics, it supersedes faith. Once, in a letter, Machiavelli wrote that he loved his fatherland more than his own soul (Parel 1992: 88). This is the type of determination which one must evoke in order to practise the Florentine's approach to strategy. One may find irony in the fact that Machiavelli referred to the combination of personal qualities which allow one to overcome Fortuna as '*virtu*'.

Although none of this explains what kind of society the Florentine ultimately hopes to create, Machiavelli's writings on God and fortune do clarify the principle which he intends for strategists to follow when making more immediate decisions. What others might see as moral dilemmas, the Florentine sees as opportunities to exploit changes of circumstance (Machiavelli 1950: 65). The reason why he favours militia over mercenaries is that foreign troops will never fully share one's interests, and thus will never be completely trustworthy. Citizen soldiers, whatever their shortcomings, are of one's own (Machiavelli 1950: 44). Such soldiers fight knowing that, if their ruler loses in war, their homes will be overrun.

Since republican governments – by definition – rule on behalf of their people, the folk of a properly functioning republic will share the interests of their state to an even greater degree than the subjects of a monarch. If people are wealthy and secure, they may prefer to pursue their private interests, but, when they are poor and in jeopardy, they will cling to the government that pursues the collective interest for them. Therefore, just as rulers who conscript their people into militia forces are in a better position to resist misfortune than those who put their faith in mercenaries, a republic composed of impoverished citizens who feel united against a common threat will be able to field a more reliable army than the most prudent prince.

De re militari addresses many of the same issues. Vegetius, however, treats them as separate problems which might potentially have separate solutions. The Roman Empire's auxiliary units, for instance, had much in common with fifteenth-century mercenaries. Vegetius criticized the auxiliaries, as previously noted, but his concerns centred on their inability to fight in a coordinated way. If, hypothetically, Rome had introduced a new training regime which overcame this difficulty, Vegetius would presumably have been satisfied.

The professional mercenaries of Machiavelli's time were, if anything, more likely to have mastered the arts of organized fighting than the newly conscripted soldiers of a newly organized militia. Nevertheless, Machiavelli rejected foreign troops, no matter how capable, on the broader principle that they were potential sources of misfortune. In a similar vein, *De re militari* notes the difficulties of raising an army in a society where people have grown accustomed to affluence. Vegetius recommends solving this problem by seeking recruits from the countryside, where young men are likely to be hardier (Vegetius 1993: 4–5). Machiavelli, by contrast, wished to keep the entire population in poverty, a measure which assures the government a greater degree of control (Machiavelli 1950: 109).

Machiavelli analyses problems in domestic politics and foreign affairs in the same meticulous way that Vegetius analyses the problems of forming effective military forces. Those who wish to understand the Florentine's approach to strategy would do well to read his writings on these topics in depth. This book notes only that the theme of mastering fortune runs throughout his discussions of strategy and politics at every level. For Machiavelli, potential enemies are the political equivalent of turbulent rivers, and much of his advice consists of measures for co-opting or destroying possible rivals before they can become dangerous. Within a state, this may mean carrying out purges while, in external relations, it must ultimately mean conquest and empire.

Not only does Machiavelli extend his strategic ideas to matters of high policy, he returns them to the minutiae of military operations. As previously noted, much of *The Art of War* comes directly from *De re militari*. One must assume that Machiavelli largely shares Vegetius' opinions about the most effective methods for waging war. Nevertheless, where the Roman assesses issues narrowly, the Florentine continually returns to his broader principles.

At times, the difference between Machiavelli and Vegetius is mainly one of detail. Both authors agree, for instance, that commanders should keep some of their forces in reserve. Vegetius explains an assortment of specific reasons why this may be useful, noting that one may deploy reserve forces in order to adopt the formations known as the 'wedge', the 'saw' and the 'pincer', and also that one can dispatch them to screen one's flanks (Vegetius 1993: 94). Machiavelli explains the value of keeping two rows of reserve troops behind the front line in the initial phases of a battle by returning to his more general theme. Since reserves provide one with resources for responding to unexpected crises, they reduce one's exposure to fortune (Machiavelli 1950: 328).

On other occasions, Machiavelli seems to work at cross purposes from Vegetius – and from anyone else who places a high value on technical competence in war. *The Art of War*, for instance, downplays the importance of gunpowder weapons. Indeed, when Machiavelli describes a hypothetical battle, he almost seems to ridicule them. 'The signal is given. Do you not hear our artillery? It has fired but done little damage to the enemy . . . The enemy's artillery has discharged its volley, but their balls have gone over the heads of our infantry without doing any harm' (Machiavelli 1965: 92–3).

Machiavelli deprecates artillery at greater length in his *Discourses on Livy* (Machiavelli 1950: 331–8). Prominent historians have also complained that he grossly underrated small arms (Machiavelli 1950: 331–8; 1965: xxvii). To Machiavelli's harsher critics, this indicates that the Florentine was blind to the importance of the weapons which were soon to dominate war. One notes, however, that when Machiavelli actually took part in organizing an army, he lobbied to equip a respectably large proportion of its troops with the matchlock shoulder pieces known as *scoppietteri* (Gilbert 1971: 275). The Florentine seems to have understood that the new weapons were valuable – he simply chose not to advertise their value to his readers.

Historian Ben Cassidy argues that Machiavelli downplayed gunpowder weapons because fifteenth-century firearms were most useful for defensive tactics (Cassidy 2003: *passim*). Cassidy rightly notes that the Florentine preferred an aggressive approach. Although Cassidy provides considerable evidence for this position, illuminating important elements of Machiavelli's military thought in the process, this argument fails to explain why the Florentine also underrated cavalry. *Discourses on Livy* allows that mounted troops are indispensable for a variety of specialized functions but holds that, in combat, disciplined infantry will always be superior (Machiavelli 1950: 339). Machiavelli wrote this at a time when, in the persuasively researched opinion of military historian F. L. Taylor, mounted troops were 'unequalled for shock tactics' and, thus 'essential in every battle' (Taylor 1921: 62). Cavalry was, in other words, vital for precisely the sort of offensive action that Machiavelli normally seemed to favour, and the field commanders of Machiavelli's time were in the process of discovering potent new ways of using it (Taylor 1921: 62–3).

In a similar vein, Machiavelli's advice about fortification seems inconsistent at best. *The Prince* questions the value of defensive works.

In that book, Machiavelli concludes his discussion of the topic on an ambiguous note, praising both those who build fortresses and those who do not (Machiavelli 1950: 81). Later, in *Discourses on Livy*, Machiavelli denied that fortresses offered any advantages whatsoever (Machiavelli 1950: 365).

Nevertheless, when Machiavelli wrote *The Art of War*, he provided detailed information about the art of building and defending fortresses, seeming to forget that he had previously described them as useless. Later in his career, he accepted a position as secretary of the committee charged with improving the walls of Florence (Machiavelli 1965: xvi). Many regard his report on the committee's findings as a work of genius, and recent historians have entertained the idea that Machiavelli may qualify as the first truly modern writer on fortification techniques (Wood 1965: xxix). Again, there seem to be discrepancies between what the Florentine advised his readers and what he actually did.

Firearms, cavalry and fortresses were all invaluable in fifteenth-century warfare. Nevertheless, all shared what Machiavelli would have seen as a common set of defects. All heightened the user's dependence upon engineers, trained gunners, experienced riders, fortress garrisons and other potentially disloyal cliques of specialists. All were of limited use under unfavourable conditions. All put commanders under pressure to base other plans around their use. Therefore, all compromised Machiavelli's principle of minimizing one's liability to fortune.

Although Machiavelli does not sum up these points in a general statement, he repeatedly offers them in passing. When he lists the drawbacks of fortresses in the *Discourses*, his first point is that they are vulnerable to treason from within their own garrisons; when he praises infantry over cavalry, he notes that foot soldiers can operate in terrain which would be inaccessible to mounted troops; and when he writes of firearms, he winds up his discussion with an intimidating list of measures a commander must take if he intends his artillery to inflict meaningful numbers of casualties upon the enemy (Machiavelli 1950: 365, 339, 337–8).

From a twenty-first-century perspective, the Florentine appears to be making a sophisticated attempt to balance the different levels of strategic planning. Machiavelli clearly recognized that firearms, cavalry and fortresses were indispensable at the level of tactics. Nevertheless, he recognized that all had the potential to undo his work at the levels of strategy and grand strategy. Therefore, one may surmise that he provided his audience with a certain amount of information about how to use guns, mounted troops and defensive works in order to ensure that readers could use these instruments when necessary, but that he coloured his advice in ways which discouraged readers from becoming excessively reliant on these troublesome technologies. Machiavelli implicitly asks readers to forgo the immediate benefits of using such tools more enthusiastically in order to maintain stronger defences against eventual changes in fortune.

Whatever Machiavelli actually thought about these topics, he does not clearly explain his reasoning. Instead, he writes as if the issues were relatively simple. Trusting readers could easily assume that he has told them all they need to know – which he most certainly has not. This may mean that Machiavelli himself was confused about these matters, but it may also suggest that he was trying to manipulate his audience. If he had admitted that he was sacrificing tactical advantages in order to pursue grand strategic objectives, readers might have decided that they had different priorities, particularly since guns, cavalry and fortresses all had attractions which went beyond their military utility. Machiavelli had encountered just such a problem when he attempted to organize infantry forces for Florence, and his potential recruits used their influence as Florentine citizens to demand more glamorous and comfortable assignments in the cavalry (Wood 1965: xiv).

Vegetius also found certain forms of military technology problematic. Like Machiavelli, he based his strategic methods upon infantry forces, and, like Machiavelli, he lived in an era when heavy cavalry seemed to offer an alternative approach. The Roman also found that his concepts of naval warfare failed to account for the increasing importance of inland campaigns involving armed river boats. In these cases, Vegetius simply confesses that he does not fully understand these matters and that newly emerging practices might be more effective than any methods he could suggest (Vegetius 1993: 142).

Like Socrates, Vegetius finds wisdom in admitting his own ignorance. Machiavelli indulges in no such humility. *The Art of War* paraphrases *De re militari* on the subject of mounted troops (Machiavelli 1965: 205). Nevertheless, at precisely the point where the Roman defers to cavalry experts, the Florentine takes the opportunity to put those experts in their place.

Vegetius ends his discussion of this topic by confessing that the cavalrymen of his day have made such progress in armaments, horse-breeding and methods of training that they need no advice from him (Vegetius 1993: 111). Machiavelli admits only that fifteenth-century cavalry methods are relatively free from corruption (Machiavelli 1965: 205). The Florentine goes on to remind readers that the true strength of the army consists of its foot soldiers and that the combination of military and civic discipline which produces strong infantry forces is the key to fielding an effective cavalry as well (Machiavelli 1965: 205). Where *De re militari* invites readers to seek the truth for themselves, *The Art of War* directs its audience towards the author's favoured conclusions.

Thus, Machiavelli rejects several popular approaches to the problems of waging war. When raising and equipping military forces, Machiavellians will resist all temptations to make war 'with gold instead of with iron', even when investing in elite units such as mercenary cavalry might actually save government funds (Machiavelli 1950: 310). Wherever possible, the Florentine's disciples will reject small forces with specialized capabilities in favour of mass armies which can fight under the widest possible variety of circumstances. For practical purposes, this means that Machiavellians will base their military organizations upon infantry.

Since Machiavellians refuse to rely on specialists, they must forgo methods which depend upon elite forces' signature capabilities. Those who follow the Florentine's advice will not hope to outwait hostile forces behind castle walls, nor will they count on obliterating their foes with firepower, nor will they expect to outmanoeuvre opponents with mounted troops, nor will they depend on armoured cavalry to crash through the enemy's lines. Instead, Machiavellians will think in terms of using their foot soldiers to do what infantry has excelled at throughout time, which is to engage the enemy in close, sustained combat. This is a bloody process for all concerned, which places a high premium on the number of troops both sides can commit, and an even higher premium on those troops' mental preparation to fight on doggedly in the face of hideous casualties.

Naturally enough, Machiavelli emphasizes both the desirability of raising large infantry armies and the importance of, to paraphrase his words, animating their valour (Machiavelli 1965: 37; 1950: 338). Having established his priorities, the Florentine can then integrate technology into his preferred methods of operation. Like Vegetius, he recommends dressing foot soldiers in body armour to enhance both their physical protection and their morale (Machiavelli 1965: 44–5). Machiavelli also suggests ways in which gunpowder weapons may turn out to be useful after all – not as a substitute for mass infantry forces, but as a tool for helping those forces gain a psychological advantage over their opponents (Machiavelli 1950: 338).

In *The Art of War*, Machiavelli develops his concepts of military operations by offering a case study of a hypothetical battle. Although the business of fighting is implicitly central to any work on strategy, the Florentine is among the first to dissect what happens when opposing armies meet in combat so thoroughly and in such detail (Gilbert 1971: 16–18; Wood 1965: xxi). Since the battlefield is the place in which large, well-disciplined infantry forces realize their potential to grind up their enemies, Machiavelli's affection for the topic is logical. Nevertheless, his enthusiasm is audacious, particularly for one who is so acutely aware of the power of chance.

For Sun Tzu, who urged strategists to minimize their exposure to the hazards of war, the ideal strategy is one of winning victories without needing to fight (Tao 1987: 99). Vegetius also advised readers to treat large-scale engagements as a last resort. In battle, the Roman warns, 'fortune tends to have more influence than bravery' (Vegetius 1993: 108). Machiavelli apparently agreed with *De re militari* on this point, since he repeats Vegetius' warning almost word for word (Machiavelli 1965: 202).

Nevertheless, when the Florentine describes his archetypal battle, fortune seems to play favourites. Both sides make mistakes and both suffer from accidents, but, as the opposing armies exhaust their opening gambits and the fighting reaches its climax, Machiavelli invites us to behold the ruin that his side's heavy infantry inflicts upon its enemies (Machiavelli 1965: 94). 'The enemy is embarrassed and falling into confusion; their pikes are too long to do any further work and their swords are of no service against men who are so well protected by their armor. What carnage! . . . They are beginning to flee. . . . We have won a glorious victory' (Machiavelli 1965: 94).

The Florentine knows that this account may sound simplistic. Machiavelli wrote *The Art of War* in the form of a conversation involving the renowned general Fabrizio Colonna and a number of Florentine gentlemen. (Some version of this conversation may have actually occurred, but Machiavelli almost certainly rewrote the details in order to bring out his own arguments; Gat 1989: 4.) After Fabrizio describes how he would lead troops to glorious victory in a notional battle, Machiavelli has a listener named Luigi Alamanni respond: 'You have carried everything before you with such amazing rapidity that I cannot very easily tell whether I ought to state any objection or not. However, with submission to your superior judgement, I will make so bold as to ask you a free question or two' (Machiavelli 1965: 94).

Luigi goes on to note numerous places at which he wonders whether Fabrizio's methods would actually work as smoothly as they worked when Fabrizio told the story. The fact that it is Luigi who raises these doubts indicates that Machiavelli himself takes them seriously. Earlier in the text, Fabrizio observed that Luigi is the youngest participant in the conversation, and that 'young men are best qualified to discuss the duties and exercises of war, as they are the readiest and fittest to put them into execution' (Machiavelli 1965: 83). *The Prince* adds, perhaps significantly, that Fortuna admires youth (Machiavelli 1950: 94).

Machiavelli uses Luigi to remind readers that real-life victories never come easily. Fabrizio is not describing an ordinary battle of his time. He is describing what one might achieve after one has adopted such measures as are necessary to 'improve our present system of military discipline' – in other words, once one has put Machiavelli's entire programme into effect (Machiavelli 1965: 83–4). Even those who wish to do this may have to struggle to achieve a position from which they can. Many of the best-remembered parts of Machiavelli's writings consist of advice on how to proceed when one is too weak or unprepared to do what one might like and must survive by playing the fox (Lukes 2001: 562).

Machiavelli prefers, however, to play the lion. Where other strategic thinkers hoped only to avoid the vagaries of battle, Machiavelli looked forward to mastering them. Fabrizio turns out to have anticipated Luigi's concerns and devised ways of addressing each one. He has built dykes and barriers. Readers should view this as an ingenious accomplishment. Fabrizio overwhelms the competent Luigi when he describes his battle plan because he is ready to overwhelm Fortuna herself.

Readers of *The Prince* will recall that Fortuna appreciates a man who can overpower her and will, in fact, coyly yield to him (Machiavelli 1950: 94). The fact that Machiavelli gives pitched battles – where Fortuna is at her strongest – such a prominent place in his strategy suggests that he believes his approach has put her on her knees. This would be a bold claim for him to make under any circumstances and it is bolder still when one recalls that the Florentine equates Fortuna with God. Machiavelli aims at nothing less than readjusting the balance of power between humanity and its creator, or, in secular terms, *homo sapiens* and the cosmos. To free people from external domination, he proposes a comprehensive system by which they are to dominate one another.

The Florentine opened his *Discourses on Livy* with these lines. 'Although the envious nature of men, so prompt to blame and so slow to praise, makes the discovery and introduction of any new principles and systems as dangerous as the exploration of unknown seas and continents, yet . . . I have resolved to open a new route . . .' (Machiavelli 1950: 103).

Here, Machiavelli seemingly compares himself to Columbus. Prometheus might have been equally appropriate.

Further reading

Machiavelli, Niccolò (1950) *The Prince and the Discourses*, trans. Luigi Ricci, E.. R. Vincent and Christian E. Detmold. New York: The Modern Library.

Machiavelli, Niccolò (1965) *The Art of War*, trans. Ellis Farneworth. New York: Bobs-Merrill.

Shrader, Charles R. (1981) 'The Influence of Vegetius' *De re militari*'. *Military Affairs* 45(4) (Dec.): 167–72.

Skinner, Quentin (1981) *Machiavelli*. Oxford: Oxford University Press.

Vegetius, Renatus Flavius (1993) *Vegetius: Epitome of Military Science*, trans. and annotations N. P. Milner. Liverpool: Liverpool University Press.

4 SUMMARIZING WAR

If Machiavelli is the Columbus of strategic theory, the early nine-teenth-century Prussian general and author Carl von Clausewitz is strategy's equivalent of Martin Waldseemuller – the cartographer who literally put the newly discovered continents on the map. Clausewitz's admirers might respond that, unlike the cartographer, the Prussian was himself an explorer in his own right. Nevertheless, the metaphor remains appropriate. Waldseemuller did not merely sketch a few previously unfamiliar coastlines – he addressed deeper questions about how a New World might fit into the Old. As a result, his most famous work is festooned with captions, portraits, diagrams, smaller inset maps and depictions of the winds (Hébert 2003). Just as Waldseemuller's attempts to explain what he drew made his map ornate, Clausewitz's attempts to describe war fully and in its proper political context produced a notoriously complicated work.

This chapter examines the ways in which Clausewitz developed the themes which earlier strategic thinkers had begun. The Prussian was hardly the first to notice that chaos reigns in war, or that warfare is intimately related to politics, or that, in his words, 'the best strategy is always *to be very strong*' (Clausewitz 1976: 204: italics in original). Clausewitz is, however, unsurpassed for his achievement in thinking through what these and other crucial observations about war actually mean, and how they connect to one another. As he considered such issues, he found that even the most basic ones were problematic. Where Machiavelli, for instance, continually pushes readers towards his preferred intellectual destinations, Clausewitz continually reminds them that the ultimate answers to his questions are as mutable as the human beings who wage war. The Prussian's map, in other words, does not come with a compass.

Box 4.1   Who was Clausewitz?

In 1780, when Carl von Clausewitz was born, his home country of Prussia enjoyed a reputation for having the best army in Europe. Sixty-seven years earlier, Frederick Wilhelm I had become king of Prussia and begun the process of drilling the small country's army for maximum efficiency. Frederick Wilhelm's son, now known as Frederick the Great, used the reformed Prussian army's exceptional discipline, mobility and musketry skills to hold off the combined forces of Russia, Austria, Sweden and France. Indeed, he subjected Austria to several sharp defeats. Carl von Clausewitz's father became a lieutenant during the second of Frederick's wars, and Carl himself obtained a commission in Prussia's 34th infantry regiment at the age of 12 (Howard 1983: 5). A year later, Carl experienced war for the first time, when Prussia contributed forces to a coalition formed to suppress the newly established government of revolutionary France.

Despite their service, the Clausewitzs remained social outsiders within the Prussian army. Their family had middle-class origins, and this distanced them from the aristocrats who dominated the military hierarchy. Moreover, Carl's quiet personality and appetite for books won him little favour from the bluff, confident soldiers around him. His skills brought him staff positions, but not the combat command which he, like most military professionals, craved (Howard 1983: 5–6).

Carl did, however, find friends and mentors, notably the military reformer General Gerhard Scharnhorst. Meanwhile, in 1803, he fell in love with Marie von Bruhl, the daughter of a count (Howard 1983: 8). The two married seven years later. Their correspondence suggests that they enjoyed an unusually tender relationship by early nineteenth-century standards, and that they shared many interests, including an intellectual interest in war.

In 1806, Prussia joined yet another coalition against France. On this occasion, the French struck first. Napoleon Bonaparte, who had crushed the Austrian forces at Austerlitz the previous year, marched France's army deep into Prussia. This threw the Prussian commanders' plans into chaos.

In the days of confusion which followed, Napoleon defeated the Prussians in simultaneous battles at Jena and Auerstadt. Clausewitz fought at Auerstadt and was taken prisoner. Napoleon went on to chase the Prussian army to the borders of Russia, overrunning all Prussia in the process. The French then fought the Russian army to a standstill. Napoleon and Russia's tsar negotiated a peace treaty on a raft while King Frederick III of Prussia stood powerlessly on the riverbank, waiting for them to decide his country's fate.

Napoleon's pact with the tsar allowed Prussia to survive as an independent nation but forcibly allied it to France. Clausewitz returned from captivity and worked with Scharnhorst to reconstitute his country's army. Nevertheless, when Napoleon called on Prussia to honour the terms of its surrender by helping him to invade Russia, Clausewitz resigned his commission and took service with the tsar's army instead. Just as Clausewitz had witnessed the collapse of the once-mighty Prussian forces in 1806, he witnessed the disintegration of Napoleon's Grande Armée in 1812, this time from the victorious side.

As Napoleon's power waned, Prussia broke its alliance with France. Clausewitz returned to his homeland, regained his commission, fought in the final campaigns against Bonaparte and eventually achieved the rank of general. Although he served in such distinguished roles as chief of staff, he never received direct command of combat units, and his defection in 1812 did little to endear him to those who had stayed behind.

Clausewitz devoted increasing amounts of time to the manuscript which would become *On War*. Meanwhile, in 1830, Prussia mobilized forces for a potential campaign to suppress an uprising in Poland. The following year, a cholera epidemic upstaged the political crisis. As Clausewitz worked to organize a quarantine along the Polish border, he contracted the disease himself and died of it. His widow edited his notes for *On War* and published them in their current form.

Clausewitz opened his masterpiece *On War* by investigating what war itself actually is. This chapter begins with a section which considers the same topic. The second section notes that Clausewitz's attempt to understand war led him to two apparently incompatible conclusions. On the one hand, he found that the word 'war' could mean entirely different things in different political contexts but, on the other hand, he argued that there are logical consequences to introducing force into human affairs, and that strategists must never let anything – including politics – distract them from those consequences. The third section notes that although Machiavelli offered readers simple advice on making politics compatible with warfare, Clausewitz refused to do so, and that although other thinkers would have concluded that no advice on this issue is possible, the Prussian also refused that extreme.

Clausewitz did try to explain how such seemingly contradictory principles could interact to shape the reality of war. War, the Prussian wrote, is a 'trinity' of primal emotion, the military art and rational planning. The fourth section of this chapter explores the implications of this idea and the fifth suggests one way in which the trinity concept may help one to read the rest of *On War* more productively. A sixth section considers Clausewitz's attempts to explain how strategists might apply his theories in practice. The conclusion notes that, despite all the difficulties of resolving the ambiguities in Clausewitz's work, those very areas of uncertainty make *On War* useful for a particularly wide range of readers with a particularly wide range of purposes.

Beginning at the beginning

Although Clausewitz admired Machiavelli, there is no particular reason to believe that he based his own ideas on the Florentine's works. Nevertheless, Book One of *On War* carries on themes which Machiavelli's readers may find familiar. The Prussian begins by attempting to define his terms – something which the Florentine habitually and notoriously declined to do. The first concept which Clausewitz tries to explain is that of war itself.

Machiavelli, one may recall, embraced battle as the defining feature of warfare and the climax of successful strategy. For the Florentine, such ideas were bold and potentially dubious. Machiavelli expected intelligent readers to challenge them. Clausewitz, by contrast, initially suggested that these points were self-evident. To him, the word 'war' clearly meant a physical struggle – a 'duel on a larger scale' (Clausewitz 1976: 75).

A sentence later, however, Clausewitz finds that this may not be the heart of the matter after all. War does not consist merely of one fight; it consists of many, and whereas duels typically end abruptly with death, first blood or some other clearly established point of resolution, war is more often an extended process (Clausewitz 1976: 75). Facetious readers may note that there are actually many different ways of fighting duels, some of which may have more in common with warfare than others, but Clausewitz decides that a wrestling match would be a better analogy.

By depicting war as a wrestling match, Clausewitz introduces at least two of the concepts which dominate his work. The first of these is the distinction between means and ends. Wrestlers spend much of their time attempting to throw one another to the ground, but this is not actually the object of wrestling – it is simply a way of gaining an advantage, and of preventing one's opponent from gaining an advantage over you. The next step in wrestling is to pin one's opponents shoulders to the ground, and in war, the ultimate goal is to get one's way in some dispute (Clausewitz 1976: 75).

This raises the questions of precisely who Clausewitz believes he is writing for, and precisely what kind of disputes he believes they are trying to win. Clausewitz chooses not to address those issues at this point since, in his view, one will not have the opportunity to accomplish anything else anything until one achieves the intermediary goal of incapacitating one's enemies by destroying their military forces in battle (Clausewitz 1976: 75). One achieves this – in war as in wrestling – by exerting as much force as possible (Clausewitz 1976: 75). Meanwhile, Clausewitz stresses, your enemies will face the same imperatives to bring the maximum possible force to bear against you. One must expect a period of pushing back and forth in which, for all practical purposes, means prevail, ends become irrelevant and the only thing which matters is strength. This is the second critical concept to emerge from the wrestling match analogy.

Clausewitz realizes that he has been making the dynamics of conflict sound cool and abstract. The Prussian hurries to remind readers that actual warfare is anything but. Human beings, no matter how advanced their society, are capable of fury and hatred. In Clausewitz's view, this bitter determination to prevail is as essential to military effectiveness as bullets (Clausewitz 1976: 76–7).

In principle, Clausewitz adds, this angry competition to obliterate one's enemies before they can do the same to you must drive both sides to extremes (Clausewitz 1976: 77). Clausewitz's critics have warned that this may be a self-fulfilling prophecy. The twentieth-century British strategic thinker B. H. Liddell Hart, for instance, famously blamed *On War* for encouraging the opposing generals in the First World War to send millions to futile deaths in frontal attacks against entrenched enemies, assuming that major battles with the strongest opposing forces were the only route to victory. Hart himself acknowledged that this was probably not what the Prussian actually had in mind (Bassford 1994: 334).

Indeed, scarcely a page later, Clausewitz reflects that this theory can never be more than a 'logical fantasy' (Clausewitz 1976: 78). To accept it as an accurate description of reality – or, worse, to base plans on it – would be absurd. Nevertheless, although Clausewitz rejects his model's conclusions, he does not feel that he can dismiss the process by which he reached them. Surely war is a matter of fighting, surely a strong fighter will overwhelm a weaker opponent and surely the combatants will feel enraged.

Since the theory seems to make sense but fails in practice, the Prussian reviews his own ideas, trying to identify the factors which complicate them in real life. Clausewitz organizes the text of *On War* into books, chapters and shorter sections. The titles of his next few sections sum up the main issues he encounters. A wrestling match is a distinct event which takes place in a ring, independently from any other sporting contests which might have taken place in the past, or which might be going on elsewhere. War, by contrast, never occurs in isolation (Clausewitz 1976: 78).

Moreover, war is a complex process which takes time to unfold (Clausewitz 1976: 79). Even when one side surrenders, it may later resume the fight in one way or another (Clausewitz 1976: 80). For these reasons, Clausewitz continues, the opposing commanders must make complex decisions involving intangibles and unknowns. One cannot deduce infallible solutions to such problems through pure logic – one must use one's own subjective judgement, and one must allow for an element of the unknown (Clausewitz 1976: 80).

Meanwhile, now that commanders are making subjective judgements, they must think about what they are fighting for, and what it is worth. Earlier in his thought process, Clausewitz decided to ignore the ends of warfare and focus only on the means. Now, he realizes, one must consider both. Since he views the issues people fight over as inherently political, he concludes that strategists must take political factors into account (Clausewitz 1976: 80). More subtly, he notes that political judgements involving unquantifiable factors concern specific human beings, whose personalities and relationships have suddenly become important.

Clausewitz continues to criticize his original theory for the better part of a chapter. Even the military means of warfare, he concludes, are less like a wrestling match than his original theory suggested. In games, both sides follow the same relatively clear set of rules. War is neither simple nor symmetrical.

The logistics of mobilizing and manoeuvring armed forces complicate the process of waging war, affecting different combatants in different ways at different times, and for different periods of time. Combat itself involves unequal factors – attackers and defenders do different things with different chances of success, and, again, they typically proceed at a different pace. The psychology of warfare is no less variegated. As war drags on, those who remain alive remain free to reconsider the judgements they once made, so that those who began playing by certain sorts of rules may end up playing by very different ones (Clausewitz 1976: 83–5). Emotions ebb and flow along with reasoned assessments, changing both what participants at every level will want to do and what they will be able to get others to do.

These reflections and more like them lead Clausewitz to his famous conclusion that 'war is merely the continuation of policy by other means' (Clausewitz 1976: 87). The emphasis is on the word 'merely'. According to Clausewitz, there is no one thing which we can call war. There is only an effectively infinite variety of situations in which 'governments and peoples' supplement their relations with violence (Clausewitz 1976: 605). The social, mental and material circumstances under which this takes place shape virtually everything about what those 'governments and peoples' will be able to do, how they will understand the things which they are doing and how their actions will turn out for them.

This leads Clausewitz to give strategists a strongly worded piece of advice. In his view, the supreme judgement that the 'statesman and commander' have to make 'is to establish . . . the kind of war on which they are embarking' (Clausewitz 1976: 88). To confuse it with anything else, or to try to make it into something which it is not, is to court disaster. Therefore, it is ironic, at the least, when writers condescendingly stereotype Clausewitz as purely a theorist of the openly conducted state-to-state wars which so many thinkers throughout the past century have so frequently declared to be obsolete. Scholars who believe that the twenty-first century is to be an era of terrorism, insurgency, ethnic conflict, wars-for-profit, wars-for-public-opinion and other continually evolving species of New War commonly claim to be knocking Clausewitz from his pedestal, but they might just as well celebrate him as one of the original advocates of their approach.

Box 4.2   Reading Clausewitz

First, some good news. One need not master every nuance of Clausewitz's argument to benefit from reading *On War*. The exercise of considering the Prussian's ideas and trying to work out what they might mean in real-life situations may often be as valuable as wrestling with unanswerable questions about what Clausewitz might have had in mind. *On War* compares learning strategy from books to practising swimming strokes on dry land. The movements themselves may not be particularly useful, but the process of going through them helps one develop a sense of what one might actually do when immersed in a different element.

For those who wish to probe the Prussian's thought in greater depth, there are more complex factors to consider. To begin with, Clausewitz died with *On War* unfinished. His notes indicate that he was in the process of reconsidering numerous portions of his work (Meilinger 2007: 119). Happily, Book One, Chapter One, in which he sets out his fundamental ideas about the discrepancy between what logic suggests war should be and the reality of what war actually is, appears to be one of his most finished sections (Handel 1998: 3).

Another issue to consider in studying *On War* is the fact that Clausewitz wrote in an archaic style. Contemporary scholars cannot agree on precisely how to translate his expressions into twenty-first-century English (Meilinger 2007: 119). Indeed it may even be difficult to capture their original meaning in twenty-first-century German. Those who have prepared Clausewitz's manuscript for English-speaking readers have had to make arbitrary judgements about which versions of the text to present (Meilinger 2007: 119). Thus, much of *On War* remains forever open to debate.

Nevertheless, when strategic thinkers discuss the meaning of *On War*, Clausewitz himself joins in the conversation. Although the Prussian found many of his own ideas unsatisfactory, he reflected throughout his work about the problems he encountered as he worked to refine them. Clausewitz went into particular detail about the difficulties of using the language of theory to describe the hard reality of war. The Prussian was as scornful of intellectual affectations as he was of military sloganeering.

Contemporary social scientists typically envision theory as a tool for explaining complex realities in a more manageable way. This approach does not require theory to account for all the details of real life. Indeed, by this reckoning, a theory which conformed too closely to reality would be useless since it would be as messy as the problems it purported to solve. Thus, for example, the school of thought known as Realism traditionally models every issue in world politics in terms of states contending with other states, not because realists are unaware of non-state actors, such as international terrorist organizations, but because they think that focusing on state-to-state competition helps one to organize one's thoughts in a useful way.

On War challenges this approach. Where contemporary theorists would simplify, Clausewitz tends to elaborate, and where contemporary theorists prize generality, he consistently treats abstract generalizations with suspicion. The Prussian asks readers to make sense of warfare, not by applying a formula but through a continual process of informed judgement. Since neither conceptual modelling nor human intuition is completely trustworthy, contemporary strategic thinkers must decide which method frightens them more.

Poet or grammarian?

Christopher Bassford, Antulio Echevarria and Bart Schuurman, among others, have written extensively defending Clausewitz from those who overlook the richness within his concept of war (Bassford 1994: *passim*; Echevarria 1995–6: *passim*; Schuurman 2010: *passim*). One recalls, however, that Machiavelli actually did steer readers towards a vision of strategy dominated by large battles between state-sponsored armies. The Florentine promoted this type of warfare, not because he was ignorant of others but because he believed that it was the optimum military tool for taking charge of one's political environment. Machiavelli and Clausewitz agree that there is a symbiotic relationship between war and politics, but where the Prussian warns readers never to try to transform a war into something other than what it is, the Florentine urges them to consider the possibilities of doing exactly that.

Clausewitz understood that Machiavelli had a point. Battle offers enemies the opportunity to destroy one another. None of the factors which complicate warfare trump physical destruction. Normally, the mere threat of obliteration will frighten likely victims into changing their behaviour. Therefore, those who can put themselves in a position to make such threats have gained a tool with which to adjust both their tactical and their political relationships. These adjustments may be as immediate as the artillery barrage which drives enemy troops from their positions or as far-reaching as the string of victories which persuades those who might otherwise have joined forces with one's opponents to remain neutral. War is far more than a simple test of strength – but it includes many such tests, and the outcomes matter.

Thus, Clausewitz compares war to language. One may use language as a medium for compositions as diverse as love letters and office memoranda, but if one wishes to express any coherent idea, one must follow certain rules. War has a 'grammar', and that grammar consists of the practicalities of doing harm. Clausewitz assumes that those who use the language of war will have coherent ideas which they wish to express (Clausewitz 1976: 605–7, 86).

Here, theorists who favour a New Wars approach might claim that Clausewitz is being narrow-minded. Perhaps some terrorists, militia leaders and even cynical western politicians use the language of war to write experimental poetry. Historians such as John Keegan and Martin van Creveld have observed that people fight for cultural and psychological reasons which persist even after more rational motivations have evaporated. The scholar Mary Kaldor adds that 'violence is a way in which groups win political power not through defeating the enemy but through mobilising support on the basis of fear' (Kaldor 2010). (Machiavelli, one notes in passing, would have agreed, since he recommended using violence for precisely that reason.)

Although those who wage war for irrational or narrowly selfish reasons will probably try to justify their acts in political terms, they may not be particularly interested in what Clausewitz called 'policy'. Therefore, they may reinterpret the grammar of war to the point at which it becomes incomprehensible. Kaldor, for instance, notes that the very idea that enemy forces are working against each other may be unwarranted. Warring bands may actually be engaged in 'a profitable, mutual enterprise' which permits both groups to maintain power and prestige within their own communities (Kaldor 2010). Outsiders who try to end such wars by working to resolve the political issues that the combatants claim to be fighting over are unlikely to accomplish anything useful because neither side actually wants the issues resolved.

Clausewitz seems to have expected his claim that war has a serious, political end to be controversial but for almost the opposite reasons. The Prussian was prepared for readers to respond that the logic of superior force is so merciless that the 'grammar' of kill or be killed must surely replace all other considerations. Clausewitz counters by reiterating that, no matter how persuasive this absolute position may sound in theory, reality is simply not like that (Clausewitz 1976: 87). In Clausewitz's view, a focus upon the political motivations for war opened intellectually challenging but undeniably real possibilities, whereas for his twenty-first-century critics it closes them.

Critics and admirers alike must agree that this is an area of tension within Clausewitz's work. No sooner does the Prussian declare that politics are all-important than he stops short and reminds readers that one must modify one's political aspirations to account for the realities of combat, and that this may alter them dramatically (Clausewitz 1976: 87). Even his metaphors shift back and forth between these conflicting lines of thought. At one point, he reflects that political considerations may transform the 'battle-sword that a man needs both hands and his entire strength to wield' into a 'handy rapier' or even a mere 'foil for the exchange of thrusts, feints and parries' (Clausewitz 1976: 606). Here, the Prussian presents this transformation as a simple fact which strategists must recognize and adapt to. Elsewhere, he advises readers to regard the same process as a dangerous temptation to be avoided. If we give up our most lethal weapons in favour of those we find more pleasing or convenient, he warns, someone will eventually come along with a sword which is sharp and 'hack off our arms' (Clausewitz 1976: 260).

The fact that Clausewitz vacillates on these issues need not mean that he has failed to think them through. As the Clausewitzian scholar Michael Handel has noted, war itself is paradoxical, and, as Handel also notes, Clausewitz deliberately adopts a form of argument which contrasts a theoretically pristine 'ideal type' with messy reality (Handel 2005: 303, 327). Nevertheless, even Handel finds unconvincing the Prussian's attempt to reconcile the rigid grammar of violent conflict with the flexible possibilities which emerge when one views war as a mere political instrument (Handel 2005: 7).

Readers are also entitled to ask how Clausewitz – who so often emphasizes that strategic theory is worthless unless it addresses practice – intends them to choose between these conflicting ideas in real-life situations. The scholar Philip S. Meilinger has compiled a list of successful leaders, respected scholars and victorious commanders alleged to have chosen wrongly, presumably because they misread *On War*. This list includes Vladimir Lenin, T. E. Lawrence, Douglas MacArthur and 'virtually' the entire German General Staff throughout the nineteenth and early twentieth centuries (Meilinger 2007: 124–5). Meilinger goes on to suggest that the fact that so many otherwise capable strategists have failed to understand *On War* may tell us more about Clausewitz's work than it tells us about those strategists (Meilinger 2007: 125).

Making history

Meilinger's remark bites deeply, particularly when one considers the fact that other strategic thinkers offer readers clearer guidance on these issues. Machiavelli, for instance, suggests a formula for combining 'laws' with 'arms'. For him, the mind-boggling possibilities of what Clausewitz called political intercourse would surely have been a part of Fortuna's realm, and the mind-concentrating impact of physical force would surely have been one of the tools mortals may use to scrape away at her power. Machiavellians use violence to increase their control over their political situation and then use their newly won political influence to enhance their capabilities for using violence. Moreover, the Florentine advised both the Medici rulers of Florence and his own republican-minded friends about how this might actually be done.

If war is a language, Machiavelli constructed a sentence in which leaders constitute a republic, suppress its internal conflicts, instil discipline among its people, mobilize those people into the type of military forces best suited to such a society's martial virtues and send those forces out under a spirited leader who will seize opportunities to annihilate potential rivals. Clausewitz lived in a time when revolutionaries in France pronounced a similar sentence and, as *On War* noted, swept the armies of Europe's monarchies from one side of the continent to the other (Clausewitz 1976: 219).

Clausewitz himself attributed France's victories to its new system of government and to that government's new ways of waging war (Clausewitz 1976: 609). Nevertheless, unlike Machiavelli, Clausewitz did not present this as a recipe for others to follow. *Discourses on Livy* warns that founding new political orders is more perilous than exploring new continents, and *On War* adds that one must always regard such revolutionary accomplishments as extraordinary. One would be unreasonable to demand them and unwise to depend upon them. When Clausewitz considered the reasons why Europe's monarchies floundered so badly in their attempts to combat revolutionary France, he reflected that it would have been unfair to expect them to perform any differently.

'The military art on which the politicians relied was part of a world they thought was real,' Clausewitz reflects (Clausewitz 1976: 610). One could hardly advise them to plan on the basis of anything other than reality. Even if some far-sighted person had perceived that the common understanding of the real was founded upon politically inspired premises which were, in fact, malleable, Clausewitz did not expect entire communities instantly to adopt successful new strategies in response to such ideas (Clausewitz 1976: 610). Columbus cannot sail until he can persuade a Queen Isabella to bankroll him. Thus, *On War* suggests that even the most insightful attempts to harness the military possibilities of social and political change must normally involve a period of uncertainty and experimentation.

Clausewitz could have taken this argument even farther. A strict follower of the intellectual movement known as Historicism might say that it is impossible for anyone to see outside the beliefs of his or her time. *On War*'s 'thoughtful strategist' could not exist. Instead, such a theorist might argue, the wise and the foolish alike have no choice but to follow the script which previous generations have written for them and face the humanly unforeseeable consequences. In the process, they modify the script they leave to their descendants, perhaps guiding humanity towards some ultimate destiny – but they will only realize what they have done in hindsight, if ever.

Clausewitz lived at the same time as the influential historicist Georg Hegel. Hegel exulted in the triumphs of revolutionary France, viewing them as the splendid and inevitable culmination of history's processes (Aron 1985: 372). Clausewitz was probably familiar with Hegel's work, and certainly shared many of the historicist's interests. Nevertheless, as intellectual Raymond Aron has explored in detail, Clausewitz rejected the idea of grand and predetermined patterns to human affairs (Aron 1985: 223–30).

On the contrary, Clausewitz credited people with the capacity for independent critical thought and the ability to act productively upon it (Aron 1985: 223–30). Warfare, the Prussian notes, deals not with impersonal historical movements but with 'living and with moral forces' – forces which can only arise from living and thinking individuals (Clausewitz 1976: 86). Clausewitz is sober about the difficulties which people who wish to assert control over their own political and military destinies must face, but he respects their efforts, and he encourages them to hope (Clausewitz 1976: 86).

Moreover, Clausewitz hated the politics of revolutionary France. When his own king made peace with Napoleon, he went to Russia so that he could go on fighting his enemies from there. Clausewitz even criticized France's brutal system of conscription, despite the fact that it undoubtedly helped the French create their powerful armed forces (Paret 1976: 130). Just as the Christian Vegetius may have hesitated to advocate a general return to the ways of the pagan Roman Republic, the Prussian patriot Clausewitz could hardly have wanted future strategists to model themselves on Robespierre, or even Bonaparte. Since he believed in free will but doubted Machiavelli's formula for expanding upon it, he was in a position to tell readers that they had alternatives.

Clausewitz's trinity

Clausewitz does, in fact, try to help readers make sense of the apparent discord between the rich possibilities of war's sociopolitical 'logic' and the austere demands of its 'grammar'. The concept of politics is broad, and Clausewitz finds that different aspects of political activity play distinct roles within war. Therefore, *On War* invites readers to look at warfare as a trinity composed of violent emotions, the 'play of chance and probability in which the creative spirit is free to roam' and the rational thinking process which tempers primal emotion and gives creativity its direction (Clausewitz 1976: 89). *On War* elaborates that the passions which inspire war arise from the general population, that creativity rests with the commanders who express popular feeling in the language of military operations and that rationality comes from the institutions of government, where administrators and political leaders consciously determine how to respond to public sentiment and what orders to give the military commanders (Clausewitz 1976: 89).

Clausewitz's attempt to operationalize the trinity may well have created more problems than it solved. Scholars have been particularly critical of the Prussian's sharp division between rational authorities and the emotional populace. Handel, for instance, reminds us that those who believe in democracy would maintain that the population has a right to participate in policy making, and that ordinary citizens may well think as clearly as those who presume to rule them (Handel 1998: 15–16). Those who fear international terrorism might add that angry people can go to war without their government's permission. One might also object to Clausewitz's claim that the emotions which drive warfare need to emerge spontaneously from the population – surely it is possible for leaders to stimulate such passions through propaganda (Clausewitz 1976: 89).

Indeed, several contemporary scholars have argued that, since *On War*'s assertions about the relationship between the people and the government seem short-sighted, the entire treatise is irrelevant (Villacres and Bassford 1995): 11). Readers may decide how harshly to judge this alleged flaw in Clausewitz's work. One may note that the Prussian himself qualified several of his most problematic claims. Clausewitz does not, for instance, insist that only the people are emotional, or that only state officials should make policy or that only uniformed soldiers can practise war as a form of art – he merely says that this is typically the way of things (Clausewitz 1976: 89). More significantly, his deeper point is that, although the three elements of the original trinity – feeling, creative capacity and reasoned planning – shape all wars, the relationships among them are unique to each case, and these relationships are in a continual process of readjustment (Clausewitz 1976: 89).

One may, for instance, imagine a war in which one side is a state which possesses a great advantage in terms of firepower, but in which policy makers keep their armed forces under careful control for fear of losing support from a dubious population. The state may be fighting an insurgent movement led by a charismatic revolutionary who both plans policy and leads his forces in combat. The revolutionary leader may seize the opportunity to take advantage of the state forces' hesitancy in some spectacularly 'creative' way – which may motivate others to join his organization – at a moment when some unrelated scandal causes the state's governing politicians to lose an election – after which the new administration appoints new policy makers who give the state armed forces more permissive instructions. The revolutionary leader may then have to cope with fact that his new supporters expect him to provide more easy victories – at a time when he can no longer use the tactics which once proved so successful. Clausewitz's argument is that, as the military and political situation in this imaginary war or any real one changes, with all that implies for participants at every level, the shifting balance among war's three essential 'tendencies' will drive the process.

Strategic patterns

Clausewitz compared war – as it actually is at any moment – to an 'object suspended between three magnets' (Clausewitz 1976: 89). Although his attempt to explain the trinity in prosaic terms may have been awkward, this simile was close to prophetic. Approximately sixty years after Clausewitz's death, as military writer Barry Watts has noted, the mathematician Henri Poincaré demonstrated that, when an object comes under the influence of three or more forces, its movements become unpredictable (Watts 1996: 113). This is not to say that they are nonsensical – each of the three magnets, to repeat Clausewitz's example, will continue to attract ferrous metals in the same way as before – but the interactions among the forces will cause the object between them to weave in a varied pattern which no mathematical approach can determine. Moreover, seemingly small changes in any part of the system can have cataclysmic consequences elsewhere, while apparently major alterations may fail to produce meaningful results.

The study of such problems has become known as chaos theory. Clausewitz's simile suggests that the continuation of politics with the admixture of military means is chaotic in something close to the mathematical sense, and that none of Machiavelli's 'dykes and barriers' can alter that. The Prussian himself refers to the capricious qualities of warfare as 'friction'. Friction, in his view, is the critical factor which separates the realities of warfare from pure theory (Clausewitz 1976: 119). As previous sections have noted, this distinction between practice and theory is basic to his thought, and therefore no one should be surprised that most of *On War* revolves around the problem of how to succeed in an enterprise where accidents and intangible factors conspire to make the most basic activities difficult (Clausewitz 1976: 119).

One may still hope to be an effective strategist. Even the mathematical version of chaos theory permits this. Human beings, Watts notes, can find and exploit patterns within chaotic systems, even if they cannot reduce those systems to formulae (Watts 2005: 109–10). This suggests that those who wish to become better strategists would be wise to begin by cultivating their ability to pick out useful – or ominous – patterns as they emerge and dissipate within their unpredictably fluid medium.

On War offers similar advice. 'A good general', in Clausewitz's view, is one who can cope with friction through 'instinct' and 'presence of mind' at 'every pulsebeat of war' (Clausewitz 1976: 120). *On War* compares this feat to steering a ship past reefs in an uncharted sea – in the dark (Clausewitz 1976: 120). The Prussian adds that one acquires the ability to overcome such challenges from experience, and, perhaps, from theoretical explanations which help to bring out the significance of more intuitive forms of knowledge (Clausewitz 1976: 120).

To recognize patterns, one must recognize the components which form them. If one reads *On War* as an aid to pattern recognition, one finds that Clausewitz has, indeed, devoted much of his work to familiarizing readers with the most common components of 'politics by other means'. Seekers after patterns must also learn to identify the ways in which the various components combine. Once again, Clausewitz addresses precisely this issue. The Prussian sets himself the task of balancing all three elements of his trinity throughout his writings – for 'a theory which ignores any one of them or seeks to fix an arbitrary relationship between them would conflict with reality to such an extent that for this reason alone it would be totally useless' (Clausewitz 1976: 120).

Clausewitz did not intend *On War* as a treatise on pattern recognition, and he did not systematically structure his writings around the trinity. Nevertheless, these concepts may help a reader to navigate what the Prussian actually did produce. *On War* not only works its way through a prodigious number of the issues which come together to make up armed conflict, it periodically returns to earlier discussions, often reconsidering them from new angles. Clausewitz's changing perspectives typically represent the three factors which his trinity describes.

Thus, for example, Clausewitz devotes an early chapter to one of the most universal features of armed conflict – danger. The first aspect of the trinity is, loosely speaking, emotional experience, and the

Prussian begins this chapter by discussing what it feels like to risk one's life in battle (Clausewitz 1976: 113). Those who have never actually had to face this danger may find the excitement of combat alluring. Clausewitz adds that there are moments when the experience of warfare is every bit as thrilling as such an innocent might wish it to be, but those moments are far from normal.

For one who imagines war as a great adventure, reality will come as a shock. Clausewitz continues in vivid, personal terms. He describes the sound of passing cannonballs and the odd behaviour of men under stress. If he intends readers to recognize the emotions of danger when they encounter them as components of larger patterns, this is the way in which he must encourage them to think and the kind of language he must use.

The second aspect of the trinity is the creative use of war's violent tools, and Clausewitz goes on to explain how the scenario he has been describing affects the officers' ability to direct their forces. The third aspect of the trinity is logical planning at the highest levels, and Clausewitz's chapter on danger proceeds to explore the broader issues which planners need to consider. Although he continues to refer to his story of the novice on the battlefield, he writes in a different style. Now, he discusses his topic in general terms, maintaining the detached tone which supports objective analysis. Clausewitz concludes that soldiers in battle think differently from people in calmer circumstances and that one cannot thoroughly follow their thought processes unless one is with them at the time.

Clausewitz habitually explores points in great depth, and this one is no exception. Having told us that human psychology changes in dangerous situations, he goes on to note that one can recover one's composure over time, and to identify factors such as courage, ambition and experience which may help combatants retain their mental agility (Clausewitz 1976: 113–14). Such ideas reappear with new twists in such chapters as 'Boldness', 'Perseverance', 'The Principal Moral Elements' and 'Military Virtues of the Army', among other places. This helps to explain why even those who have studied Clausewitz for many years still find themselves discovering new dimensions to the Prussian's thought – and why those who have less time to devote to reading *On War* can so easily miss important points.

Clausewitz ends his initial reflections on peril by summing up the reasons why planners must consider the topic in order to assess military situations rationally. Danger and its effects on the people who experience it are, in his view, essential parts of friction. Since, to Clausewitz, friction is the defining characteristic of war, one cannot think sensibly about warfare until one comes to grips with the psychology of mortal peril. One notes that the Prussian has gone from pure narrative specificity to pure theoretical generalization, with a transitional discussion of practical considerations in between. In the process, he has shown how the three aspects of his trinity come together around the issue of danger, and, perhaps, how danger might fit into larger patterns involving the same three elements.

One also notes that Clausewitz implies even deeper theoretical arguments than he explicitly states. Strictly speaking, the first aspect of the trinity is not merely emotion in a general sense. The first aspect of the trinity is the murderous enthusiasm which moves entire communities to kill. *On War* associates this enthusiasm with the population as a whole, which consists largely of civilians.

In 'On Danger in War', Clausewitz argues that this enthusiasm is naive. It will not survive its first battle. Nevertheless, it is one of the three intrinsic elements of warfare. One cannot have war without it. This suggests that, all other things being equal, war will turn out badly for everyone who takes part in it. Combatants, faced with an experience they could never have fully imagined, will lose their nerve. Civilians, indignant at the horrible and unexpected realities of what they have entered into, will panic, revolt, clamour for a hasty peace or, perhaps, press for an equally hasty escalation to yet bloodier extremes. Elsewhere, Clausewitz speaks of a balance to the trinity, and his chapter on danger implies that the trinity is lopsided. Left to itself, it will topple.

For those who remain resolved to fight, Clausewitz's concept of the trinity also suggests both theoretical and practical responses. The balance among the trinity's three elements shifts, and if one threatens to drag it over, the others may still pull it upright. Those who exercise creativity and logic in war may use these abilities to rally hesitant combatants, lead fractious populations, train recruits to be as resilient as the inexperienced can realistically become, plan in the knowledge that fresh troops are unreliable, and so forth. Readers who have followed the argument to this stage must then decide how to apply these ideas to particular wars and particular circumstances. Those who interpret *On War* in the light of chaos theory will also recall that those who meddle with the dynamics of three-body systems will often be surprised by the results.

Related ideas appear throughout the works of most strategic thinkers. Vegetius, for instance, warns commanders to blood fresh troops in skirmishes before committing them to a major battle (Vegetius 1993: 83). Sun Tzu advises commanders to force troops to be courageous by putting them in situations in which they must fight fiercely to survive (Tao 1987: 120–1). Thucydides focuses on Pericles' efforts to temper the moods of the Athenian people. What Clausewitz does, or seems to attempt, is to show how such advice might fit into an overall concept of war.

In this case, Clausewitz implies that the problems of initiating fresh troops and the problems of leading fractious populations are connected. *On War* also suggests that such problems are rooted in the make-up of war itself, and that one must regard them as universal. Ultimately, one must also regard them as insoluble. One may cope with their immediate manifestations at any particular time – a commander may turn recruits into seasoned fighters and a gifted leader may restore his people's confidence – but in the very process, these commanders and leaders will produce unintended consequences which will then present them with further challenges. Sun Tzu, one recalls, appears to have embraced Lao Tzu's principle that weapons are, by their very nature, inauspicious instruments. Clausewitz's chapter on danger explains one reason why both ancient Chinese thinkers appear to have been right.

The practical sceptic?

The fact that Clausewitz explores so many profound theoretical issues in even the shorter sections of an infamously long book makes his work intellectually stimulating, but it may also leave strategists wondering how they are supposed to apply such ruminations in practice. The Swiss strategic thinker Antoine Henri Jomini (1779–1869) concluded that Clausewitz had let his pen run 'vagrant' (Jomini 2005: 42). To this, Clausewitz would be entitled to counter that he follows his theoretical sections with increasingly practical ones. Although Books 1–2 of *On War* focus on the abstract problems of understanding war as a concept, Books 3–7 address concrete issues ranging from the most effective methods for exploiting numerical superiority to the defence of swamps. Book 8 concludes the work by considering the topic of strategic planning, which presumably requires both theoretical knowledge and a sense of how to act upon it.

Jomini acknowledged that *On War* took up such topics. Nevertheless, he did not think that Clausewitz dealt with them constructively. In the Swiss author's view, the Prussian's corrosive and nearly universal 'scepticism' merely undercut serious efforts to improve practice (Jomini 2005: 42). Jomini also suggested that the Prussian's critiques

were self-serving. Clausewitz, the Swiss remarked, 'believes in the effi-
cacy of his own doctrines if he does not believe in those of others'
(Jomini 2005: 42).

For better or for worse, Clausewitz was certainly a sceptic. Where
followers of Sun Tzu might seek clever ways to win battles without
fighting, *On War* reminds us that the persuasive 'grammar' of direct
physical violence is liable to reassert itself before long and, where
Machiavelli's Fortuna coyly yields to those with the manly *virtu* to
force themselves upon her, Clausewitz's friction remains eternally
implacable. Thus, although Clausewitz acknowledges that it is practically impossible to gain any strategic advantage unless one manages
to take the enemy by surprise, he warns that surprise moves will rarely
be sufficient to achieve truly significant victories (Clausewitz 1976:
198). Although he salutes the strategists who exceed reasonable expectations through 'genius', he offers little encouragement to artistes – a
Clausewitzian genius is likely to be staunch and 'inquiring' rather than
impetuously brilliant (Clausewitz 1976: 112). (Clausewitz's chapter on
boldness, which he views as 'a genuinely creative force', encourages a
more Machiavellian approach: Clausewitz 1976: 190.)

In this spirit of sceptical enquiry, the Prussian demystifies popular
strategic concepts. For instance, many military writers of his day were
captivated by the idea that the secret of successful strategy might lie
in a commander's talent for deploying forces in well-chosen places at
well-chosen times. The expression 'space and time' had become a
catchphrase. *On War* tells us that some authors went so far as to
speculate that the most gifted generals had a special organ in their
brains which helped them to make space-and-time calculations more
effectively (Clausewitz 1976: 196).

Clausewitz agrees that space and time are important factors in
all physical undertakings. In that sense, they are basic to strategy
(Clausewitz 1976: 196). Nevertheless, Clausewitz notes, there are few
historical examples of generals who suffered serious defeats because
they failed to calculate space-and-time relationships effectively. History
provides numerous examples of leaders who won victories through
effective positioning and timing, but Clausewitz suggests that we
can understand such achievements more fully if we set the concept
of 'space and time to one side and look deeper into the details of
what these commanders actually did and how they actually did it'
(Clausewitz 1976: 197).

Despite Jomini's accusations, the Prussian attempted to build as
well as to tear down. Although Clausewitz questioned the ways in
which his contemporaries understood a wide range of prominent

strategic concepts, he often made great efforts to explain what those concepts actually meant, and one might apply them more productively. Clausewitz also tried to explain why he felt his critiques were fair and necessary. For an example of how Clausewitz attempted to justify his scepticism – and a clearer idea of how his advice on practical issues contrasted with that of other influential thinkers – one might look at the way he treated the concept of holding forces in reserve.

Vegetius and Machiavelli, one may recall, were both enthusiastic about reserves. The Roman author detailed a variety of tactical situations in which having a reserve could prove useful. The Florentine also found that maintaining a reserve upheld the concept of building dykes and barriers to redirect Fortuna's turbulent rivers – a principle which he advised readers to apply in whatever ways they could, whenever they could create the opportunity. Clausewitz agreed with both of them.

Like *De re militari*, *On War* lists examples of situations in which commanders might find reserves indispensable. Like Machiavelli, Clausewitz connects these examples by noting that all reflect the principle that it is wise to have forces available to deal with the unforeseen. Indeed, this concept can help one decide how large a force to hold back. The more uncertain the situation, he suggests, the greater the need for reserves (Clausewitz 1976: 210). This means, for instance, that one will normally need larger reserve forces when rough terrain limits visibility. This also means that commanders on the defensive will normally need to maintain particularly large reserves, since they cannot know when or where their opponents will strike.

Nevertheless, Clausewitz's overall theory of war also warns that, no matter what form the military instrument assumes, its special power lies in its potential to harm. We forget that at our peril. One of the reasons why Clausewitz is so critical of so many worthwhile strategic concepts is that he fears they may distract us from this truth. Having detailed numerous ways in which commanders might use reserves productively, Clausewitz reminds readers that, no matter how valuable reserve forces can be, one cannot realize that value until one sends them against the enemy.

If one continues to hold troops back after a battle has passed its critical point, one has wasted them. To commit one's reserves at the right moment requires perceptive decision making. Theories which reduce the problem of using reserves effectively to glib abstractions tempt us to abdicate that judgement. This problem, Clausewitz adds, is all too common. During Prussia's 1806 war with Napoleonic France, he notes, Prussian commanders kept over 45,000 of their troops out of the fighting, with no particular purpose in mind (Clausewitz 1976: 211–12). Clausewitz found it unnecessary to add that, while approximately one third of the Prussian army waited in reserve, Napoleon overran Prussia (Parkinson 1970: 50).

Clausewitz's sceptical approach led him to take a particularly provocative position on the subject of intelligence. Where Sun Tzu – like most contemporary strategic thinkers – saw information as a tool for gaining control of situations, Clausewitz feared that it would become the opposite. To begin with, the Prussian noted that friction affects information-related activities as much as it affects every other aspect of war. Most intelligence reports, in his view, are confusing, ambiguous or simply wrong (Clausewitz 1976: 117). Not only are such reports misleading, they are all too likely to shake one's confidence. Thus, they undermine the resolve and cultivated intuition which are a commander's only real tools for prevailing amidst the chaos of war. Clausewitz goes so far as to suggest that commanders should count themselves lucky when their intelligence reports contradict one another because then, at least, they will find it easier to ignore them (Clausewitz 1976: 117).

As usual, Clausewitz thought the issue through in greater depth than his more curmudgeonly comments seem to suggest. Contemporary researcher John Ferris, for instance, reminds readers that the Prussian was primarily warning field commanders about the risks of overreacting to tactical reports in the midst of battle (Ferris 2005: 241). According to Ferris, Clausewitz understood that higher-level planners have both greater requirements for information and a greater ability to use it effectively. Readers of earlier paragraphs may recall that Clausewitz attributed certain famous victories to the fact that the triumphant generals had made a 'correct appraisal' of the opposing commanders – a feat which must have demanded some data about what the opposing commanders were like.

Handel, meanwhile, notes that On War's derision of wartime information was justified in the early nineteenth century (Handel 1989: 26). Since then, Handel observes, technological advances have made intelligence reports more reliable. Strategists now can – and must – make greater use of them. Handel's arguments about intelligence, however, raise a broader point about Clausewitz's work. Many other aspects of warfare have changed since the 1800s as well.

For this reason, many scholars have concluded that all of Clausewitz's writings on practical issues are obsolete. Meilinger, for instance, declares that '[n]early half of On War is now of little use' (Meilinger 2007: 119). Bernard Brodie and Michael Howard agree

that the practically oriented sections of Clausewitz's work will appeal
more to historians than to modern students of war, although Brodie
adds that historians should find them very interesting indeed
(Brodie 1976: 672; Howard 1983: 4). At a certain level, Meilinger and
Brodie are obviously right. Only historians are likely to be directly
interested in *On War*'s discussion of the number of hours an early
nineteenth-century division consisting of eight to ten thousand men
could hold off superior enemy forces in particular types of terrain
(Clausewitz 1976: 238).

Clausewitz, however, was not primarily interested in such details
himself. Early in his writings on the theory of war, he notes that he
does not intend to repeat points which troops learn in their training
(Clausewitz, 1976: 131). All a theorist needs to know about such subjects, he continues, is 'the end product' (Clausewitz 1976: 132).

When Clausewitz turns to more technical issues in Book Three, he
assures readers that he still has the end product in mind. Indeed, he
notes, an attempt to catalogue isolated details about the methods of
waging war without reference to their deeper significance would be an
exercise in pedantry (Clausewitz 1976: 183). When Clausewitz tightens
his focus to examine battlefield tactics in Book Four, he reaffirms that
these details are, indeed, indispensable. He does not include them
simply because they are part of warfare; he includes them because one
needs to understand them in order to understand more fundamental
principles of strategy (Clausewitz 1976: 225).

Clausewitz found inspiration in practice, claimed to justify his ideas
using evidence taken from practice and explained his subtler points
using illustrations based upon practice. Moreover, throughout his
work, he emphasizes the importance of viewing all the diverse aspects
of strategy as a unified whole. Accordingly, it seems unlikely that one
can properly understand the apparently timeless sections of *On War*
without also considering the ones in which Clausewitz related his theoretical concepts to war as he knew it. Readers may recall that fifteenth-
century readers of Vegetius encountered a similar problem. Those who
used the Roman's ideas most successfully tended to take the earlier
author's entire work, including his superficially outdated thoughts on
practical issues, into account.

Twenty-first-century readers may attempt to use Clausewitz the
same way. Certainly, some of Clausewitz's own concepts seem to
support such an approach. If all war shares the same underlying
'grammar', one can presumably learn the principles of this grammar
from the Prussian's reflections on nineteenth-century European
warfare and then adapt those principles to war in different settings.

Nevertheless, even Clausewitz continually found himself forced to distinguish between what the logic of war seems to imply in theory and what one actually needs to know to engage with the reality of the thing.

From time to time, latter-day strategists may indeed be attracted to the practical chapters of *On War* for guidance on contemporary military operations. If the Prussian's work has value, this would appear to be a reasonable way to use it. Nevertheless, those who wish to use *On War* this way would be wise to keep the author's many caveats in mind. Applying Clausewitz, like waging war itself, appears to be a matter in which the simplest thing is difficult.

Conclusion

Readers of *On War* continually discover that the author comments on issues which might interest them, and just as often discover that he leaves them to decide what to do with his thoughts. Clausewitz understood that he was putting his audience in this position. Early in *On War*, as the Prussian revealed how difficult it is to define the most basic strategic concepts, he reflected that, although this difficulty may frustrate theorists, it may inspire and encourage the rest of us (Clausewitz 1976: 86). People, he tells us, find uncertainty fascinating, not merely for its own sake but because it provides opportunities to those with the courage to seize them (Clausewitz 1976: 86).

What Clausewitz here calls uncertainty, others call freedom. Historian Azar Gat has noted that Clausewitz's challenge to those who would reduce human affairs such as strategy to fixed concepts and formulas is a significant part of what distinguishes *On War* from the dominant eighteenth-century writings on the subject (Gat 1989: 139–40). The Prussian's faith in unquantifiable human potential is no less controversial today. This faith remains attractive for the same reasons which Clausewitz described – it accounts for reality as we experience it, and it offers us some control over our destinies. Indeed, it offers us more independence than Machiavelli's programme for mastering Fortuna, since Machiavellians achieve freedom only through a long collective struggle, whereas Clausewitz's possibilities may open at any time for anyone.

The fact that possibilities always exist does not mean that all things are possible. Clausewitz continually warns readers of that, as well as confronting them with the duty to pursue opportunities responsibly. Most often, this means paying due respect to raw power, but it has many other meanings as well, possibly including moral ones. Although

Clausewitz emphasizes that 'war is such a dangerous business that the mistakes which come from kindness are the very worst', he also allows that the horror of war 'must make us take war more seriously' (Clausewitz 1976: 75, 260).

Clausewitz does not spell out what taking war more seriously actually involves. One could easily infer that it means that those who have a choice in the matter would be well advised to think carefully before going to war at all. One must hasten to add that the Prussian was no pacifist. Not only did he warn against misplaced compassion, he actively glorified war (Clausewitz 1976: 192). Nevertheless, the liberating uncertainty within his concepts allows his ideas to guide prudently peaceful strategies as robustly as it guides more bellicose ones.

One also recalls that Clausewitz's own wartime career was primarily one of defending things he cherished from a conqueror, not one of gratuitously seeking conflict. On the contrary, he observed that rashness can be as naive as humanitarian sentimentalism. 'Would Prussia in 1792 have dared to invade France with 70,000 men' he reflected, 'if she had had an inkling that the repercussions in the case of failure would be strong enough to overthrow the old European balance of power?' (Clausewitz 1976: 581).

Sun Tzu might well have made similar points. To accept war is to accept all that the logic of war may imply. That includes the moral responsibility for inflicting tremendous suffering, and it also includes the virtually unlimited perils of friction. *On War* teaches us to think of war as a political instrument, and it reminds us of precisely what that instrument can do, but there are other instruments as well, and, although Clausewitz does not discuss them at any length, his ideas suggest that we would be wise to use all of them.

Further reading

Aron, Raymond (1985) *Clausewitz: Philosopher of War*, trans. Christine Booker and Norman Stone. Englewood Cliffs, NJ: Prentice-Hall.

Bassford, Christopher (1994) 'John Keegan and the Grand Tradition of Bashing Clausewitz: A Polemic', *War in History* 1(3) (Nov.): 319–36.

Clausewitz, Carl von (1976) *On War*, trans. Michael Howard and Peter Paret. Princeton, NJ: Princeton University Press.

Strachan, Hew and Herberg-Rothe, Andreas (eds) (2007) *Clausewitz in the Twenty-First Century*. Oxford: Oxford University Press.

5 RIGHT PLACE, RIGHT TIME, RIGHT TECHNOLOGY

Despite the many differences between Sun Tzu, Machiavelli and Clausewitz, critics of these thinkers find that all three have at least one thing in common. All allegedly overlook the significance of technology (Van Creveld 1991: 321). Throughout military history, the importance of technological mastery has been particularly obvious in naval warfare. Therefore, it may be more than a coincidence that Sun Tzu, Machiavelli and Clausewitz seem to have ignored maritime issues as well.

Thucydides, by contrast, reminds us that maritime power – and the technology that makes it possible – plays a distinctive role in strategy. Not only can it help to win wars, it helps in its own way. The fact that Athens began the Peloponnesian War with a superior fleet whereas Sparta began with superior ground forces did not mean that the enemy cities were evenly matched – it meant that strategists on the opposing sides had different options, confronted different challenges and sought different goals. Indeed, the differences between land power and sea power conditioned the way Spartans and Athenians understood the most basic concepts of politics and war.

This invites us to expand our understanding of strategy to account for the special role of maritime power. Moreover, just as technical acumen allows strategists to exploit the seas, human ingenuity opens other new venues for strategic action. For over a century, to pick the most notable example, aircraft have extended conflict into a third dimension. Technology changes people's relationship to their environment and this affects strategy at a fundamental level.

This chapter introduces this issue by examining the long-established and deeply studied implications of air and maritime power. It focuses on methods of using these types of power to achieve relatively well-defined objectives in the short to medium term. Alfred Thayer Mahan and Julian Corbett stand out for their writings on maritime strategy. Thus, the first main section of this chapter explores their works, while a second contrasts their positions with Giulio Douhet's influential arguments about war in the air.

Clausewitz, as is so often the case, proves resilient in the face of his critics. Mahan, Corbett and Douhet alike find themselves attempting to balance the apparent simplicity of war's theoretical 'grammar' with the complexity of actual wars which take place within the larger context of the real world. Indeed, one of the greatest attractions of extending conflict into new environments is that this can be a way to change the context of a dispute. Nevertheless, as the chapter's conclusion notes, strategists are well advised to consider the possibility that such attractions may prove treacherous.

Location, location, location

One can sum up the strategic value of maritime power with a single word. That word is 'transport'. Ships allow one to go to a greater number of places along a wider variety of routes. Often, those routes will be shorter than the land alternatives. Even when they are not, water transport is dramatically more efficient than any other method of moving large cargoes long distances.

Thus, strategists who control adequate numbers of ships and enjoy the ability to use them freely can typically deploy larger forces than those who cannot. Those forces will normally be ready for action sooner. Moreover, those forces will normally be better able to sustain themselves throughout the course of an extended campaign. For those who share Clausewitz's views about the self-evident advantage of being stronger than one's enemies, the implications could not be more profound.

Admirers of Sun Tzu should be equally impressed. Those who control the seas will typically be able to attack their enemies from many directions and may choose the one that seems most favourable. Those who do not must fear attack from all sides and prepare accordingly. As this ancient Chinese thinker noted, such situations allow attackers to concentrate their forces while forcing defenders to disperse their troops over wide areas (Tao 1987: 106). This virtually ensures that the attacker will enjoy numerical superiority.

The American admiral, author and president of the US Naval War College Alfred Thayer Mahan, active in the late nineteenth and early twentieth centuries, opens his best-known work by exploring such points. Readers are entitled to feel that he is stating the obvious, but he takes this approach in order to develop a deeper argument. His insight is not merely that these things happen to be true; it is the extent of their consequences. Mahan never wrote a book entitled *The Convenience of Sea Power for Logistics*; instead, he called his most famous work *The Influence of Sea Power upon History*. (In fact, Mahan wrote several volumes in the *Influence of Sea Power* series, the most famous of which is undoubtedly *The Influence of Sea Power upon History, 1660–1783*; Sumida 1997: 120.) Mahan encourages readers to understand this influence as 'but one factor in that general advance and decay of nations which is called their history' but adds that its role is 'immense' (Sumida 1997: 27).

If the value of sea power was as simple to grasp as the fact that more than 70 per cent of the world's surface consists of water, one would expect all strategists to exploit it as energetically as their circumstances allowed. Instead, some communities have consistently made more of their maritime opportunities than others. Although *The Influence of Sea Power upon History 1660–1783* inevitably contains a great deal of material on the naval triumphs of Great Britain, historian Jon Tetsuro Sumida observes that Mahan was perhaps equally interested in the relatively lacklustre exercise of maritime capabilities in France (Sumida 1997: 28). The fact that Mahan's own country had suffered badly from its lack of naval preparedness in the War of 1812 undoubtedly sharpened his interest in such issues, as did the fact that he was writing at a time when the US navy was expanding, and when, thanks in part to his own efforts, its role in national life was a matter of increasing public debate.

Just as Vegetius, Machiavelli and Clausewitz found it necessary to ground their broader ideas in detailed considerations of weapons, training and tactics, those who wish to use maritime forces to influence history must consider the details of how they are going to go about it. Mahan addressed this issue from both a naval commander's point of view and from the perspective of grand strategy. Later parts of this chapter will discuss his grand strategic ideas in more detail. This section will address his approach to the more immediate problems of naval operations. Although Mahan's points on these subjects are spread throughout many writings, Sumida has compiled and analysed them in his *Inventing Grand Strategy and Teaching Command*.

Mahan, like Machiavelli and Clausewitz, advocated large battles to destroy opposing military forces as the most broadly reliable way to master the situations which arise during war. The admiral also shared Clausewitz's scepticism about alternative approaches to warfare, particularly those which come 'presented in the fascinating garb of cheapness' (Sumida 1997: 47). Mahan warned, for instance, that amphibious operations were a waste of resources and a 'fad' (Sumida 1997: 45). Once one has crippled one's enemies' navies, Mahan reasoned, one may blockade their ports and deny them the use of the sea. Meanwhile, such a victory followed by such a blockade would presumably leave one's own merchant ships free to sail in relative safety.

The admiral understood that there would be exceptions to all such rules, and that, even when particular principles happen to be relevant, commanders would still have to determine how to put them into practice. He certainly opposed 'the sterile glory of fighting battles merely to win them' (Sumida 1997: 44). Nevertheless, he continually reminded readers that one achieves strategic results through 'organized force' (Sumida 1997: 47). Fleets of warships, in his view, were the actual organized forces which made applying the concept of organized force possible. Thus, Mahan suggests, the most effective way to deploy one's own ships will normally be to concentrate them into the most powerful fleet one can assemble, and that fleet's first mission must normally be to sink the enemy navy.

One's approach to naval operations has implications for naval hardware. There are many ways to design ships, and it may be possible to invent new ones. Maritime strategists must determine which types of vessels will be most effective in the situations they envision using them in. Since building new ships practically always requires daunting amounts of time and resources, maritime strategists must also be prepared to live with their decisions for extended periods. Not only must a ship be as effective as possible for its intended use, its capabilities must be relevant to as many as possible of the situations which might arise during its lifetime.

When Machiavelli and Clausewitz considered similar problems in land warfare, both concluded that strategists should place their highest priority on creating a powerful infantry. The two authors developed this idea in different ways, but both would have agreed that one of the principal reasons why infantry is exceptionally important is that it is well suited for confronting strong enemy forces and annihilating those forces in battle. Neither author promised that this would guarantee a successful outcome to every conflict, but both agreed that it is practically always a step in the right direction.

Mahan's writings suggest that the maritime equivalent of infantry is the capital ship. The capital ships of his day were the large armoured, gun-carrying vessels known as battleships, but one could apply similar arguments to the so-called 'supercarriers' of leading twenty-first-century navies with only minor modification. For numerous reasons of engineering, big ships are both more resilient and more capable of dealing out destruction than their smaller equivalents. Infantry is dramatically more effective when combined with other arms, and capital ships may depend upon protection from support craft for their very survival, but, if one's primary goal is to sink enemy navies in major surface battles, one seems well advised to acquire the largest contingent of large fighting vessels one's circumstances allow, deploying smaller and more specialized designs primarily in order to assist them.

Nevertheless, Clausewitz also concluded that it was unrealistic to think of warfare as nothing more than a massive duel. This is as true in maritime conflicts as in any other kind. Wayne P. Hughes of the US navy notes that even navies which have no hope of winning large surface battles can serve valuable strategic purposes (Kane 2002: 45). To illustrate this point, he cited examples from both the American assault on Okinawa in the Second World War and the British campaign to regain the Falklands Islands in the 1982 Falklands War. In the first case, although the US navy had crippled Japan's fleet well before the Okinawa operation, Japanese pilots using suicide tactics managed to sink American ships at the rate of one per day (Kane 2002: 45). In the second, even after Britain's Royal Navy had driven Argentina's surface fleet from the combat zone, the Argentinians managed to hamper British operations significantly with the threat of air, missile and submarine attack. Hughes draws special attention to the point that Argentina was able to mount a credible submarine threat with just one operational submarine (Kane 2002: 45).

Sumida demonstrates that Mahan was well aware that there is more to war than battles (Sumida 1997: 44). Mahan, like Clausewitz, may have intended his propositions about organized force as starting points for a fuller discussion. Whatever the case, author Julian Corbett concentrated more explicit attention on the fact that there are actually many ways to use ships for strategic purposes. Corbett urged strategists to keep the ultimate goals of maritime power in mind.

Since people live on the land, bodies of water are primarily useful only as a way to get from place to place. Since the oceans are vast, it is rare for even the strongest navies to be able to monitor them – let alone control them – in their entirety. Therefore, although Corbett declares that the object of naval warfare must always be command of the sea, he reminds readers that command of the sea means neither more nor less than 'the control of communications' (Kane 2002: 45). Seldom will one side enjoy total command of the sea while the other completely lacks it. Instead, opposing sides will achieve different levels of command at different times and in different places.

The art of maritime strategy, Corbett suggests, consists of getting the maximum possible use out of water transportation while frustrating the enemy's ability to do the same. This may involve sinking enemy warships to enhance one's 'command' of disputed points, but it may just as well mean keeping the enemy's battle fleet occupied in one part of the ocean while routing one's own transport vessels across another. In offensive operations, raids against enemy coasts and merchant shipping may actually be more useful than showdowns with enemy navies. Opportunities to cooperate with friendly land forces are also to be prized, since the true purpose of maritime operations is not to win a contest on the waters, but to overcome land-based opponents.

Corbett's approach to naval operations inspires him to take a different view of naval technology. For him, writing at the dawn of the twentieth century, the maritime equivalent of infantry was not the capital ship, but the cruiser. The cruisers of his time were smaller and more lightly armed than battleships, but they were also cheaper and more capable of operating independently. An early twentieth-century nation which based its navy upon cruisers would have been able to build relatively large numbers of them and dispatch them throughout the oceans to discomfit its enemies in a wide variety of creative ways. Where one approach to maritime operations values smaller ships primarily as tools for supporting capital ships, Corbett valued capital ships largely as tools for keeping enemy warships from hunting down friendly cruisers (Kane 2002: 46).

Just as certain aspects of Machiavelli's enthusiasm for infantry parallel Mahan's arguments in favour of capital ships, other passages from *Discourses on Livy* foreshadow Corbett's advocacy of cruisers. Although the Florentine valued infantry for its use in winning decisive battles, readers may recall that he also paid special attention to foot soldiers' ability to carry on the fight in places where seemingly impressive forces such as cavalry cannot. Clausewitz expressed the same concept in more general terms (Clausewitz 1976: 286).

Corbett explored the various ways in which strategists might use maritime forces at length. Many other thinkers – Charles E. Callwell, a British military officer of the late nineteenth and early twentieth centuries, being an early and prominent example – have continued this effort. For those who wish to use armed forces to achieve long-term political goals, one of the most interesting points to come out of such writings is that maritime power seems to be particularly well suited for manipulating the circumstances under which conflicts take place, and thus for influencing enemy behaviour in ways which go beyond simple firepower. Corbett recalls how Sir Francis Drake boasted of his ability to 'impeach' the Spanish navy's threat to England simply by sending a relatively small number of vessels to pose a countering threat (Kane 2002: 46).

Clausewitz noted that when one has the potential to perform a certain act, one may achieve some of its effects without actually having to carry it out. He compared this situation to commerce, where one can buy goods by writing a cheque without immediately needing to produce cash (Clausewitz 1976: 97). Maritime power, to continue this analogy, may be especially useful for the strategic equivalent of trading in futures, options and derivatives. One can use it, not merely to facilitate a direct exchange of one thing for another but to arrange new kinds of transactions on newly devised terms.

Corbett used the Russo-Japanese War to illustrate how strategists may employ maritime power to set the terms for a conflict, and thus to gain advantages over apparently more powerful opponents. Japan could not possibly have destroyed the Russian army in all-out war. '[W]ho will contend that, if Japan had tried to make her war with Russia, as Napoleon made his, she could have fared even as well as he did?' (Kane 2002: 49). To make matters worse for Japanese strategists, the political leaders on both sides were, indeed, committed to fighting with all their strength.

> [E]very one felt that the real object of the war was in the abstract unlimited, that it was in fact to decide whether Russia or Japan was to be the predominant power in the Far East. Like the Franco-German War of 1870, it had all the aspect of what the Germans call 'a trial of strength'. Such a war is one which above all appears incapable of decision except by the complete overthrow of the one power by the other. (Kane 2002: 49)

Fortunately for Japan, the 'political and geographical conditions' of the conflict presented the Japanese with strategic opportunities. Readers of *The Peloponnesian War* may recall that, although Athens and Sparta also had general and long-standing motives to view one another as enemies, the rival cities did not spontaneously attack each other for that reason. War broke out only in the context of a complex political drama which began on the seemingly insignificant island of Corcyra, and Thucydides found it appropriate to narrate this episode in detail. The 'trial of strength' between Russia and Japan took shape in a specific place over a specific issue as well. Corbett continues:

> The penetration of Russia into Manchuria threatened the absorption of Korea into the Russian Empire, and this Japan regarded as fatal to her own position and future development. Her power to maintain Korean integrity would be the outward and visible sign of her ability to assert herself as a Pacific Power. Her abstract quarrel with Russia could therefore be crystallised into a concrete objective. (Kane 2002: 49)

This objective had concrete physical characteristics. The disputed area was far from the economic centre of Russia, and overland transportation networks were poor. Ground forces on both sides relied heavily on maritime transportation. This meant that if the Japanese could neutralize the Russian fleet, Japan's army could fight the Russian army on more even terms.

The Japanese succeeded at this for a variety of reasons. Mahan might have noted that the Japanese government had invested in developing a modern fleet and that Japanese sailors of every rank performed admirably. Others might note that the Japanese navy opened the war by carrying out a devastating raid on the Russian fleet at Port Arthur. This is not, however, the surprise attack that Corbett singles out for special attention. Corbett focuses on the Japanese army's equally audacious capture of Seoul, which required support from the sea, and which succeeded despite the fact that powerful Russian naval forces remained active (Corbett 1911: 82). This coup allowed Japan's ground forces to dominate the rest of Korea.

From that point on, the Japanese ground forces simultaneously drove against both Port Arthur and the Russian ground forces at Liao-yang. Under other circumstances, Japanese commanders would have had to split their forces between these different objectives, perhaps fatally weakening themselves in the process. By using maritime transport to take full advantage of the local geography, Corbett explains, Japanese commanders managed to coordinate the two campaigns in a mutually supportive way (Corbett 1911: 83). This combination of ground and naval operations ultimately allowed the Japanese to capture both Liao-yang and Port Arthur, putting the Russian forces in the theatre in an untenable position on both land and sea. In theory, Russia remained far more powerful than Japan, but its leaders could no longer bring that power to bear at anything they might have regarded as an acceptable cost.

Although the previous examples concern open warfare, fleets play similar roles in peacetime. The arrival of naval forces in a disputed region affects all parties' strategic options even if the warships never fire a shot. Naval forces also have special characteristics which make them particularly useful in situations which demand finesse. The fact that ships can reach a wide variety of destinations at relatively short notice, for instance, means that political leaders find it relatively easy to get them where they need them, even in rapidly developing situations.

Moving ships through international waters attracts less attention, involves fewer legal complications and typically proves less provocative than, for instance, marching an army into a disputed region. Moreover, ships can perform a wide variety of missions when they arrive. The same vessel may blockade a disputed waterway on one occasion, escort friendly shipping on another, bombard land targets on a third, serve as a floating headquarters for ground forces on a fourth and then go on to evacuate civilian refugees. One could list many further examples.

James Cable has written insightfully on the role of maritime forces in politically complex situations (Cable 1971: *passim*). Like Mahan and Corbett, Cable finds that his research has implications for ship design and naval budgeting. If one wishes to practise what Cable straightforwardly describes as gunboat diplomacy, one needs the 'naval equivalent' of the 'clubs and shields' which the twentieth-century British army adopted for crowd control in Ireland (Cable 1971: 170). The ability to survive collision, Cable notes, might prove more useful than sophisticated anti-ship missiles (Cable 1971: 170).

Nevertheless, Cable does not merely advise strategists to build the contemporary equivalent of Corbett's cruisers. On the contrary, he reminds them that they will have to make technological compromises in the face of tight funds and an unknowable future. It is easier, he notes, to adapt a capital ship for gunboat diplomacy than to adapt a lightly armed patrol craft for high seas combat (Cable 1971: 171). Nevertheless, he suggests, a ship's most expensive and technologically demanding capabilities may often be its least useful ones, and a single-minded effort to build the most advanced vessels possible can easily degenerate into vanity (Cable 1971: 171).

Valuable as maritime power can be, its uses vary greatly with circumstances. If Japan had confronted Russia across a differently shaped coastline, it would have had to deploy its forces in an entirely different way. Clausewitz's reflections on friction and context seem particularly relevant to maritime affairs. Cable makes this point explicit. Writing against the backdrop of the Cold War nuclear stand-off, he notes:

> The way toward megadeaths is well charted and straightforward. There is a single theory, properly worked out and coherent. Scientific man need only maintain his progress to reach his final destination. Turning aside means exploring one difficult and devious trial after another. Limited naval force is among them: an expedient with an uncertain future, neither intrinsically desirable nor generally applicable. If men were sensible, governments would resolve their disputes without the threat or use of force. If men accepted the logic of their own lunacy, there would be no need to limit the force they employed. It is in the absurd world of real life that governments sometimes impose their will through the ritual confrontation of warships, by seizing vessels, landing marines or establishing a blockade. Such devices are of interest because they have actually been used; they are of importance because their employment might be repeated; their value derives from the existence of worse alternatives. (Cable 1971: 172)

The great grammarian

Aerial warfare raises similar issues to maritime power and takes certain of them to greater extremes. Aircraft, like ships, achieve their special significance as a means of moving things from place to place. Where floating vehicles allow one to move large cargoes along water routes efficiently, flying vehicles allow one to move small cargoes in all directions fast. These small cargoes may include weapons, and powered heavier-than-air flight happened to become feasible during the same historical period that inventors perfected compact armaments ranging from machine guns to poison gas.

Just as Mahan drew attention to the simple but strategically pivotal role of the seas, early twentieth-century thinkers explored the strategic use of the air. For those who wish to explore this topic, the works of Giulio Douhet provide a useful starting point. Although Douhet did a poor job of predicting the course of future wars, he did an exceptionally thorough job of sketching out the distinguishing characteristics of air power (Kohn and Harahan 1983: viii; Watts 1984: 1). Douhet, like Clausewitz, is a mapmaker.

Douhet contrasted the free movement of aircraft to the constrained mobility of ground forces. The fact that he was writing only three years after the cruel, frustrating stalemate of the First World War gave his points special poignancy. As Douhet notes, land and maritime forces alike are limited to the frequently inconvenient contours of a two-dimensional environment – the planetary surface (Douhet 1983: 8). Both must follow the routes permitted to them by terrain.

Ships might appear more mobile on the open oceans, but the very fact that they are restricted to the water means that the principle remains valid (Douhet 1983: 8). These truths make the movements of surface forces predictable, and, under modern conditions, relatively easy for opposing forces to block. The fact that armed forces had become able to check the movements of enemy armed forces had social, political and industrial effects as well as tactical ones. Civilians had enjoyed the luxury of avoiding combat, humanitarian lawmakers had been able to implement relatively effective legislation requiring military personnel to respect civilians' non-combatant status and more militaristically minded authorities had been free to organize non-combatants to produce war *matériel* with only the occasional threat of enemy interference (Douhet 1983: 9).

Douhet goes on to declare this situation obsolete. Aircraft can fly over opposing forces to attack virtually any point in the enemy's territory. Since warplanes can generally ignore ground obstacles, they are free to travel by the shortest, fastest routes. Alternatively, fuel permitting, they may follow whatever other route they choose, increasing their chances of gaining surprise and complicating attempts to defend against them (Douhet 1983: 9–10). Civilians can no longer count on their country's armed forces to keep them safe, and strategists can no longer depend on a protected industrial base to support military operations.

Mahan presented the overall influence of sea power upon history as long term and intertwined with other factors. The influence of air power, Douhet suggests, will be singular and effectively instantaneous. A few enemy aircraft, he suggests, could cripple Italy's railways in a single day (Douhet 1983: 51–2). A small number more could strike Rome, destroying the centres of finance and government. Such a strike could also cut off the capital's communications with the outside world. Douhet expected this to provoke panic and chaos, certainly within Rome itself and presumably throughout the nation (Douhet 1983: 51–2).

Even in this scenario, Douhet lets Rome off easily. Elsewhere he notes that bomber aircraft could exterminate the populations of European capitals with chemical weapons and then use incendiaries to burn the lifeless cities to the ground (Douhet 1983: 182). The toxins, he elaborates, would make it impossible for anyone to enter the affected areas to put out the fires (Douhet 1983: 182). Douhet adds that

American scientists have experimented with poisons which would render affected areas barren for years (Douhet 1983: 182).

When Mahan considered the practicalities of how commanders might use ships to exert influence, he concluded that the most effective way to proceed would normally be to amass the strongest forces consistent with one's overall situation and employ them to cripple the enemy. This is the logic of Clausewitz's wrestling match, and also the logic which Machiavelli hoped to brandish over Fortuna. Douhet reasoned along much the same lines. The 'basic principle' of warfare in all environments, he declares, is to '*inflict the greatest damage in the shortest possible time*' (Douhet 1983: 51).

The italics are Douhet's own, and so is the urgency they imply. Douhet believed that aircraft had made prompt, concentrated attacks more decisive than ever. Not only can massed aircraft strike crippling blows, they can deliver them within a matter of hours, and they can repeat the performance regularly at virtually whatever locations their commanders choose. Many of the factors which blunt, qualify and transform the effects of offensive action in other environments lose their relevance in the air. In naval warfare, for instance, it is common for one side to achieve command over the sea in some locations while its opponents remain active in others but Douhet believed that air warfare would be practically impossible to localize (Douhet 1983: 220).

Historically, land and naval forces have been able to retreat, disperse, adopt guerrilla tactics and resort to various other stratagems in order to hold off powerful attackers. Aerial warfare offers few such options. For all their agility in flight, aircraft are completely dependent upon airfields. Moreover, the airfields themselves rely on a larger complex of factories and transportation systems to remain in operation (Douhet 1983: 222).

Enemy air offensives can strike such networks directly. To shield one's air forces from the effects of enemy attack, one would have to find some way to 'draw in' much of one's national infrastructure. Douhet acknowledges the possibility that one might disperse critical industries over wide areas and conceal key installations underground, but he does not view this as a particularly attractive option (Douhet 1983: 222). The only effective way to protect oneself, he argues, is to drive enemy aircraft from the skies, and the surest way to accomplish that will be to destroy the facilities which permit them to fly (Douhet 1983: 53).

One notes that Douhet is advising virtually everyone who takes part in aerial warfare to go about it in the same way. When war breaks out, both sides must launch bombing raids to destroy their opponents' infrastructure as quickly as possible. Once one side has rendered the other incapable of launching aircraft, it will enjoy what Douhet calls command of the air. That side may then exploit its air supremacy to attack whatever targets seem most vital to the enemy war effort. The Italian theorist notes that there are cases in which commanders may profit from alternative approaches – if, for instance, the enemy's air forces are already too weak to require such attention – but nevertheless, he portrays aerial warfare as simpler than any other kind.

Land and maritime forces also depend on support from their home country's infrastructure. Douhet warns army and navy commanders to make ready for situations in which enemy air forces may deprive them of it. He is willing to believe that adequately prepared surface forces may find ways to fight on even after their enemies have won control of the skies. Nevertheless, he is not sure it will do them much good. Those who have won command of the air may go on to destroy what they like and, under most circumstances, 'a collapse in morale of the air-dominated nation will come before the outcome of war on land and sea could be decided' (Douhet 1983: 203).

The effects of aerial bombardment challenge basic concepts of strategy. Clausewitz, one may recall, opened his principal work by imagining a war which begins and ends with one cataclysmic duel. Although he thought this scenario made sense as an abstract representation of conflict, he immediately noted a series of reasons why nothing of the sort ever happens in real life. This gap between theory and practice is the heart of his military thought. Douhet does not explicitly argue against Clausewitz, but as previous paragraphs have noted, *Command of the Air* predicts that real-life aerial warfare will actually be very duel-like.

On War notes that wartime enemies, like wrestlers, will be unable to achieve their ultimate goals until they have prevailed in an intermediary trial of strength. This trial pits one side's military against the other. *Command of the Air* points out that aircraft can fly past opposing armed forces to strike directly at the enemy's homeland, rendering the intermediary contest largely superfluous. Clausewitz also found that attack and defence are fundamentally different activities, but in Douhet's survivor-take-all exchange of bombs, offensive and defensive operations are indistinguishable (Clausewitz 1976: 83).

Clausewitz observes that war does not consist of a single short blow. Douhet finds that aircraft may inflict paralysing damage in a single bombing attack. *On War* states that the results in war are never final. Douhet counters that, for those who are willing to follow that first, devastating strike with further raids to prevent enemy forces from rebuilding their ruined infrastructure, the effects of aerial attack might as well be (Douhet 1983: 221).

Clausewitz's reflections on the factors which prevent real conflicts from unfolding as mere duels prompted his ideas about friction, the trinity and the political dimension of war. Things may go wrong in a duel, but it is war's plethora of interacting factors which make chaos an essential part of war's basic nature. These interacting factors are the forces which make different wars fought under different political circumstances almost completely different undertakings. These factors are also what moved Clausewitz to conclude that strategy depends upon such qualities as will, leadership and creativity.

Douhet never denies that these factors exist or that they are critically important. Nevertheless, his writings imply that future strategists may not encounter quite so many of them and that their relationships may become more predictable. Where Clausewitz finds that 'in war many roads lead to success', Douhet identifies one route as particularly promising, and, although Clausewitz's roads need not always lead to total victory, Douhet's certainly does (Clausewitz 1976: 94). Thus, where Clausewitz alternates between warning readers of war's violent grammar and reminding them that military action must conform to political considerations, Douhet stresses grammar alone.

Where *On War* suggests that military commanders should take direction from government authorities, *Command of the Air* urges them to provide it. Douhet presumes to instruct political leaders on no less an issue than the question of when to go to war. His normal advice would be – attack potential enemies on even the slightest provocation, as early in a conflict as possible, with the maximum possible force and preferably by surprise (Douhet 1983: 51, 59). To follow any other policy is to risk allowing one's enemies to strike first, in an environment where the first effective blow is likely to shape everything else which happens throughout whatever remains of the war. Where Clausewitz urged readers to be ready for the possibility that any conflict might escalate to extremes, Douhet takes it for granted that most future conflicts will.

Machiavelli also guided readers towards one particular road to success. His route also featured large-scale battles and an aggressive foreign policy. Nevertheless, where the fifteenth-century writer presented his method as a daring approach which demands the cunning of the fox and the courage of the lion, his twentieth-century countryman presented his principles as mere facts of life in the age of flying machines. By diminishing the importance of what *On War* called friction, *Command of the Air* seems to diminish the need for what *On War* called genius. When Douhet implies that technology has reduced basic issues in strategy to the physical capabilities of aircraft, he seems to reduce the requirement for Machiavellian *virtu* as well.

Although certain of Douhet's arguments seem to deprecate human factors, Douhet personally believed that they remained extremely important. Indeed, he wrote passionately about the need for resolute leadership and acute strategic judgement (Douhet 1983: 224). Without the former, nations might hesitate to use air power as vigorously as necessary, and without the latter, air forces might waste time attacking poorly selected targets. Nevertheless, the technology of aerial warfare seems to promise so much that it can easily overshadow the less tangible components of strategy. Whatever Douhet himself intended, later generations of air-power theorists have found it easy to overlook them.

American airman Barry Watts, writing in 1984, found that the US air force had 'systematically neglected' the factors which, in Clausewitz's view, divide theory from practice in warfare (Watts 1984: 2). Twenty-four years later, Ole Jorgen Maao reviewed the international literature on the art of command in aerial warfare and found that little had changed. Maao defined command to include both leadership and effective strategic decision making (Maao 2008: 36). Although the Norwegian air force explicitly encourages its officers to study these issues, strategic thinkers in other countries barely mention them and neither the British nor the American air force provides an official doctrine on such subjects (Maao 2008: 37).

Watts argues that air theorists are making a mistake. As he notes, those who fixate upon one dazzling new weapon but fail to study conflict 'as a total phenomenon' risk losing their ability 'to do the one thing that successful military organizations have always done: *adapt to changing conditions better than the adversary*' (Watts 1984: 1; italics in original). Ironically, those who are most fascinated by today's emerging technology may be the least prepared for technological – and other – factors which transform the strategic environment tomorrow. The fact that air forces have never succeeded in applying Douhet's formula to win a major war strengthens Watts's case. Aerial bombardment is devastating, but air forces have typically achieved their most useful strategic effects when cooperating with other branches of the armed services, and when the overall circumstances of a conflict have favoured their use.

Douhet was also blatantly wrong about several important issues. His errors reinforce Watts's points. Douhet assumed, for instance, that civilians would panic under aerial attack. Readers may recall that he expected this to generate social unrest which would force nations which lost command of the air to surrender, even while their land and sea forces remained able to fight (Douhet 1983: 203, 188).

To this, Clausewitz might have responded that although there are undoubtedly conditions under which bombing may destroy a community's collective will to resist, the elements of the trinity are constantly in motion, and there may equally well be circumstances in which it will not. In practice, just as Clausewitz might have predicted, civilians have often proven brave and resourceful in the face of aerial bombardment. This has made air raids less devastating and less certain in their effects than devotees of *Command of the Air* might expect. And this, in turn, has made air power far less challenging to the rest of *On War* than it initially appeared.

In a similar vein, national leaders have exercised more restraint than Douhet thought likely. Even in the Second World War, for instance, neither the Germans nor the Allies bombed each other's cities with poison gas. Not only has this diluted the effects of aerial attack even further, admirers of Clausewitz are entitled to note that it has also reaffirmed the bond between war and politics. Political circumstances play a pivotal role in determining what weapons air commanders will be able to use and what targets air commanders will be able to attack.

Douhet also fell into precisely the trap which Watts described. By focusing on the technology of the First World War, he failed to anticipate crucial inventions which had appeared by the time of the Second. Like Mahan, Douhet advised political leaders to acquire the types of equipment which would best support the critical offensive strike. Douhet also followed Mahan's lead in warning readers not to waste resources on secondary pursuits. Since the Italian air theorist found the fighter planes and anti-aircraft artillery of his time unimpressive, he classified air-to-air combat and surface-based air defences as dispensable luxuries.

Just as Mahan advised naval strategists to field battleships which were to operate in concentrated fleets, Douhet advised air strategists to field armed, bomb-carrying 'battle planes', which were to maximize their firepower by operating in concentrated formations. This approach always made more sense on the sea than in the air. Whereas Mahan could reasonably argue that capital ships were the best weapon for offensive operations, the best shield against enemy attacks and also the type of vessel most likely to survive combat, the physical problems of aeronautical engineering make a truly general-purpose aircraft impossible. Douhet himself admitted that those who followed his single-minded emphasis on bombers would leave their homeland vulnerable to enemy attack (Douhet 1983: 59, 194). He viewed this as a necessary sacrifice.

By the time of the Second World War, technological improvements – notably the invention of radar – had made all forms of air defence far more effective than *Command of the Air* anticipated. Shooting down enemy aircraft in flight had become as much a part of dominating the skies as bombing infrastructure targets. Aerial combat, like other forms of warfare, came to rely on mutually supporting combinations of attack and defence. Not only did air forces require both fighters and bombers, they found it continually necessary to develop new hardware and new methods to cope with ever-changing tactical situations. Clausewitz, once again, appears to have been vindicated.

Nevertheless, when the North Atlantic Treaty Organization (NATO) finished its bombing campaign against Serbia in the 1999 Kosovo War, personnel at America's Air War College famously posted a sign declaring 'Douhet was right' (Robertson 2008: 38). This is a surprising claim but, in an important sense, it is a valid one. Douhet was right in the way that Sumida argues that Mahan was right. *Command of the Air* oversimplifies, but it directs us to points which we may build upon to develop a fuller understanding of how strategists may use aircraft to change the terms of conflict.

Certainly, Douhet failed to predict the tactical details of the 1999 war. The NATO alliance did not even attempt to paralyse Serbia's armed forces and crush the morale of the Serbian people with a swift, overwhelming onslaught. On the contrary, NATO struck relatively small numbers of targets sporadically over the course of many weeks. Throughout much of the war, alliance members struggled to avoid the opprobrium of harming civilians in any way. NATO restricted its operations yet further to keep its own pilots' risks to an absolute minimum.

Douhet would almost certainly have predicted that this tentative approach would produce ambiguous results. The fact that alliance members found their attempts to use air power frustrating provides us with no particular reason to reject Douhet's theories. Nevertheless, the outcomes of NATO's campaign provide no particular support for Douhet either. *Command of the Air* depicts bombing as swift and decisive in its effects. Serbia defied the most advanced air forces in the world for almost two months. Over a decade later, alliance members still face the unwelcome task of policing the troubled region.

Air power did, however, permit NATO to act at a moment when it would otherwise have been impotent. This, in turn, permitted alliance members to maintain their accustomed degree of influence over international affairs. Machiavelli suggests that this quest for control is the essence of strategy (Machiavelli 1950: 90). Air power provided alliance members with a weapon which depended upon them alone, and thus it proved every bit as pivotal as *Command of the Air* predicted.

In 1999, one should recall, NATO's very reason for existence was in doubt. The western nations originally formed NATO to counter the Soviet Union and its Warsaw Pact allies. When the Soviet Union restructured itself between 1989 and 1991, NATO seemed to have lost its purpose. The alliance was, however, still the western nations' best-developed institution for organizing collective military operations. Meanwhile, as the decade went on, other international bodies, such as the United Nations (UN), failed spectacularly in their attempts to resolve a series of tragic and politically troublesome crises.

These crises included an ongoing string of conflicts in the Balkan region. The state of Yugoslavia, which had previously governed that part of the world, had dissolved. Organizations representing the various peoples who inhabit the Balkans were attempting to found independent republics, while the government of Serbia, which claimed to be the legitimate successor to the Yugoslavian state, attempted to keep as much of the region as possible under its own control. Balkan political movements typically coalesce around ethnic groups, and the fact that many of those groups have bitter historical grievances against each other made it easy for militants on all sides to incite their followers to violence.

Not only did the UN flounder in its attempts to respond to the Balkans conflicts, its members disagreed over what its responses should be. American policy makers, for instance, tended to view Serbia as an aggressor. Russian leaders, by contrast, demonstrated more sympathy for the Serbian government's positions. Since both America and Russia have the right to veto resolutions within the United Nations Security Council, the UN frequently proved unable to act.

In 1995, the United Nations authorized the alliance to intervene in a clash between Serbia and Bosnia. The Serbs and the Bosnians promptly reached terms. Rightly or wrongly, NATO took credit for this outcome. Alliance members went on to reinvent their organization as an enforcer of collective decisions in international affairs.

NATO seemed to have succeeded where the UN had failed. Moreover, Russia had no official voice within the alliance. Not only did that allow NATO to implement policies more efficiently, it meant that, for those who shared the American position, the alliance was more likely to choose appropriate policies in the first place. Other NATO states viewed Balkan issues from other perspectives, but the alliance seemed to represent its members' shared aims more effectively than the available alternatives. Although certain alliance members might have found the European Union (EU) more simpatico, the EU's mechanisms for undertaking military endeavours were rudimentary at that time.

Meanwhile, the Balkan crises rekindled in what was then the Serbian province of Kosovo. A militant faction of Kosovo's Albanian ethnic group clashed with government forces and with ethnically Serbian civilians. On 20 March 1999, the Serbian army attacked the villages where Kosovo's Albanians lived, killing, setting fires and driving thousands into exile (Anonymous 1999). The same pattern of events which had recurred throughout the decade seemed to be repeating itself, and, once again, the United Nations Security Council offered no decisive response.

This was an unmistakable test of NATO's ability to perform its new mission. The Kosovo conflict was important in its own right and also because of its broader implications. The alliance needed to succeed to justify its own survival. Its member states needed it to succeed in order to preserve what was then their most effective instrument for imposing their will in international conflicts.

Although NATO had no choice but to respond, it did not have many actual responses available. Despite the fact that Serbia is geographically part of Europe, it shares no borders with NATO countries. Moreover, the Kosovo region is landlocked. In other words, NATO armies and navies had no direct access to the crisis area.

If NATO had hoped to deploy surface forces in March 1999, it would have had to begin by persuading conveniently located countries to permit its troops on their territory. NATO political leaders would also have had to convince their own constituencies to support a long, costly war. The United Nations, which many perceived as the only institution with the legitimate right to authorize armed interventions, had not granted NATO permission to use force in the Kosovo crisis. This would have compounded alliance members' diplomatic and public relations difficulties even further.

Even if one overlooked the political obstacles to a surface campaign, NATO would have needed considerable time to collect, equip and deploy its forces. In May, when alliance members actually did contemplate ground operations, French authorities estimated that the preparations would take until winter (Priest 1999: A1). Air power, by contrast, allowed NATO to mount its intervention within four days. Neither geography nor controversy stopped it.

Serbia eventually accepted a settlement on the alliance's terms. Watts and Clausewitz would be entitled to note that NATO did not achieve this result through bombing alone. The Serbian government did not concede until the alliance signalled that it might be ready to supplement its air operations with an overland invasion. The fact that Russia shifted its position and pressed for an end to the conflict was probably even more significant.

Kosovo remains violent, impoverished and politically contentious. Still, over a decade has passed since Balkan affairs have presented a dangerous challenge to NATO or its members. To adapt Machiavelli's metaphor, NATO piled a few sandbags along the banks of a flood-prone river. What Douhet called air power's 'freedom of action and direction' made this possible.

This freedom was more than the physical freedom to fly over obstacles. Air power also freed NATO members from many of the political constraints which would otherwise have forced them to delay, to compromise and quite possibly to fail. Although it is arrogant for air power theorists to neglect the social, political and psychological aspects of strategy, it is not completely groundless. Human factors remain fundamental, but air power can provide strategists with a temporary and provisional ability to sidestep them.

To this extent air power, like maritime power, can be a tool for remaking one's strategic environment. Aircraft are not, however, as versatile as Corbett's cruisers. Ships routinely perform a wide range of strategically useful functions without ever firing a shot. Douhet focuses almost exclusively on air power's value for direct, physical attack.

NATO's experience in Kosovo suggests that Douhet was correct to emphasize this aspect of air power. Having noted this, one should also note that there are also many other ways in which aircraft prove strategically useful. In the Kosovo campaign, for instance, NATO forces depended heavily on air assets for transportation, reconnaissance and electronic warfare. Indeed, the 1999 war drove home the lesson that many alliance members needed to invest greater sums in developing such capabilities (Anonymous 2000: 17–18). Nevertheless, the primary way in which aircraft exert direct pressure on opponents remains the use – and seldom the mere threat – of their weapons systems. There may be occasions in which the simple possibility of aerial bombardment will frighten prospective victims into surrender, but the 1999 Kosovo war was not one of them.

This means, among other things, that the technical capabilities of aerial weapons systems play an exceptionally large role in shaping the strategic potential of air power. One of the reasons why NATO political leaders felt able to wage war in 1999 was that its more technologically blessed members possessed precision-guided munitions which allowed them to destroy their chosen targets while reducing the so-called collateral damage to civilian bystanders to a historically unprecedented minimum. One of the reasons why NATO members were unable to resolve the war as quickly or as cleanly as they might have liked is that even the most accurate aerial munitions can only strike targets which their users can distinguish from the air. This meant, for instance, that Serbia's armed forces were able to continue their campaign against Kosovo's ethnic Albanians throughout the war since even the best technology available in 1999 did not allow pilots to pick off soldiers raiding homes in a crowded residential neighbourhood from 15,000 feet in the air without also massacring the civilians whom NATO forces were presumably trying to save.

The fact that air power is mainly – although not entirely – a means for delivering firepower also suggests that Douhet's emphasis on what Clausewitz called the 'grammar' of force is correctly placed. Clausewitz's 'grammar' underlies all forms of conflict, but, in aerial warfare, its influence is particularly close to the surface. Therefore, much of Douhet's advice about organizing and deploying air forces remains well taken. Just as theorists such as Corbett and Callwell reformulated Mahanian concepts of sea power to account for the richer possibilities of real life, strategic thinkers such as US Air Force officer John Warden have reformulated Douhet-esque concepts of air power to account for such factors as changing technology, a wider variety of political situations and, perhaps most crucially, the fact that aircraft typically prove more useful for their ability to support joint efforts by all branches of the armed forces than for their alleged potential to win wars on their own. Nevertheless, the gap between the original and oversimplified concepts and their more realistic successors tends to be smaller in aerial warfare than in maritime strategy.

Conclusion

This chapter's introduction notes that, although Clausewitz may not have explicitly discussed the use of technology to exploit new strategic environments, his ideas prove salient to the thinkers who do. In conclusion, one may add that Sun Tzu also remains relevant. Much of Sun Tzu's thought concerns the art of engineering situations in which one's preferred methods for solving problems will work and work well. Air power and maritime power are both tools for engineering situations – figuratively, by engaging one's opponents in new settings, and literally, by optimizing one's hardware for the types of operations one plans to carry out.

Sun Tzu also tells us that one can create an infinite variety of situations using merely two types of materials – the ordinary and the extraordinary forces. As discussed in chapter 1, Sun Tzu seems to assume that any particular weapon and any particular type of military organization can serve as either one, depending on what commanders choose to do with them. Corbett, to a certain extent, might agree. Certainly, he expected navies to support decisive land campaigns at certain times while armies supported decisive fleet operations at others and he urged commanders to use all their assets flexibly. Warden, among others, might accept comparable principles for conflicts involving air power.

Nevertheless, ships and aircraft are more than clay for strategists to sculpt with. Their peculiar capabilities favour some uses over others. Moreover, to have an effective navy or air force, one must invest in it – generously, consistently and well in advance. Mahan and Douhet both stress this point. The more resources – material and psychological – a community entrusts to fighting in a particular environment, the more it commits itself to a certain strategic approach. Machiavelli was sensitive to the fact that the various types of land forces each had their own effects upon a society's *virtu*, and similar principles apply here.

Maritime forces accentuate what international relations theorist Joseph Nye might call the softer forms of power (Nye 2004: *passim*). Despite the awesome power of naval munitions, even the relatively bellicose Mahan values sea power as much for its long-term economic benefits as for its immediate use in battle. Air power, by contrast, tends to be hard and direct. It is a weapon, and it appears to achieve its greatest effects when used as a weapon of first resort.

A mutually supporting collection of technological improvements permits air strategists to wield their weapon in increasingly discriminating ways. This may palliate some of the ethical problems of air strategy. Political leaders in contemporary liberal democracies certainly seem to find that this makes it easier to justify air operations to voters at home and allies abroad. The fact that, as of 2013, those democracies are not confronting enemies who can shoot down substantial numbers of their pilots makes it even easier for such leaders to use air power aggressively.

A weapon which minimizes the cost and peril of direct action is obviously invaluable. The fact that this weapon can strike in so many places so swiftly with so few short-term complications makes it even more precious. Nevertheless, a Pericles, a Sun Tzu and perhaps even a Machiavelli might warn that it also presents policy makers with dangerous temptations. For all its advantages, air power has proven more effective as a tool for opening wars than for resolving them satisfactorily, and even its alleged victory in Kosovo reminds us that those who wish to profit from its use must be prepared to follow it up with more arduous operations on the ground. The ongoing war in Afghanistan, which began for its western participants with a seemingly triumphant air campaign in 2001 and continues for them as a bloody counter-insurgency in 2013, provides a crueller example of a similar point.

Further reading

Callwell, Charles E. (1996) *Military Operations and Maritime Preponderance: Their Relations and Interdependence*. Annapolis, MD: United States Naval Institute Press.

Douhet, Giulio (1983) *The Command of the Air*, trans. Dino Ferrari. Washington, DC: Office of Air Force History.

Falk, Kevin (2000) *Why Nations Put To Sea: Technology and the Changing Character of Sea Power in the Twenty-First Century*. London: Routledge.

Mahan, Alfred Thayer (1890) *The Influence of Sea Power upon History, 1660–1783*. Cambridge, MA: John Wilson and Son.

Sumida, Jon Tetsuro (1997) *Inventing Grand Strategy and Teaching Command: The Classic Works of Alfred Thayer Mahan Reconsidered*. Washington, DC: Woodrow Wilson Center Press.

Warden, John A. (1989) *The Air Campaign: Planning for Combat*. Washington, DC: Pergamon-Brasseys.

Watts, Barry D. (1984) *The Foundations of US Air Doctrine: The Problem of Friction in War*. Maxwell Air Force Base: Air University Press.

6 HEAVY METAL

The strategy of crushing one's enemies with brute force may not be particularly humane or efficient, but at least it seems as if it ought to be simple. Raw combat power appears easy to recognize and even easier to wield. Few could disagree with the remark that God is on the side of the biggest battalions. The observation implies that, if one can only amass superior forces, one can achieve gratifying results merely by hurling them against one's enemies and letting God's will prevail. Since war is so arduous and ridden with uncertainty, any approach which promises to simplify the process of achieving victory demands attention.

Accordingly, strategic thinkers throughout history have pondered the issue of mass. Sun Tzu warned readers to avoid basing their plans on material strength alone, but he seems to have feared that they would find the apparently simple approach seductive. Machiavelli, by contrast, appears to have believed that the strategy of overwhelming opponents with potent forces actually was the surest route to success, and that his capricious goddess would swoon before those who followed it. Clausewitz reminded readers that one must assess military means in their political context, but he urged them never to forget what physical power can do.

Vegetius, however, noted that achieving victory through physical might may not be as straightforward as it sounds. Large numbers of troops, for instance may actually be a handicap (Vegetius 1993: 63). Although the Roman believed that it was possible to construct objectively superior military forces, he felt compelled to write three entire books in order to explain how. Careful readers of Machiavelli and

Clausewitz will note that they also devoted many chapters to exploring the numerous problems of realizing combat potential in practice.

Not only has the strategy of annihilating one's enemies through superior force always been problematic, the nature of combat power has become increasingly complicated over time. This became obvious in the land campaigns of the First World War. The first years of that conflict demonstrated that the simplest version of the simplest strategy – the one in which opposing commanders use the best troops they can field in the largest numbers they can assemble to assault strong enemy forces directly – had become little more than a suicidal exercise in futility. As the struggle went on, inventors and tacticians developed a panoply of ways to carry out offensive operations with some hope of success, but the new methods introduced new complications into the eternally formidable challenge of achieving one's ends through war.

In the 1920s and 1930s, a variety of thinkers explored ways to integrate the new tactics and new equipment into an effective approach to strategy. The Second World War seemed to winnow the well-conceived theories from the less promising ones. The success of Germany's so-called blitzkrieg campaigns of 1939–41 inspired later generations of strategists to return to the ideas which appeared to have made the Germans' early victories possible, with a view to achieving similarly dramatic results in more recent political and technological environments. This process of updating mid-twentieth-century thought on combined arms warfare continues to this day.

The next section of this chapter summarizes the developments which forced mid-twentieth-century theorists to rethink strategy. A third section reviews the insights they achieved and the deeper issues they raised, focusing on the works of B. H. Liddell Hart and J. F. C. Fuller. The chapter's conclusion considers how these ideas recur in the strategic theory of the 1990s and 2000s. Although twentieth- and twenty-first-century strategists have developed compelling ideas about how to direct the increasingly complicated machinery of modern land warfare towards coherent strategic ends, none of their suggestions have proved to be panaceas. Creative thought and an accurate appreciation of political circumstances remain fundamental to achieving victory in war.

Never more into the breach: the triumph of defensive warfare

Those who hope to win simple victories by attacking in overwhelming strength face an equally simple obstacle. Frontal attacks against prepared defences have been slow and bloody since the dawn of war. Strategic thinkers throughout history have understood this point. Sun Tzu warned that assaults on walled cities could embroil armies for months (Tao 1987: 99). Clausewitz, who held that defence is the most potent form of warfare, sketched out the tactics of defensive battle in terms which would have seemed up to date a century later on the River Somme, where over half a million attacking Allied soldiers died to capture stretches of territory which were commonly measured in yards (Clausewitz 1976: 390–2).

The power of defensive warfare, Clausewitz noted, goes beyond the fact that troops who enjoy the luxury of choosing strong positions and awaiting their enemies there typically inflict proportionately more casualties than they suffer. An army on the defensive is free to take up many such positions, one behind the other, so that attackers who manage to overcome the first line of defence merely come up against a second one, and then another and another, suffering delay and disruption at every stage of the process. Since the attacking force is unlikely to advance everywhere at once, the most successful attackers are likely to find that they have merely pushed forward into exposed positions in which the majority of their comrades can no longer support them. Hurt, exhausted and with enemies on all sides, they are vulnerable to counter-attack.

Just as Clausewitz does not expect defenders to be content with a single strong position, he does not expect attackers to give up simply because the first push proves difficult. The Prussian assumes that armies on the offensive will make repeated efforts to overcome the enemy's defensive lines, ideally by going around them. Nevertheless, he notes, the attackers' attempts to carry out such flanking manoeuvres invite defenders to strike back by outflanking the outflankers. For a time, at least, the opposing sides' efforts will neutralize each other, and deadlock will prevail (Clausewitz 1976: 391).

For a strategist, deadlock is always unwelcome. Moreover, only a few years after Clausewitz raised these points, Jomini observed that advances in firearms technology were strengthening defenders even further, thus compounding the situation. Jomini suggested that attackers might respond by using armoured cavalry to overrun otherwise invincible defensive positions. Readers may decide for themselves whether he deserves credit for predicting the invention of the tank.

Over the next ten decades, military thinkers with similar concerns developed the tactics which make offensive operations possible in land warfare today. Most of these methods are based upon the fact that, even when it is impossible for one entire army to overcome another, small groups of enterprising soldiers may still be able to find vulnerable points in the opposing side's defences and work their way through. Such small-unit infiltration tactics matured during the First World War, but the logic behind them is as old as the Trojan Horse, and the need for them had been apparent throughout most of the nineteenth century. Historian Stephen van Evera cites the American Civil War, the Russo-Turkish War, the Boer War and the Russo-Japanese War as experiences which should have warned Europeans what the industrial-age battlefield had become, and his list could easily have been longer (Van Evera 1984: 59).

Nevertheless, commanders continually returned to the practice of sending large units to attack strong enemy positions en masse. There are a variety of reasons why such methods remained popular. One is that military thinkers, notably in France, believed that bold offensive manoeuvres would inspire troops to equal levels of boldness. Another is that small-unit tactics did not always appear particularly promising – often, they led only to the annihilation of the small units. Another is that officers may have doubted that their troops were intelligent or reliable enough to trust with the level of autonomy which small-unit methods require.

Moreover, by fragmenting every battle into a multitude of skirmishes, a system of warfare based upon small-unit tactics exponentially increases the difficulty of coordinating military operations to achieve one's overall purpose. An attack which strikes only at the unpredictable points where groups of perhaps ten or twenty troops manage to out-manoeuvre ten or twenty of their opponents leaves the overall situation between the opposing armies unchanged. Thus, it scarcely counts as an attack at all. Van Evera suggests that an irrational 'cult of the offensive' blinded the military leaders of the early twentieth century to the fact that large-scale frontal assaults had become obsolete, but even commanders who understood the state of affairs could reasonably have concluded that direct attacks remained a grim necessity (Van Evera 1984: *passim*). Despite all the advantages of defensive warfare, Clausewitz also reminds readers that a strategy which fails on the offensive is passive, and that passivity accomplishes nothing on its own (Clausewitz 1976: 358).

By 1914, when the First World War broke out in Europe, the necessary had ceased to be possible. Jomini had been correct when he noted that progress in firearms technology would permit defenders to mow down attackers ever more efficiently. Over the course of the nineteenth century, weapons designers refined the rifle and introduced the machine gun. Perhaps of even greater significance, artillerymen developed improved procedures for carrying out indirect fire. This made it practical for gunners to lob shells over friendly troops and intervening terrain to hit targets that would otherwise have been immune.

This also reduced the value of covered defensive positions. Nevertheless, attacking troops advancing across open ground have virtually no protection against bursting shells, whereas properly entrenched defenders can often survive a nearby blast. Moreover, troops on the defensive typically find it easier to identify the avenues that attackers will need to follow to reach their lines than troops on the offensive find it to pinpoint the sites at which their enemies have chosen to dig in. This was particularly true in the early years of the First World War, when wireless communications technology was unavailable and troops on the front line normally relied on field telephones to request fire from distant artillery. Neither side's communications networks tended to survive for long in battle, but defenders had marginally greater opportunities to lay telephone lines and to bury them for protection from enemy shells.

The improved infantry weapons and the improved methods of using artillery complemented one another. Commanders who positioned their forces intelligently could use indirect artillery fire to drive enemies into exposed areas where friendly troops armed with direct-fire weapons could finish them off. An assortment of other inventions provided further ingredients for the brew. Barbed wire, for instance, gave defenders a new way to slow down their opponents. The longer attackers need to cross the battlefield, the longer they must suffer the effects of weapons of every type, and the harder they will find it to manoeuvre for any sort of advantage.

Numerous other tactical and technological factors intensify the lethality of the defence in modern land warfare. Moreover, social, economic and political developments have produced an environment in which these factors can easily become insurmountable. Clausewitz expected the impasse between attackers and defenders to dissolve when the victorious commander worked troops around the enemy's lines to strike from the flank and the loser could no longer muster the means to respond in kind (Clausewitz 1976: 391). On the First World War's Western Front, modern states proved capable of raising enough troops to extend their lines hundreds of miles from one impassable geographical obstacle to another and of continually reinforcing such armies for years, if not indefinitely. As long as this situation endured, neither side could outflank the other on land, both sides enjoyed an effectively unlimited ability to turn back the enemy's advances and Clausewitz's scenario remained stalled in its most tragic and strategically frustrating phase.

As previous paragraphs have noted, responses to such problems have existed throughout military history. The opposing armies of the First World War rediscovered many and invented more. Not only did both sides institutionalize small-unit infiltration tactics, they introduced new types of armaments so that forces of all sizes could go into action with the widest possible range of independent capabilities. Just as a British general of that period would have supported his infantry brigades with indirect fire from howitzers of the Royal Field Artillery, his brigade commanders acquired the ability to support smaller infantry formations with indirect fire from trench mortars, their platoon commanders acquired the ability to support seven-man sections with indirect fire from other sections armed with rifle grenades and individual soldiers carried hand grenades to obtain a modest indirect-fire capability of their own. Similar logic led armies to introduce the flamethrower, along with an increasing range of lighter automatic weapons.

Even as armies reconfigured infantry units to carry out successful offensive operations in microcosm, they sought ways to break defensive stalemates on a larger scale. One promising method was ancient – even when there is no way to circumvent the enemy's defensive lines on land, it may still be possible to get around them by sea. The Allies attempted this multiple times during the course of the First World War, most notably in the Gallipoli campaign of 1915–16. Germany was not in a position to carry amphibious assaults on a comparable scale, but it used its High Seas Fleet to attack enemy coastlines and enemy commerce.

The submarine gave navies more options than ever. Emerging technology opened fresh possibilities for other branches of the armed services as well. Aircraft, for instance, offered strategists yet another way to bypass land defences. Meanwhile, ground forces introduced new hardware of their own. Poison gas promised to inflict casualties across unprecedented swathes of the battlefield. Armoured tanks had the potential to penetrate stronger defensive positions than small infantry units could infiltrate on their own, and to do more damage after they broke through. Although the actual tanks of the First World War were slow, mechanically temperamental and easily stopped by unfavourable terrain, motorized fighting vehicles had the potential to be faster than soldiers on foot and to maintain high rates of speed over greater distances.

By 1918, the enemy nations of the First World War had introduced all these innovations and more. Many worked spectacularly, especially while they remained new. When German forces first used poison gas on a large scale, to pick one example, they managed to depopulate the opposing Allied positions along four miles of the front (Hart 1930: 83). Nevertheless, even this massacre was insufficient to alter the course of the war, and both sides went on to introduce countermeasures against chemical weapons, making it far harder for anyone to achieve such results with poison gas again.

This pattern repeated itself with virtually every novel offensive method. Even by 1918, when the warring armies had mastered numerous techniques for breaking through trenches in a literal sense, the enemy forces continued to push each other back and forth across France and the Low Countries without achieving any clear resolution. Germany was impoverished and in political turmoil by the time it surrendered, but its army remained capable of fighting and its borders remained nearly intact. Despite all the advances in offensive tactics, deadly equilibrium remained the normal condition of war.

The difficulty of exerting force on the modern battlefield had receded as a problem of tactics but resurged as a problem of strategy. Throughout the decades which followed, strategic thinkers sought a coherent method for applying what the military art had become to increase their control over the course and outcome of wars. Just as the first campaigns of the First World War had exposed the folly of persisting with traditional approaches to warfare, the first campaigns of the Second World War winnowed promising attempts to update those methods from certain obvious failures.

Experienced soldiers whose previous careers had earned them a reputation for brilliance had concluded that, if the tendency towards deadlock in warfare had increased, the wisest response must be to accept what was and seek, wherever possible, to capitalize upon the development. Better to conserve resources, delay confrontations and induce enemies to break themselves against one's defences than to squander forces in aggressive campaigns which, all too probably, would come to naught. Since Americans and Western Europeans found resources scarce and the prospect of another world war appalling, this approach to strategy seemed to suit their needs. In the early 1930s, perhaps, it did. By the end of that decade, however, the growing strength and obvious malice of Imperial Japan and National Socialist Germany had outmoded it.

Between 1939 and 1941, Japan and Germany repeatedly demonstrated what a well-conceived offensive can achieve in modern war.

German troops overwhelmed Poland, the Low Countries and France in rapid succession. Japan crushed British and American forces throughout the Far East with similar audacity. Those who had based their strategies on resigning themselves to seemingly inexorable trends had proved not worldly wise but the opposite.

Which way is up? Fuller and Hart reappraise strategy

For a strategist, the German offensive triumphs seem particularly revealing, both because they involved the same opponents as the stale-mates of the previous war, and because they seemed to revive the principles of mass and manoeuvre which industrial-age warfare had threatened to negate. Although the practice of throwing the bulk of one's forces into head-on assaults remained unacceptably costly at the level of tactics, the Germans profited from their decision to concentrate their tanks and mechanized support forces into dedicated panzer (armoured) divisions, whereas the western Allies suffered for dispersing their armoured fighting vehicles in so-called penny-packets spread out among infantry units. Since the panzer divisions were able to bring significant numbers of tactically powerful assets to bear in a small area, they had an enhanced ability to overwhelm enemy defences. Since the panzer divisions enjoyed relatively lavish access to motorized transport, they could move swiftly to strike the enemy's most vulnerable points. Once the panzers had got past the enemy's defences, they could out-race counter-attacking infantry to encircle opposing forces in flanking movements reminiscent of the ones described in *On War*, but on a grander scale than Clausewitz could have envisaged. Clausewitz expected such manoeuvres to decide battles, and the German coup of 1940 threatened to decide the entire war.

Numerous military thinkers had considered the possibilities which the German army exploited so successfully. Soviet ideas regarding armoured warfare were, if anything, more advanced than German concepts, and if Josef Stalin had not devastated his own country's military command structure by purging the officer corps over the course of the 1930s, the Red Army might have demonstrated this several years earlier. In the West, the British writers B. H. Liddell Hart and J. F. C. Fuller stand out for their success at explaining the factors which shape modern land warfare. Not only did these authors' early studies influence the German generals who won the victories of

1939–40, their later and more widely accessible books outline contrasting approaches which continue to define the problems and possibilities of land warfare.

One may begin with Hart, whose basic argument, whatever its weaknesses, is both straightforward and radical. Hart, like Machiavelli and Clausewitz, suggests that there is a relatively simple logic underpinning strategy. The British author, however, derives this logic from a different source. Where the Florentine and the Prussian invite us to analyse armed struggles in terms of the opposing forces' physical strength, Hart invites us to analyse them in terms of the opposing strategists' imaginations.

Hart begins his argument by noting the consequences of failing to wage war imaginatively (Hart 1991: 4–5). To settle for unimaginative approaches is to be predictable, and to be predictable is to enhance one's enemies' ability to prepare. This principle applies in both a material sense and a psychological one – enemies who know what to expect may be able to find a way to counter it, and enemies who know what to expect may also be able to steel themselves to stand up to it. At a minimum, they will not be surprised. Thus, the more innovative side always has the opportunity to outperform stodgier opponents, even if it is too weak to overcome them completely. The most satisfactory victories, Hart suggests, come from approaches which simultaneously undermine the enemy's material capabilities and the enemy's mental capacity to respond (Hart 1991: 4–5).

This led Hart to reconceive yet another basic aspect of classic strategic thought. Clausewitz warns readers that every action in warfare encounters the smorgasbord of difficulties which he describes as friction, and that pushing one's actions forward against unpredictable obstacles is the essential challenge of waging war. As readers may recall, one of the main reasons why commanders throughout history have so doggedly returned to strategies based on brute strength and frontal assaults is that they have shared Clausewitz's pessimism and seen these methods as the surest way to persevere in an environment of incomprehensible chaos. Hart, by contrast, specifies one particular type of friction as critical. This, in his view, is the enemy's opposition (Hart 1991: 323). Where Clausewitz asserts that a strategist must struggle against resistance in an imponderable variety of forms, of which enemy activity is but one among many, Hart suggests that it is possible to identify the main obstacles to success and bypass them (Hart 1991: 323).

Hart was also acutely concerned with the possibility that one might win battles and still lose wars – or that one might prevail at such a cost that victory becomes hollow. Therefore, he directed his thought towards the higher realms of strategy, grand strategy and politics (Hart 1991: 338). Where Clausewitz, for instance, took a curmudgeonly view of scruples and sentiment, Hart responded that one's ethical standing could be a source of immediate psychological leverage, not to mention its deeper importance as part of what makes one's case worth fighting for (Hart 1991: 322). Where other military thinkers had reconfigured small military units to seize local opportunities on the battlefield, Hart imagined reconfiguring the largest units to achieve similar levels of independence and flexibility throughout the entire theatre of war (Hart 1991: 332–3).

Fuller shared many of Hart's aspirations. Like Hart, he encouraged strategists to win wars through ingenuity (Fuller 1942: 17). Like Hart, he cherished the hope that swift, well-placed blows could decide wars with minimal casualties and cost (Fuller 1942: vi). The two men also came to agree that emerging technology – notably the tank – offered land forces a particularly valuable tool for waging this type of warfare. Both recognized the importance of comprehensively structuring and equipping military organizations to use armour, aircraft and other new technology as efficiently as possible for these purposes.

The two men knew each other, and corresponded throughout their lives. Details of their agreements, disagreements and mutual influence might fill volumes. Nevertheless, their approaches differed in significant ways, and from the perspective of the early twenty-first century, one contrast between their approaches stands out as particularly revealing. Where Hart inclined his thoughts towards grand strategy, Fuller declared that 'the bottom is the top' (Fuller 1942: 7). In this statement, he suggests that the practicalities of tactics and operations define the possibilities of strategy at its higher levels.

Fuller despised this state of affairs. Indeed, he railed against the trends which he believed had made human beings slaves to their own inventions (Fuller 1942: 19–26). Nevertheless, where Hart sought human solutions to strategic problems, Fuller focused on optimizing the application of material resources. As a young man, Hart cherished the idea that a suitably clever general could practise strategy effectively with traditional forces (Mearsheimer 1988: 34–5). Fuller persuaded him that even the most intelligent commander would need the emerging technology of the tank (Mearsheimer 1988: 34–5). Where Hart insisted on the importance of ethical and political issues, Fuller declared himself to be a ruthless, apolitical pragmatist (Fuller 1942: 8–10). When Fuller concluded that a dictatorship which subjected all of society to the military chain of command would be the most efficient

– and hence the most desirable – system of government, he did not hesitate to say so (Fuller 1942: 8–10).

Leaving broader political issues aside for the moment, Fuller's emphasis on practical detail makes his work more immediately useful for those who wish to apply his ideas in military planning. Where Hart, even in his more technical works, tends towards grand concepts, Fuller, even when writing for more general audiences, proposes specific manoeuvres and tactical formations. Hart may reveal something vital about the essence of successful strategy, but one cannot even begin to put his theory into practice until one has performed an original feat of creative genius. Fuller, by contrast, tells readers how to get started.

Although Hart focuses on the conceptual level of strategic planning while Fuller begins with battlefield technicalities, their ideas converge. Hart considers the problems of putting his strategic ideas into practice. Fuller, for his part, considers the higher-level preparations which military forces and, indeed, entire nations must make in order to employ his tactical suggestions systematically at the most useful times and places. Thus, both authors draw attention to the middle levels of strategic planning.

In this, Hart and Fuller echo Soviet military theorists such as A. A. Svechin, who suggested that the 'operational art' of orchestrating mid-level military activity is the key to overcoming the problems of industrial-age war (English 1996: 13). Soviet thinkers developed this idea with exceptional clarity. As Hart himself noted, Germany's triumphs of 1939–40 mask the fact that, by that time, German concepts had already grown stale (Hart 1960: 177). In a similar fashion, the USSR's near-collapse in 1941 obscures the fact that Soviet theoretical works had already outlined more sophisticated concepts which permitted the Red Army to recover, regain the initiative and break its enemies apart.

Like Hart, Soviet military thinkers emphasized the art of unhinging enemy armies at the highest levels of strategic planning. Soviet doctrine aimed to achieve this by striking rapidly and unexpectedly with overwhelming force. Like Fuller, Soviet military thinkers hoped to realize these concepts by mastering the 'science' of combining different weapons systems for maximum efficiency and organizing military units to give higher-level commanders maximum control over their forces. Soviet theorists understood efficiency in terms of using tanks, aircraft, long-range artillery and whatever new weapons systems might become available to press the enemy relentlessly over extended periods of time throughout as large an area as possible.

Since the Second World War, concepts such as operational artistry have waxed and waned in popularity. During the 1950s, strategic thinkers in both the USSR and the West tended to assume that intercontinental ballistic missiles bearing nuclear warheads could inflict devastation on such a scale that all other forms of warfare would decline in significance. One might still win nuclear wars by crippling one's enemies through overwhelming shock, but one would not need to carry out bold ground offensives to do so. As increasing numbers of strategists recognized that the apocalyptic consequences of a global nuclear exchange would almost certainly outweigh the possible gains of initiating one, military thinkers returned to the themes which Hart, Fuller and the Soviet thinkers had raised.

Wheel of strategy?

Meanwhile, just as the evolution of small arms, railways and techniques of indirect fire and a host of related technologies progressed throughout the second half of the nineteenth century, electronics, satellites, concepts of information management and a similar collection of related fields progressed throughout the second half of the twentieth. The first set of technological developments had combined to demand – and, more gradually, to enable – new methods of waging war. As early as the 1970s, Soviet military thinkers began to explore ways in which the second set might do the same (Krepinevich 2002: i).

Soviet theorists presented their ideas in the language of communist ideology. Marx held that human progress exposes the injustices and inefficiencies of primitive systems of social organization. Eventually, Marxist theory predicts, societies based on obsolete models succumb to revolution. The victorious revolutionaries then establish more productive – and, in Marx's view, ultimately more humane – ways of living. In this spirit, Soviet military thinkers described the emerging possibilities in warfare as a military–technical revolution (MTR).

Other writers on this topic found the term 'MTR' too limiting. These authors referred to the ongoing developments in the art of war using the more sweeping expression 'revolution in military affairs' (RMA). An RMA presumably includes social, political and organizational issues which go beyond mere technical advances. One might participate in an MTR simply by outfitting one's forces with superior equipment, but those who hope to be on the winning side of an RMA must rethink fundamental issues about their approach to waging war.

One of the ironies of history is that although Soviet theorists took the lead in developing these ideas, the United States and its allies took the lead in fielding the technology which had originally made an MTR seem possible. In the process, western military thinkers adopted a wide range of Soviet ideas. During the 1980s, for instance, the states which made up NATO sought ways to use their advantage in advanced technology to counter Soviet numerical superiority. American commanders came up with a doctrine for fighting future wars known as AirLand Battle, while their European counterparts came up with a similar approach known as Follow-On Forces Attack (FOFA). Both approaches featured many of the same ideas as earlier Soviet writings on engaging enemy forces simultaneously in three dimensions throughout as large an area as possible. Thus, both approaches also echoed the writings of J. F. C. Fuller.

The similarities between AirLand, FOFA, the Soviet concepts and Fuller may have been largely coincidental. In the early 1990s, however, western strategic thinkers explicitly adopted Soviet ideas. During the Gulf War of 1990–1, a coalition consisting primarily of US and Western European forces defeated the large and reasonably well-equipped army of Saddam Hussein's Iraq rapidly and with minimal casualties. Afterwards, American military theorists sought to understand how they had won this victory and how they might repeat the performance. Andrew Krepenivich and Andrew Marshall of the US Center for Strategic and Budgetary Assessments suggested that the 1990–1 Gulf War had been an early step towards a coming RMA.

As previously noted, an RMA may involve changes that go far beyond technology. Nevertheless, the Soviet version of RMA theory developed from MTR theory. Whatever the deeper reasons for the coalition's victory in 1990–1, advanced western weapons systems played a particularly visible role. Therefore, one should not be surprised that the many influential writers on contemporary military transformation have followed Fuller's example and raised the 'bottom' of technical planning towards the 'top' of strategy itself.

The Soviet MTR and RMA concepts emphasized the integrated functioning of three sets of machines: the 'reconnaissance' equipment which provides accurate information; the communications and data-processing equipment which allows forces to access useful facts in a timely fashion; and the long-range precision weapons which allow those forces to 'strike' the most valuable targets their sensors can find (Vego 1990: 1–7). Just as early RMA theorists explored the possibilities of assembling different kinds of hardware into these so-called 'reconnaissance-strike complexes', thinkers such as Admiral William

Owens of the US navy have noted that one can understand larger organizations such as military forces as yet more complicated networks of systems, each nested within a greater one (Owens 1996: *passim*). Owens published his initial paper on this topic in 1996. As the admiral himself observed, this was a period of history when the American government was cutting military spending and defence policy makers were reconsidering the way in which they would invest the funds remaining to them (Owens 1996: 1). Naturally enough, Owens emphasized the ways in which planners could use his ideas to structure their own forces for increased economy and maximum combat efficiency.

Owens intended his concept to be a guide for waging war, as well as preparing for it. In his words, he hoped that forming the US armed forces into a unified 'system of systems' would enable American commanders to 'match the right force to the most promising course of action at both the tactical and operational levels of warfare' (Owens 1996: 2). Those who have read Clausewitz may find this idea excessively optimistic. Therefore, it is noteworthy that Owens echoed Hart in explicitly claiming that his approach could partially reduce one's exposure to 'the fog and friction of war' (Owens 1996: 4). Nevertheless, where Hart urged commanders to disperse the proverbial fog of war by out-thinking their opponents, Owens focused on the more Fullerian challenge of coordinating surveillance and communications assets to provide commanders with useful information in a timely fashion.

Hart would certainly have appreciated Owens's aspiration to hone his country's forces into a 'smaller' but 'far sharper' spear that could 'pierce the opponents' jugular vein on the first throw' (Owens 1996: 4). Owens wisely acknowledges that different enemies will have different characteristics and, presumably, different points of vulnerability (Owens 1996: 4). Again, however, his concepts and language suggest a Fullerian approach to identifying what those points might be. If it is useful to understand one's own military establishment as a 'system of systems', this is presumably also a useful concept to apply when attempting to understand one's enemies.

If one can deduce how an opposing system works, one may target its most vital components. Precision weapons and twenty-first-century surveillance technology seem to offer newly effective ways to accomplish both. Harlan Ullman, James Wade and their co-authors took up this theme in their work *Shock and Awe: Achieving Rapid Dominance* (Ullman et al. 1996: *passim*). The challenges of configuring one's own networks to disrupt opposing 'systems of systems' can easily resemble problems of engineering. Researchers at Johns Hopkins University's Applied Physics Laboratory thought so, and responded to Owens's writings by establishing a programme intended to 'change warfighting' by applying the techniques of 'systems engineering' throughout the US military establishment (Manthorpe 1996: *passim*).

This approach to strategy has implications which extend far beyond military operations. Vegetius, one recalls, also focused on equipment, organizations and techniques. Machiavelli emphasized the same factors throughout most of his *Art of War*. As both authors understood, a technocratic approach to warfare demands a literally technocratic approach to politics. For a government to organize efficient military forces, it must first organize itself to mobilize its society's resources with equal efficiency, regardless of who this might offend or what cherished principles this might threaten. Fuller, as previously noted, reasoned along similar lines.

Moreover, the works of these three thinkers suggest an ominous trend. Vegetius' fourth-century calls for reform appear relatively benign. When Machiavelli returned to these ideas at the dawn of the modern period, he advocated aggressive foreign policies and a harshly disciplined society. Even Machiavelli, however, wished for that society to be a republic. Fuller openly called for military dictatorship. Readers can only speculate about the reasons why Machiavelli took more brutal positions than his predecessor, but Fuller explicitly argued that technological advances made totalitarian government continually more necessary. If the Soviet RMA theorists were sincere Marxist-Leninists, they associated progress with dictatorship as well.

More recent western thinkers have taken almost the opposite point of view. Alvin and Heidi Toffler outlined this contrasting approach in their 1993 work *War and Anti-War: Survival at the Dawn of the 21st Century*, which argues that emerging methods of waging war are part of a more general trend towards a society organized around the exchange of information (Toffler and Toffler 1993: 69–71). In such societies, the Tofflers suggest, decentralized networks can often act faster and more appropriately than rigidly structured institutions (Toffler and Toffler 1993: 77–8). Where Fuller argued that governments must maximize their efficiency by managing every aspect of national life, the Tofflers argued that they might – for better or for worse – maximize their efficiency by outsourcing strategically important activities to the various local and transnational groups which may become at least temporarily better qualified to perform the state's traditional roles (Toffler and Toffler 1993: 179–89).

The Tofflers are persuasive, but their arguments offer no excuse for complacency. Although the popular revolutions which swept the Middle East in 2011 appear to bear out the libertarian promise of *War and Anti-War*, this appearance is potentially misleading. Information technology, international commerce and the spread of transnational political organizations weaken certain authoritarian regimes, but the same factors can strengthen tyrants of other kinds. Activist Naomi Klein, among many others, has written eloquently about how powerful states and powerful corporations exploit such trends (Klein 2008: *passim*). Klein suggests that these states and corporations practise all the familiar cruelties associated with old-fashioned dictatorships, from mass surveillance to mass murder.

Even those who find Klein's writings one-sided might note that it is possible to do the types of things she describes, whether or not contemporary western governments and contemporary western businesses are particularly guilty of doing them. One may wield power ruthlessly in a globalized and information-dominated political environment. Lenin expected communist revolutionaries to operate through loose transnational networks, and Nazi minister of propaganda Joseph Goebbels was fascinated by the political uses of the radio. Moreover, those who would emulate Lenin and Goebbels have at least one advantage over those who hope that twenty-first-century technology has outmoded twentieth-century repression. As chapter 8 notes in its discussion of twenty-first-century insurgency, strongly led organizations have a special ability to act purposefully over extended periods.

Since strategy is presumably about planning one's actions in order to achieve one's goals, this virtue is supremely important to any strategist. Therefore, if we adopt a technical understanding of war, we must concede that Fuller's political arguments may yet turn out to be right. Even if decentralized and globally integrated societies have some assortment of advantages in principle, authoritarian control retains indispensable uses in practice. The fact that some despots have proved inept should not obscure the possibility that others may apply despotic policies more intelligently.

Thus, liberal democrats must continue their age-old struggle to reconcile kindly ideals with harsh realities. For this reason, liberals may take perverse comfort in the fact that the technical problems of strategy remain unsolved. Twenty-first-century equipment and twenty-first-century methods of using it provide strategists with formidable new capabilities, but they offer no guarantee of success. Ironically, perhaps, prominent democracies such as Great Britain and the United

States have been among the first to neglect this principle and among the first to pay the price. These two countries and their supporters attempted to substitute technology for numbers in their 2003 invasion of Iraq, only to learn that small armies configured for information-age warfare were poorly equipped to take control of the country once they had conquered it.

Indeed, all the lessons of the First World War notwithstanding, brute force retains its age-old appeal. As the wheel of strategy goes through its revolutions, the principle of mass remains near the hub. When western forces attacked Afghanistan's Taliban regime in 2001, the US air force used technologically sophisticated munitions to pick off Taliban armoured vehicles with great precision and efficiency. Taliban soldiers promptly learned to sleep outside their tanks and, since land warfare in the Afghan mountains favours infantry, they were able to go on fighting without them. Only when the USAF resorted to less technologically elegant tactics of area bombing did Taliban forces retreat (Cobain and Evans 2001: 8).

The US army had a similar experience during its 2003 operations against Iraq. This campaign took place in open terrain, where tanks can bring more of their advantages to bear. Certain American units came equipped with lighter vehicles designed to use superior intelligence and superior technology to outperform traditional heavy forces. Whatever the theoretical virtues of agility and information dominance, the advantages of armour and large-bore guns proved more certain (Gordon and Pirnie 2005: *passim*).

None of this should have been particularly surprising. Although military writers of the late twentieth and early twenty-first centuries have flirted with a techno-centric approach to warfare, many of the same authors have also recalled the enduring importance of old-fashioned forces and old-fashioned force. Ullman et al., among others, noted these very issues (Ullman et al. 1996: 34). If US military planners neglected the human dimension of warfare in 2003, they cannot blame these theorists.

This emphasis on psychology returns us to Hart's vision of winning wars by devising innovative measures which simultaneously invalidate the enemy's material and mental preparations to resist. Thus, the emphasis on psychology also seems to vindicate Hart's celebration of creative thought at the highest levels of strategic planning. Hart assumed that this creativity would prove inseparable from the other intangible faculties of conscious beings, including the full range of human feelings and perhaps even the capacity for moral reasoning. Optimists still have cause to hope that he was right.

Further reading

Fuller, J. F. C. (1928) *On Future Warfare*. London: Sifton Praed & Co.

Fuller, J. F. C. (1942) *Machine Warfare: An Enquiry into the Influences of Mechanics on the Art of War*. London: Hutchinson & Co.

Guderian, Heinz (1992) *Achtung-Panzer: The Development of Tank Warfare*, trans. Christopher Duffy. London: Cassell.

Hart, B. H. Liddell (1991) *Strategy*. London: Faber & Faber.

Hooker, Richard D., Jr (ed.) (1993) *Maneuver Warfare: An Anthology*. Novato, CA: Presidio.

7 THE ONCE AND FUTURE ATOM

The threat of hanging, Samuel Johnson tells us, concentrates the mind. One might assume that the threat of a nuclear war would have a similar effect upon entire nations. This would, as it happens, be a convenient assumption for strategic theorists. If we posit that all responsible people make avoiding global annihilation their highest priority, we can go on to work out how all responsible participants in a potentially nuclear confrontation will understand their circumstances. We can detail the various ways in which they might respond, and in which their counterparts might respond to their responses. We can even factor in the possibility that some of them may turn out not to be so responsible after all, or, perhaps, that they may feign irresponsibility in order to unnerve their opponents. By allowing us to foresee the situations which may emerge in future struggles and the ways in which human opponents may respond to them, this assumption demystifies many of the greatest unknowables in the art of strategy.

Since the Second World War, such thinkers as Bernard Brodie, P. M. S. Blackett, Albert Wohlstetter, Herman Kahn and Thomas Schelling have used this assumption to construct detailed models of possible conflicts and their possible outcomes. Although most of these models seem at least tacitly based on the nuclear stand-off between the western powers and the USSR, they reveal important dynamics operating within other types of disputes as well. Nevertheless, as thinkers have developed these concepts, they have found themselves returning to the intangible considerations which have characterized strategy throughout history. Meanwhile, the end of the Cold War, the restructuring of many communist states and the subsequent realignments in international politics have presented theorists and practising strategists alike with a wide range of new situations to contend with. In the early twenty-first century, the classic works on nuclear strategy remain enlightening but not definitive.

This chapter explores what selected works on nuclear confrontations reveal about strategy, and how their insights fit into the contemporary world. The next section examines some of Bernard Brodie's basic observations about the significance of nuclear weapons. A third section takes up Albert Wohlstetter's point that, although the logic of nuclear confrontation may be simple in principle, it depends on a 'delicate balance' of technical capabilities in which the operational details of waging nuclear war are critical. A fourth section goes on to show how Kahn and Schelling, among others, developed these ideas into more comprehensive models of possible conflicts, while a fifth notes how such thinkers as Colin Gray found the delicate balance of human minds and human societies so critical as to call such models into question. The sixth and final section considers the ways in which these debates may – or may not – inform us about the contemporary international environment.

Clausewitz regained?

In 1946, strategic thinker Bernard Brodie and four co-authors published a volume entitled *The Absolute Weapon: Atomic Power and World Order*. This very title expressed the fundamental idea which has shaped western thought on nuclear strategy. An absolute weapon is more than just a particularly powerful weapon. It is a perfect weapon, a weapon which fulfils its purpose so completely that it erases the distinction between theory and practice.

Readers of previous chapters will recall that Clausewitz based his understanding of warfare on the idea that the realities of combat will always diverge from our ideas about how violent conflict ought to work in principle. Brodie, who later wrote the introduction to an influential English translation of *On War*, almost certainly understood that the existence of an absolute weapon would force us to revisit Clausewitz's propositions. Certainly, Brodie found that nuclear weapons challenged his own ideas about warfare. The day that the existence of the atomic weapons became public knowledge, he told his wife that his previous books on strategy had become obsolete (Booth 1991: 20).

Some might assume that an absolute weapon would transform what Clausewitz described as ideal war into reality. War would, indeed, become a single great test of force. The US air force's early plans for a campaign against the USSR reflect such an idea. Where Clausewitz compared ideal war to a wrestling match, American air force commanders preferred boxing. During the early phases of the Cold War, the USAF prepared to knock a future enemy out of the fight with a nuclear 'Sunday Punch'. USAF commanders later reconsidered this approach, and Brodie rejected it as well. Although Brodie did not slavishly present his ideas in Clausewitzian terms, his core arguments follow the logic of *On War*. Clausewitz's wrestlers were not merely attempting to hurt each other. Rather, each wrestler was trying to render his opponent incapable of hurting him.

Clausewitz's analogy of the wrestling match explains certain aspects of nuclear confrontations accurately. One can easily imagine a scenario in which opposing sides use nuclear weapons to destroy each other's military forces, thus rendering those forces incapable of doing harm. Indeed, throughout the Cold War, member states of NATO based their plans for resisting a potential Soviet attack on the possibility that, if necessary, they would do exactly that. Since the Soviet Union and its allies would probably have been able to concentrate greater numbers of aircraft and non-nuclear ground forces against defenders in the critical regions of north-west Europe, NATO members viewed nuclear weapons as one of their most promising instruments for beating back an otherwise unstoppable foe.

Not only can one use nuclear weapons to sink enemy ships and devastate opposing armies, one can use them against an opponent's nuclear weapons. The technical term for this method of waging war is 'counterforce', and writers on the subject normally contrast it with the 'countervalue' approach of targeting the opposing nation's people and industry. A 'counterforce' strike might well destroy the best part of the opposing side's nuclear arsenal, particularly if one managed to launch it by surprise. Douhet, readers of chapter 5 will recall, advocated bombing raids against enemy airfields as the most promising method for achieving command of the air, and a similar principle might seem to apply.

Brodie found this possibility compelling. Indeed, during certain phases of his career, he endorsed Douhet's *Command of the Air* as a guide to nuclear strategy. Strategic thinker Barry Watts reminds us that Douhet and Clausewitz are incompatible (Watts 1984: 43–58). Where *Command of the Air* encourages strategists to behave as if Clausewitz's idealized concept of war was the real thing, the Prussian warned that friction, among numerous other factors, would make such an approach dangerously ill conceived. On the occasions when Brodie endorsed Douhet, he was implicitly suggesting that nuclear weapons had transformed strategy into something radically different from what Clausewitz described.

Brodie did not, however, settle on this conclusion. Although he was sensitive to the likelihood that more effective weapons of mass destruction would make Douhet's ideas more feasible, he was also sensitive to the economics of nuclear procurement. In proportion to the damage they can do, nuclear weapons are cheap. Therefore, under most circumstances, industrially capable nations will be able to build considerably more of these devices than their opponents can expect to neutralize. As a bumper sticker popular in the 1980s observed, even one nuclear weapon can spoil your whole day. Even the nominal loser of a nuclear war would almost certainly have the opportunity to retaliate with a dying blow against the nominal winner, and this blow would almost certainly be ruinous.

Therefore, Brodie concluded, nuclear-armed opponents will be exceedingly reluctant to wrestle. Nevertheless, he did not harbour much hope that human beings would abandon their differences, or even that they would make significant progress at resolving international disagreements through any form of world government. Instead, he expected opposing communities to coexist in their hostility. Enemies in such a relationship would exploit each other's fear of nuclear destruction to the maximum degree that they found possible, while trying to avoid any action which might precipitate an actual war.

For Brodie, Clausewitz's basic concepts remained relevant in much the same way that *On War* presented them. The wrestling match analogy would continue to illustrate a critical dynamic in armed confrontations, but it would remain inadequate to explain how such confrontations will actually unfold. Enemies would continue to express the political logic of their disagreements using the grammar of their material capabilities. Nevertheless, to stretch the metaphor further, the vocabulary of this dialogue would come to consist primarily of euphemisms. The conversation of war would acquire rules of etiquette.

Wohlstetter's ruler: the operational analysis of strategic logic

Brodie personally expected strategy to remain a human drama, with all the fluid complexity that implies. Nevertheless, as war acquires rules, it would seem to become more predictable. If one views these rules as reliable, one can base plans upon them and this simplifies the process of making strategy. Moreover, the idea that one might use nuclear weapons to deter one's enemies from attacking and perhaps even to intimidate them into complying with one's wishes while reducing the need to prepare for the full range of military undertakings has obvious appeal for policy makers.

Policy makers tend to be busy people with concerns that go far beyond military affairs. For these reasons – and others – policy makers throughout history have not only gravitated towards simple, appealing ideas, they have tended to take these ideas too far. In 1948, British strategic thinker P. M. S. Blackett published his own early thoughts on the significance of nuclear weapons in a book entitled *Military and Political Consequences of Atomic Energy*. At that time, Blackett rejected the propositions that the atomic bomb would either vindicate Douhet at his most extreme or force nations to treat each other with exaggerated circumspection. The British writer aimed his criticism not at Brodie's scholarly reflections but at oversimplified versions of similar ideas which appeared to influence the US government.

In 1946, for instance, the American State Department had proposed a plan under which all nations would surrender their atomic arsenals to the United Nations. Blackett viewed this as naive at best (Blackett 1948: 155). He viewed it as equally naive to assume that atomic weapons would prove so frightening that one could base one's strategy on the mere possibility of their use, and he doubted that an actual bombing campaign using such munitions would be sufficient to decide a major war (Blackett 1948: 155). Moreover, he was concerned that sensational ideas about the apocalyptic potential of the new weapons would confuse people and their elected leaders about a wider range of seemingly related issues, such as the use of nuclear power to generate electricity (Blackett 1948: 7).

Blackett based his arguments on a detailed study of the effects of aerial bombing in the Second World War and the explosive power of the atomic weapons available in the late 1940s. In this study, he attempted to make his case in 'as numerical a form as possible' (Blackett 1948: 4). This represented more than a historian's appreciation of specific detail. Blackett was, in fact, an innovative practitioner of the analytical technique known as operational research, which attempts to identify optimum methods for performing selected activities by formulating questions of practice in quantifiable terms and then collecting data to answer those questions. Although Blackett's 1948 work consists mainly of textual argument, a rigid approach to operational research reduces problems like those encountered in military strategy to mathematical equations.

If the data change, the results of a study based on operational research presumably change as well. Less than four years after *Military and Political Consequences* appeared in print, the United States tested a new technology which made it practical to construct explosive devices hundreds of times more devastating than the atomic bombs that Blackett had factored into his calculations. Accordingly, Blackett revised his view. The new weapons, he concluded, certainly would force even such bitter opponents as the western powers and the USSR to treat each other with a degree of discretion unprecedented in the history of world politics (Baylis and Garnett 1991: 14–15). Strategy had acquired rules of etiquette after all.

Meanwhile, another specialist in operational research took similar ideas farther, and in a different direction. This was Albert Wohlstetter, an American analyst at the research institute known as the RAND Corporation. Wohlstetter accepted the premise that nuclear strategy was primarily a matter of manipulating what he described as the balance of terror. Like Blackett, he believed that the dynamics of this balance depended on the technical details of what weapons can do and how the opposing sides might use them.

Blackett concluded that a war fought with fusion weapons (see Box 7.1) would be so catastrophic that the only wise strategy was to maintain sufficient retaliatory forces to deter potential enemies from launching one. More elaborate plans based on more extensive arsenals

---

Box 7.1   Bomb and Superbomb

In the 1950s, as the main text notes, researchers perfected a new and far more devastating type of nuclear weapon. An extended technical discussion would lie beyond the scope of this work but, for those who are unfamiliar with the issue, the earlier bombs relied exclusively on nuclear fission, while the newer ones used the energy released by a fission explosion to trigger a far more powerful fusion reaction. Writers on such subjects commonly refer to fission devices as 'atomic' and fusion devices as 'nuclear', although since both types of reaction take place within the nuclei of atoms, there is a logical case for using these expressions interchangeably. This book uses the word 'nuclear' as a general term for weapons of mass destruction based on both principles, while reserving 'atomic' for fission devices.

of weapons, the British thinker noted, could well prompt potential opponents to respond with more aggressive policies of their own. Excessive preparations for nuclear war risk increasing the chances that there might actually be one.

Wohlstetter believed that the new weapons opened a wider range of possibilities. The American thinker emphasized the point that if your enemies do not believe that you are capable of using your armaments, the simple fact that they exist as physical objects will not deter anything. Indeed, if you appear unprepared, either in a psychological or in a material sense, your rivals might conclude that it is rational for them to attack pre-emptively, before you actually become as dangerous as your weapons might make you. Since one cannot afford to behave irrationally in matters involving nuclear war, your potential enemies might feel obliged to carry out this pre-emptive attack, whether they truly wish to or not. A strategic etiquette exists, but, like social etiquette, its rules vary according to context.

Clausewitz also depicted strategy as contextual. The Prussian, however, maintained that the context of war would remain eternally in flux. Wohlstetter suggested that the parameters of nuclear deterrence were more rigidly fixed. Whereas the total phenomenon of warfare might dance among the largely intangible and broadly defined forces which make up the Clausewitzian trinity, deterrence rests on the anticipated material consequences of using clearly identified weapons in clearly identified ways. Operations research purports to analyse such consequences precisely and reliably.

Precision and reliability are invaluable in any practical activity. In other branches of strategy, planners may supplement analytical techniques, such as operations research, with historical studies of comparable conflicts and often with the direct experience of veterans. Since there has never been a conflict which seems analogous to nuclear war, Wohlstetter's approach appears to fill a vital niche for those who make contemporary strategy. Certainly the RAND Corporation's studies – and Wohlstetter's personal contributions to them – have had considerable influence on American government policy.

Although the first aim of nuclear strategy must be that of dissuading enemy attack, strategists may wish to influence their opponents in other ways as well. Moreover, even the logic of dissuasion may not be as straightforward as it initially appears. The most basic version of deterrence theory notes that if one country attempts to obliterate another, it is probably reasonable to assume that the victim will strike back as vigorously as it can, and therefore it is equally reasonable to assume that if the potential victim enjoys the undisputed ability to launch a devastating retaliatory strike, its enemies will refrain from all-out attack. A nuclear war might, however, unfold in many other ways.

When, for instance, one country threatens another with anything less than absolute destruction, it is far less obvious that the victim will be willing to respond with a large-scale nuclear strike. Indeed, since one's enemies are likely to retaliate for one's retaliation, the logic of deterrence may come to favour the aggressor. Those who strike second may have to restrain themselves for fear of what their opponents have the undisputed ability to do when they strike third. Since the western powers relied on nuclear weapons to counter the Soviet Union's advantage in non-nuclear forces during the Cold War, this was more than a hypothetical scenario.

One can imagine innumerable other variations on the basic deterrence relationship. Nevertheless, as long as opponents must structure their critical decisions around one another's perceived capacity for revenge, one may use operations research to establish their military capabilities and similarly formal methods of analysis to model their policy options. In this spirit, Herman Kahn, among others, explored the foreseeable permutations of nuclear confrontation, famously engaging in dark humour along the way, but emphasizing his commitment to consider even the most horrible possibilities with thoroughly dispassionate rationality. The process of logical reasoning achieves particularly high levels of purity in the realm of mathematics, and Kahn co-authored an early paper promoting the mathematical technique known as game theory as an aid to strategic analysis (Kahn and Mann 1957: *passim*).

Kahn's RAND colleague Thomas Schelling applied game theory to nuclear strategy even more extensively. These thinkers' approaches promoted the idea of potentially violent conflict as a form of bargaining, in which opponents balance threats against demands in the attempt to convince one another to modify their behaviour. If this concept models actual conflicts accurately, successful strategy requires both the readiness to carry out one's threats and the corresponding will to restrain one's actions rationally, even in the midst of carnage. Those who are not willing to hurt their opponents – perhaps using nuclear weapons – will have no bargaining power, but those who overreact will merely provoke their opponents to respond in kind, achieving nothing but senseless mutual destruction. Indeed, this model suggests that it may actually be a mistake to hurt one's opponents too severely since this produces a situation in which they may feel that they have nothing left to lose.

Although this view of conflict calls upon strategists to exercise what may be an inhuman degree of sangfroid, it paradoxically suggests that it will often be useful to convince one's enemies that one is reckless. An opponent who understands the dangers of war but fears that you do not will presumably feel compelled to treat your threats with an otherwise unnecessary degree of caution. Schelling noted that one can achieve a similar effect by deliberately leaving one's plans to chance (Baylis and Garnett 1991: 11–12). Such ideas inspired the automatic Doomsday Machine featured in Stanley Kubrick's film *Dr. Strangelove*. This idea also suggests that it may be useful for a government to promote the idea that it is prepared for war and expects a considerable portion of its population to survive, even if its leaders secretly know that their plans are dubious. Khan often seems to downplay the horrors of a nuclear exchange, and his critics have suggested that he was deliberately trying to encourage this kind of perversely useful overconfidence (Menand 2005).

Kahn and Schelling's concept also suggests that it is wise to prepare to attack one's enemies in a succession of different ways, each harsher than the one before it. This allows one to extend the process of threat and counter-threat for as long as possible, increasing the chances that opponents will be able to negotiate a settlement before either side finds it necessary to launch an all-out nuclear strike. Thus, the idea of conflict as a bargaining process provides one rationale for maintaining strong non-nuclear forces and an arsenal of smaller so-called tactical nuclear weapons, as well as a more devastating strategic force. Kahn and Schelling's theoretical works on these subjects appeared during the same period of Cold War history that military authors throughout the western countries were also reasserting the utility of possessing a wide range of strategic options. General Maxwell Taylor, for instance, famously developed this theme in his work *The Uncertain Trumpet* (Taylor 1960: *passim*).

On a more reassuring note, the model of conflict as negotiation suggests that even bitter enemies may find it mutually advantageous to bargain over the circumstances under which future bargaining will take place. Opponents may, for instance, voluntarily accept a situation in which they feel less capable of attacking their opponents, as long as they feel that the same situation renders their opponents less capable of attacking them. They may, in other words, agree to enforceable arms control treaties. Neither side is likely to give up its weapons entirely. Indeed, since the entire process depends on mutual deterrence, complete disarmament might actually increase the chances of war. Nevertheless, just as Kahn and Schelling's models provide an intellectual basis for aggressive behaviour and high levels of military spending, they also support the hope of moderating both through diplomacy.

Although Kahn and Schelling were particularly interested in potential nuclear conflicts, these ideas can apply to disputes of any kind. US Secretary of Defense Robert McNamara, for instance, drew on conflict bargaining theory when he advised American President Lyndon Johnson's administration on the Vietnam War. Johnson's successor Richard Nixon earned a reputation for being more forceful, but he also used bombing campaigns largely as a tool to pressure his opponents into modifying their negotiating positions, and he may have even cultivated a reputation for psychological instability in order to make his threats more frightening. Nevertheless, even as American presidents were applying the conflict bargaining concept with some degree of success, a new generation of strategic theorists were starting to question its fundamental premises.

But is it strategy? The cultural critique of deterrence theory

The structured approach featured in formal analytical techniques such as operations research and game theory exposes the oversimplifications which find shelter beneath purely impressionistic theories of conflict. Nevertheless, these techniques introduce oversimplifications of their own. Since these approaches aim to reduce the impossibly complex problems of real life to manageable conceptual models, they force modellers to leave out complicating factors. Some of these factors may turn out to be important. Kahn himself noted similar points in his early writings on the subject (Kahn and Mann 1957: 1–2). In these writings, he advocated game theory as a mental exercise and a supplement to other ways of studying nuclear issues, not as a replacement for the free-flowing process of creative reflection which has characterized strategy throughout human experience, and which Clausewitz attributed to genius.

Formal methods do, however, seem to provide definite answers to important questions. Since these methods purport to offer a logical account of logical behaviour, their results seem exceptionally persuasive. Certainly, by the 1970s, the Cold War appeared to be unfolding in roughly the ways that a casual reader of deterrence theory might have expected. The opposing superpowers were stockpiling tens of thousands of nuclear devices designed for an increasingly imaginative range of possible uses while simultaneously discussing complex treaties to adjust the course of these preparations. Both sides regularly engaged in what former American Secretary of State John Foster Dulles had called brinksmanship, but, nevertheless, both had apparently acquiesced to the state of cordially negotiated rivalry known as détente.

The strategic thinkers of earlier eras tended to be suspicious of appearances, particularly when those appearances seem to make perfect sense. Sun Tzu, for instance, claimed that all war is based on deception. Thucydides provides example after example of the paradoxes which reverse rational expectation in strategy, even when neither side has a particularly well-conceived scheme to outwit the other. In this spirit, researchers from several branches of strategic studies and the social sciences began to ask whether the seemingly simple logic of deterrence theory is the actual logic of the Americans, Soviets, British, French, Chinese, Israelis and others who incorporate nuclear weapons into actual strategy, and whether the seemingly simple problems that deterrence theory models are the actual problems which real-world strategists are attempting to solve.

Psychological research suggests otherwise. The brain does not seem to function according to the principles of pure logic. Actual human reasoning deviates even further from abstract rationality when people collaborate in groups. Robert Jervis and Irving Janis stand out for their work on these topics. Since human cognition seems consistent enough for one to generalize about the ways in which people actually do solve problems, Jervis, Janis and others were able to critique traditional deterrence theory on a variety of points. This, in turn, suggested that those who assumed that the Cold War was going as expected and would continue to conform to theoretical predictions indefinitely might be risking a fatal mistake.

Jervis, for instance, noted that human beings appear to have a tendency towards overconfidence, a tendency to overlook factors which may complicate their preferred solutions to problems, a corresponding tendency to interpret new information in ways that support their preferences and an inclination to screen out information they find upsetting (Jervis 1982–3: 20–30). Such observations indicate that once one's opponents have made up their minds to do something, even a credible retaliatory threat may not stop them. This suggests, at a minimum, that nuclear-armed opponents would be wise to handle each other more cautiously than purely rationalistic versions of deterrence theory seem to imply. Sun Tzu's proposition that one should always leave one's opponents a way to escape may have acquired fresh relevance.

These types of psychological insights challenge specific models of deterrence relationships, but most of them remain fundamentally compatible with the general concept of deterrence modelling. As Schelling has noted, game theory can accommodate as much human complexity as one is prepared to specify and account for (Schelling 1984: 239). The same is true of most other formal analytical techniques. Moreover, strategists may look for ways to coax people out of their idiosyncrasies. Scholar Lawrence Freedman provides a historical example of an occasion when American policy makers may have attempted to do this in a particularly ambitious way. According to Freedman, Robert McNamara and his admirers recognized that the USSR was irrationally aggressive by the standards of deterrence theory but hoped that the United States could coax the Soviet leadership into adopting more considered policies by setting a good example (Freedman 1981: 257).

Meanwhile, writers such as Jack Snyder, David Jones, Carnes Lord, Colin Gray and Kenneth Booth noted that, even when one takes cognitive biases into account, strategists from different cultures seem to reason in different ways. A rationalist might respond that some of these ways must be more logical – and thus more effective – than others, but the strategic culture theorists could counter that strategic planners from different origins have such different goals, expectations, capabilities, physical environments, economic systems, political systems and other background circumstances that there will often be no meaningful way to compare their problems and thus no meaningful way to judge between their solutions, except perhaps in hindsight. Certainly, it is a mistake to assume that one's opponents will change. (The Soviet Union, as Freedman noted, adopted only a handful of the lessons which McNamara was allegedly trying to teach: Freedman 1981: 260–1.) It is also a mistake to assume that others' methods will not work for them. On the contrary, as Gray points out, cultures typically evolve their distinctive approaches to strategy because those approaches allow them to compensate for their own distinctive weaknesses and exploit their own distinctive advantages (Gray 1999a: 14).

It is difficult to reduce cultural influences on strategy to simple propositions. Gray, in particular, emphasizes that cultural knowledge is only useful when one integrates a thorough knowledge of the numerous issues which commonly contribute to strategic culture into an even broader understanding of other strategically relevant issues. Those who merely assume that others will behave in stereotypical ways risk lapsing into mere prejudice. For these reasons, deterrence theorists cannot fully account for the concept of strategic culture merely by adjusting models of rational decision making to include a few additional variables. Where the psychological insights of writers such as Jervis suggest that we need to modify traditional deterrence theory, the broader insights of writers on strategic culture stress that we need to think about nuclear confrontations in a far more flexible way.

Conclusion

While theorists sought to make sense of strategy in the nuclear age, the world of international politics changed around them. From the time when Blackett challenged the convenient assumptions of American statesmen to the beginning of the strategic culture debate, the Marxist-Leninist states organized around the Soviet Union and the western powers had engaged in the so-called Cold War. The opposing sides in this struggle not only competed for goods such as resources and access to militarily advantageous territory, they professed fundamentally incompatible ideas about how human beings should live. These enemies were the greatest military powers of their time in terms of both nuclear and non-nuclear weapons.

Few writers on nuclear strategy limited themselves to discussing the East–West dispute, but most oriented their ideas around it to one degree or another. For operations researchers, the Cold War was, at a minimum, the richest available source of data. The concept of deterrence is at its clearest when two implacably hostile opponents confront each other directly over an irreconcilable issue. Even the early literature on strategic culture tended to focus, quite sensibly, on the most strategically relevant cultures of its time. The title of Jack Snyder's pioneering work on this topic begins *The Soviet Strategic Culture . . .* (Snyder 1977: *passim*).

Beginning in 1989, Moscow permitted its allied states to abandon their constitutional commitments to Marxism-Leninism, break their military ties with the Soviet Union and, ultimately, to realign themselves with the West. Between 1990 and 1991, the USSR offered similar autonomy and ideological flexibility to its constituent republics, including the Russian Republic itself. This transformation may not have ended Russia's rivalry with the western powers, but it ameliorated the conflict's former intensity. As the 1990s progressed, largely or partially unrelated issues ranging from Baathist Iraq's bid to dominate the Middle East to India's dispute with Pakistan to al-Qaeda's global terrorist movement gained prominence. Despite rhetoric from both supporters and critics of American President G. W. Bush's promise to wage a global war on terrorism, none of the disputes of the late 1990s or early twenty-first century dominated international affairs as comprehensively as the Cold War dominated the politics of the previous forty-odd years, and none of them have been remotely as dangerous.

Brodie's absolute weapon probably contributed to this transformation. Nuclear deterrence presumably played some role in preventing the Cold War from becoming an actual war for long enough for such changes to take place. Some have suggested that American President Ronald Reagan brought down the USSR by raising US defence spending. According to this argument, Soviet leaders felt compelled to outdo the Americans and bankrupted their country in the process. The Reagan administration's most technologically ambitious new project was its Strategic Defense Initiative (SDI) to develop defences against nuclear-tipped ballistic missiles, and this was presumably the programme which gave the Soviet Union the most trouble. Those seeking a detailed account of why the USSR might have found SDI exceptionally problematic may consult Dmitry Mikheyev's work *The Soviet Perspective on the Strategic Defense Initiative* (Mikheyev 1987: *passim*).

One may debate the merits of such arguments, but one fact is relatively well established. Whatever role nuclear weapons played in the restructuring of the Soviet Union and its alliances, they were but one factor among many. Culture also was no more than one aspect of this process. Nevertheless, the strategic culture theorists reminded their readers that even nuclear strategy is a multi-dimensional affair and that those who wish to understand it must rediscover Clausewitz's respect for holistic and intuitive thought.

The end of the Cold War suggests that this reminder was worth heeding. Therefore, it may be noteworthy that one of the more influential writers on strategic culture, Colin Gray, has since written a particularly comprehensive study of the role which nuclear arms might play in twenty-first-century strategy, entitled *The Second Nuclear Age* (Gray 1999b: *passim*). Where previous writers on such topics based their ideas on the physical effects of the weapons, Gray organized this study around the political context in which such devices appear (Gray 1999b: 17). Gray suggested that the end of the Cold War had given way to a period in which increasing numbers of actors would acquire nuclear weapons, but the West would continue to dominate global affairs and the United States would remain the West's pre-eminent power.

Gray added that this period, which he called 'the second nuclear age', would almost certainly give way to a third, in which the United

States acquires a significant nuclear rival (Gray 1999b: 25). In his view, the People's Republic of China is a likely candidate (Gray 1999b: 33). During this period of transition, Gray tells us, the United States will need nuclear weapons for at least five different reasons (Gray 1999b: 120). The first of these reasons is simply that they symbolize its status, while the second two involve deterrence in various forms (Gray 1999b: 120). Gray's fourth reason is that nuclear weapons provide their owners with distinctive military options, such as an enhanced ability to destroy targets buried deep underground, and the fifth is that such weapons offer a form of insurance if other types of military force fail (Gray 1999b: 120).

Although Gray focuses on the United States, one may assume that other powers will find even more ways to exploit nuclear capabilities, certainly to intimidate, and perhaps as an actual weapon of war. The strategic applications of nuclear arms will proliferate even faster than the weapons themselves. At this point, it is worth noting that few among the earlier generations of nuclear theorists would have been surprised. The writers of the early Cold War commonly explored what they called the *nth* country problem, which was the question of how strategic relationships might change as new states acquired nuclear weapons, and Schelling has argued that formal deterrence modelling provides insights into the circumstances under which non-state actors such as terrorists might acquire nuclear weapons (Schelling 1984: 309–27). Schelling even suggests that terrorists may be cautious about using them (Schelling 1984: 309–27). Classical deterrence theory continues to provide provocative ideas regarding the possibilities of nuclear strategy, as long as one understands that its view of the topic is not definitive.

Further reading

Baylis, John and Garnet, John (eds) (1991) *Makers of Nuclear Strategy*. London: Pinter.

Freedman, Lawrence (1981) *The Evolution of Nuclear Strategy*. Basingstoke: Macmillan.

Gray, Colin S. (1999) *The Second Nuclear Age*. Boulder, CO: Lynne Rienner.

Kahn, Herman (1962) *Thinking About the Unthinkable*. London: Weidenfeld & Nicolson.

Schelling, Thomas C. (1980) *The Strategy of Conflict*. Cambridge, MA: Harvard University Press.

8 THE WEAK AGAINST THE STRONG

War has a way of defying expectations. Thucydides' Greeks repeatedly discovered this, often at terrible cost. Clausewitz's work on the trinity suggests that it must always be so. Indeed, the very phenomenon which military writers commonly describe as 'conventional warfare' is actually a historical rarity. Researchers Gorka and Kilcullen have used figures from the Correlates of War dataset to calculate that fewer than 20 per cent of the armed conflicts which have taken place since 1815 have been open confrontations between the official armed forces of commonly recognized states (Gorka and Kilcullen 2011: 17).

The rest have been more complex disputes involving partisans, terrorist cells, criminal gangs, unofficial militias, guerrilla movements, the private armies of warlords and a kaleidoscopic variety of other so-called non-state actors. In most conflicts of this nature, some participants are far stronger than others. Typically, for instance, state security forces are larger, more skilled, more disciplined and much more lavishly equipped than any non-state organizations which might oppose them. Unsurprisingly, according to one study, states defeat non-state enemies approximately 80 per cent of the time (Gorka and Kilcullen 2011: 17).

Nevertheless, even when the stronger side prevails, the process is often slow, gruelling and uncertain. The nominal losers frequently achieve some of their aspirations. The nominal victors must normally compromise many of theirs. For many governments, the need to commit time, money, military units, political capital and human lives to such affairs is itself a strategic setback, no matter how regularly their soldiers win firefights. The longer the struggle goes on, the more profound the setback becomes.

Conflicts of this nature challenge strategic thinkers to explain how forces which appear so weak can achieve such effects against forces which appear so powerful. For such an explanation to be useful, strategists must go on to identify the ways in which those who lack the advantages traditionally associated with state armed forces can maximize their chances of achieving their political aims, and also the most efficient ways for states to suppress them. The fact that complex conflicts involving non-state actors have dominated world politics throughout the twenty-first century gives these issues special urgency.

Numerous strategic thinkers have written about complex struggles involving mismatched opponents. Although the number of works on this topic is growing rapidly, this body of literature has its classics to which other theorists and practitioners perennially return. This chapter explores the ways in which classic authors have addressed the special problems of achieving one's objectives in this type of warfare. Most of the thinkers discussed throughout this book have expressed some version of Clausewitz's dictum that war is the continuation of politics by other means, and complex conflicts seem to elevate this strategic concept above all others. Nevertheless, this observation leaves strategists to determine which other means to apply in particular situations and, there, what Clausewitz called the grammar of war remains relevant.

After this introduction, the next main section of this chapter reviews what thinkers discussed in earlier parts of this book wrote about irregular conflict. A third section explores how such classic theorists

---

Box 8.1   What is Insurgency, Anyway?

There are innumerable words for various forms of irregular warfare. None of them capture the reality of actual conflicts with any great precision. The fact that many of these terms carry legal and emotional baggage only compounds the problem. One person's terrorist, the well-worn saying goes, is another person's freedom fighter.

Moreover, this same terrorist/freedom fighter may once have been a uniformed soldier in a state army, and eventually may be again. One might also refer to the same terrorist/freedom fighter/soldier as a bandit, an insurgent, a guerrilla, a revolutionary, an illegal combatant, a member of a popular militia and many other things besides, depending on context and circumstances. Each of these terms draws attention to certain facts about what the fighter in question actually does, and each of the terms obscures others.

Nevertheless, words such as 'terrorism', 'insurgency' and 'people's war' refer to real ways of fighting, with distinctive methods, advantages, requirements and limitations. Strategists need to discuss these topics. Therefore, despite the fact that the various terms for irregular combatants and their practices are tendentious and imprecise, strategists cannot avoid using them. This book uses the word 'insurgency' as a generic word for irregular warfare.

Strategic thinkers still need a way to distinguish insurgencies from other forms of wars. Gorka and Kilcullen suggest that the best way to accomplish this is to classify conflicts on the basis of the types of actors which take part in them during a particular period of time (Gorka and Kilcullen 2011: 17–18). A struggle between recognized state forces is, by their definition, conventional. Military contests involving non-state actors are insurgencies.

This book adopts Gorka and Kilcullen's approach, not only because it acknowledges the complexities of the topic but because it suggests a focused approach for exploring recent writings on this matter. As this chapter notes, the concept of insurgency attained much of its current prominence when certain writers became interested in the problems of challenging recognized states and, indeed, the capitalist form of society which confers recognition upon them. Revolutionaries such as Lenin and Mao articulated ideas which shaped the irregular conflicts of the twentieth century and which serve as a starting point for discussions of irregular conflict today. This chapter emphasizes those ideas and focuses on thinkers who have addressed them.

of irregular warfare as Mao Zedong have developed our understanding of this topic. A fourth section notes how the various issues which arise in complex conflicts return us to the problems of establishing an effective political community – problems which also preoccupied Vegetius and Machiavelli. This chapter's conclusion draws on the ideas discussed throughout the chapter to ask whether the insurgencies of the early twenty-first century have unrealized strategic potential and whether there is a need for a new body of theory to explore it.

A weapon of the strong? Insurgency in pre-twentieth-century strategic thought

Many of the most revered strategic thinkers appear to have neglected insurgency. Sun Tzu, for instance, seems to overlook the topic. Thucydides, Vegetius and Machiavelli address it obliquely, if at all. Although Clausewitz devoted a chapter of *On War* to 'The People in Arms', many of his most prominent contemporary critics find this treatment inadequate.

The fact that so many writers who prove so perceptive on other issues appear to pass over this subject suggests that their apparent failure to give this issue proper attention is more than an oversight. One reason why these thinkers wrote so little which explicitly deals with insurgency as we understand it in the twenty-first century may simply be that people living in different historical periods have different expectations of warfare. A campaign involving mercenaries, town militias, spontaneously organized bands of religious fanatics and high-born warriors who scorn military discipline but fight to fulfil personal obligations would have been unremarkable to Machiavelli, but it would certainly rate as a complex and irregular conflict if it took place today.

Therefore, one can hardly expect strategic thinkers from other eras to address the subject of insurgency as twenty-first-century readers understand the term. Earlier thinkers routinely discuss the elements of contemporary insurgency, but it is rare for them to organize their thoughts around that concept. *The History of the Peloponnesian War*, for instance, is replete with accounts of revolts, subversive plots and street violence. Readers may recall that one of the pivotal episodes in Thucydides' account of the Sicilian campaign began when unknown conspirators provoked hysteria by systematically mutilating statues of the god Hermes, a deed which bloodlessly parallels modern acts of terrorism. Thucydides does not highlight such incidents as examples of a distinctive form of warfare, but he certainly discusses them.

Moreover, even where earlier strategic thinkers recognized hybrid forces and guerrilla tactics as noteworthy, they would not necessarily have recommended the combination as an alternative approach to strategy. These thinkers certainly valued many of the methods which twenty-first-century strategists associate with insurgency. All three praised cunning, indirect approaches and psychological warfare. Machiavelli goes into particular depth on insurgency-related topics in a chapter on conspiracy. The Florentine notes that more rulers have fallen to plotters within their own realms than to foreign armies (Machiavelli 1950: 410). Machiavelli observes that this challenges common assumptions about who is strong, who is weak and who is in a position to pursue political goals through force. Although only those who command armies can challenge opposing rulers on the battlefield, the arguably more effective tactics of conspiracy are potentially available to virtually everyone (Machiavelli 1950: 410).

These lines appear in *Discourses on Livy*. Machiavelli dedicated that book to friends who shared his republican sympathies at a time when Medici princes ruled over Florence. One might have expected Machiavelli to find the possibility of conspiracies intriguing. Instead, he goes on to point out that the overwhelming majority of all plots fail. Since the price of failure is normally torture and death, Machiavelli claims that it is foolish to become involved in such ventures (Machiavelli 1950: 410).

Cynics may suspect that Machiavelli included those lines so that he could later deny having written a book which advocated insurrection. Nevertheless, if his only goal had been self-protection, he would have been wiser to omit the chapter entirely. The Florentine may well have phrased his statements about plots to serve multiple purposes, but readers may reasonably assume that one them was to debunk misconceptions concerning conspiratorial methods. Whether one wages war openly or by stealth, he warns, the same realities prevail and the same principles of strategy apply.

Machiavelli later argued that conspiring against a state was less personally dangerous for the conspirators than scheming to murder an individual ruler, and that republics might be particularly vulnerable to subversion (Machiavelli 1950: 431). Nevertheless, plotting against entire states also raises new and more serious difficulties. To control an entire population, the Florentine notes, one normally requires an army, and, unless the plotters are in command of one, they will have to rely on outside support or on some particularly ingenious trick (Machiavelli 1950: 431). Although the Florentine presents examples of conspirators who used such methods successfully, readers may recall that he views cunning as an inferior instrument and foreign aid as a downright pernicious one. Better, one must infer, to acquire an army of one's own, formed along the lines he details so comprehensively throughout the rest of his works.

Sun Tzu, Vegetius and Machiavelli were preoccupied not with insurgency as such but with the problem of using all the instruments of strategy to best effect. All three were aware that systematically trained, equipped and structured military organizations enjoy a wide range of potent advantages in practically all situations. All three were concerned that rulers would find it cheaper, politically easier and perhaps culturally more appropriate to rely on more hybridized forces. Machiavelli also claimed to worry that dissidents of various persuasions might let romantic ideas about conspiracies tempt them into doomed adventures, suicidal for themselves and uselessly destructive for their communities. One may speculate that these authors would have been reluctant to write anything which might encourage readers in such tendencies, and one may definitively state that they viewed what twenty-first-century writers refer to as insurgency as something for strategists to assimilate and improve upon, not something for strategists idolatrously to set apart. As later sections will note, the contemporary period's most penetrating thinkers on irregular warfare would support that approach.

This brings us to Clausewitz, who addressed the concept of insurgency in something closer to its contemporary form. Clausewitz personally helped organize a popular resistance movement against French forces in East Prussia during the winter of 1812–13 (Howard 1983: 56). He discussed this aspect of warfare throughout his works. As previously noted, he collected his ideas on this topic in Book Six, Chapter Twenty-Six of *On War*.

Earlier thinkers seemed to assume that the methods currently associated with insurgencies were merely parts of a larger strategic whole. Clausewitz stated this point explicitly and explained his reasoning as follows. Since guerrillas depend on stealth to survive, they cannot hope to defeat state armies in a single battle or even in a continuous series of battles directed against a clearly established geographical objective (Clausewitz 1976: 480). Napoleon led his army to Moscow, but the Russian peasants who rose up to resist him did not even try to march on Paris.

Guerrillas, Clausewitz tells us, injure their opponents by wearing them down piecemeal over extended periods. Meanwhile, the popular forces themselves will suffer losses, which will normally undermine their capabilities more seriously and at a steadier pace than they can undermine their antagonists. Thus, although Clausewitz acknowledges circumstances in which an insurgency movement might mushroom into a force which can threaten its enemies with total destruction, it is normally more appropriate to think of insurrection in the larger context of a war in which state forces will ultimately play the decisive role (Clausewitz 1976: 480). Although Russia's partisans could not seize the French capital, Tsar Alexander's army eventually did.

Although Clausewitz notes limits to what popular movements can accomplish on their own, he portrays insurgency as a uniquely powerful form of warfare. At one point, he compares guerrillas to hot coals at the heart of a building, which can burn away supporting timbers and bring the entire structure to the ground (Clausewitz 1976: 480). Not only does he use vivid language, he suggests that irregular and hybrid forces have unique capabilities. Such forces, for instance, are far more effective than other types of military units at interdicting enemy movements, particularly in rough terrain (Clausewitz 1976: 481).

Insurgencies offer their side's strategists access to new pools of resources which would not otherwise be available (Clausewitz 1976: 479). As long as one does not sacrifice one's fighters in such numbers that the insurgency movement loses its ability to attract support, guerrillas have the advantage of being expendable (Clausewitz 1976: 482). Of even greater strategic significance is the fact that popular forces can remain active in regions under enemy occupation. This means that they will often be able to operate against the enemy's vulnerable rear (Clausewitz 1976: 481). Moreover, it means that insurgents can keep a country's cause alive even after that nation's regular armed forces have suffered the most overwhelming defeat (Clausewitz 1976: 483).

Accordingly, Clausewitz urges readers to take full advantage of insurgency warfare. Where Machiavelli feared that dissidents would naively rush into conspiracies, Clausewitz feared that state leaders would naively hold back from mobilizing their people as partisans (Clausewitz 1976: 479). Where others depict insurgency as a method of fighting which blurs the distinction between the weak and the strong, *On War* depicts it as a tool which allows whoever uses it to become stronger. This seems to imply that strong states which combine irregular warfare with other methods of fighting have even more to gain from insurgency techniques than rogue malcontents.

One might have imagined that Clausewitz would view insurgency as part of the friction which prevents real wars from unfolding as the straightforward contests of force which he views as logical in theory. On the contrary, he argued that the Europeans of his generation had turned to it precisely because of the remorseless logic that compels wartime enemies to draw on all possible resources to maximize their strength. People's wars, in his view, brought real war closer to the hypothetical ideal of a vast duel than it had ever been before. As it became increasingly common, he argued, those who wished to win wars would have no choice but to exploit it, and if this had far-reaching social consequences, humanity would have to adapt to them. Although Clausewitz himself did not develop these points any further, one might note that the same process of reasoning would presumably drive warring opponents to continue developing even more unorthodox methods of fighting. It would, for instance, seem logical for those who have exhausted the possibilities of guerrilla warfare against enemy military organizations to strike enemy civilians in spectacular acts of terrorism.

So you want a revolution?

Clausewitz's thoughts on insurgency remain incomplete, but perhaps not for the reasons his critics tend to suppose. Where contemporary commentators accuse him of failing to appreciate the possibilities of this form of warfare, he may actually fail to appreciate all of its challenges. *On War* lists five conditions which strategists must meet in order to use guerrilla forces effectively (Clausewitz 1976: 480). One of these is simply that the war must last for a sufficient length of time, and three more concern physical geography. Although Clausewitz also notes that insurgencies can only succeed in countries which have a cultural tradition of such uprisings, he generally seems to assume that when leaders resolve to arm civilians as irregular combatants, the people themselves will obligingly assume that role. *On War* does note that guerrilla movements will gain and lose followers as they win victories and suffer defeats, but it says little about more general problems of securing and exploiting popular support.

This may be a case in which Clausewitz's perceptions of his own historical period coloured his thought. Clausewitz observed that nineteenth-century Europeans were rationalizing their methods of waging war (Clausewitz 1976: 479). This had led them to expand their armed forces and to introduce more effective methods of using them. This had also led them to become ever more ruthless. Clausewitz believed that the realities of conflict made it virtually certain that such processes would accelerate, and he viewed people's wars as but one of these trends (Clausewitz 1976: 479).

The early nineteenth century also happened to be a time when many of the most widely influential political movements stressed patriotic loyalty to one's nation. Clausewitz himself was a fierce patriot, and he experienced irregular warfare amongst other patriots who had taken up arms to protect their homelands from foreign invaders. Indeed, Clausewitz classified insurgency as a form of defensive warfare. These facts may have made it easier for him to take it for granted that people's wars would, in fact, be popular, and that there would be state military organizations at hand to direct guerrilla operations.

The founders of contemporary insurgency theory lacked such luxuries. Our current understanding of this subject begins with the writings of Vladimir Lenin and Mao Zedong. Both wrote their most influential works of strategic thought while they were organizing communist revolutionary movements within their own countries. In this process, they faced many of the same difficulties as Machiavelli's conspirators and, like the Florentine, they recognized these challenges as daunting. Where Clausewitz expected outraged citizens to unite behind a universally recognized cause, Lenin and Mao had to operate within an environment in which significant numbers of people supported the very governments that they were trying to overthrow, and the overwhelming majority would have preferred not to become involved. Moreover, many of the people who were willing to oppose the government already belonged to other dissident organizations with their own goals and their own ideas about how to achieve them.

Just as revolutionaries cannot expect to begin their careers with widespread popular support, they cannot automatically turn to outside institutions to underwrite their efforts. External support may be available to some degree and in some form. Rebels may, for instance, make contact with foreign organizations that support their cause or even with sympathetic groups within their own country. Nevertheless, this sort of help is likely to be far less generous and far less reliable than Clausewitz anticipated. Moreover, those who value their independence might be cautious about accepting it.

For these reasons, contemporary insurgency theorists have emphasized the politics of irregular warfare. Many of Lenin's most influential writings address the problems of drawing the various activist groups of early twentieth-century Russia into the communist movement and using them to advance its strategies. Mao summarized the issue in more general terms when he compared guerrilla fighters to fish swimming in a sea made up of the people. If guerrillas can organize sufficient numbers of those people to join their ranks, provide them with supplies, hide them from government forces and otherwise support their movement, Mao suggests, they will thrive.

Those who have fought recent insurgency movements have noted that the opposite is also true. If one can dry up Mao's 'sea' by turning the population against a revolutionary movement and isolating its fighters from outside support, one can suffocate the insurgency. In 1966, Sir Robert Thompson, a British officer and civil servant who had directed anti-guerrilla operations in what was then the British colony of Malaya, presented his insights on this topic in a book entitled *Defeating Communist Insurgency*. This work remains basic to twenty-first-century understandings of combating irregular opponents. The US army's counter-insurgency field manual, for instance, acknowledges a substantial debt to Thompson's work (Anonymous 2006: viii). Thompson listed a series of fundamental principles for fighting insurgents, and all gave broad political considerations priority over simple combat effectiveness (Thompson 1966: 50–62).

Nevertheless, irregular warfare is more than a popularity contest. Indeed, few insurgents can afford to let it become one. There may be occasions upon which guerrilla fighters take up arms purely to win some measure of democracy for their fellow citizens without having any strong preferences about the form which democratic governance might take, but such cases are far from typical. Most politically inspired revolutionaries find themselves in the same position as Lenin, who presumably believed that his version of communism would be in the best interests of the people, but doubted that the people themselves would ever institute it on their own. Those who fight for personal gain are even less likely to achieve their goals through freely given public support.

Therefore, even the most well-meaning insurgent leaders must normally function as what Lenin called a vanguard. They must sustain a cause which even their own supporters may not fully understand. They must do so in the face of enemies who are not only better armed but are initially better organized to control the population by other means. They will need to exploit popular affection to overcome these handicaps, but they are unlikely to achieve their actual aims until they are in a position to secure those goals directly. Like Clausewitz's wrestlers, they will need to overpower their opponents in order to get to this point.

Clausewitz also noted that opponents in real-life conflicts have more options than athletes following the rules of a game. In real life, one may overpower opponents through a wide variety of means. Some of these means may be bloodless. Some may even be legal. Nevertheless, the possibility of violence remains, and neither insurgent nor counter-insurgent forces are likely to succeed in their aims until they develop the capacity to subject their enemies to unbearable physical harm.

Not only does this mean that most insurgencies will be bloody for both sides, it means that the violence is more than theatre. As Lenin observed, purely symbolic acts of mayhem are seldom enough to threaten existing political orders (Lenin 1973: 95). Lenin also doubted that such acts would inspire others to support the insurgent movement. On the contrary, he suggested, even sympathizers are more likely to 'stand by "twiddling their thumbs," watching a handful of terrorists engaged in single combat with the government' (Lenin 1973: 95).

Other insurgents have been more optimistic about the propaganda value of violence. The Argentinian revolutionary Che Guevara, for instance, inspired a school of thought known as *foco* theory. This theory holds that insurgents can arouse and even coordinate opposition to an unpopular regime simply by performing dramatic acts to show that resistance is possible (Kitson 1971: 33). Moreover, *foco* theory suggests, such acts will provoke government forces to overreact by imposing draconian security measures, squandering whatever public support they might once have enjoyed and thus contributing to their own destruction (Kitson 1971: 33–4). Thompson, for his part, warned those who are responsible for planning counter-insurgency campaigns to be wary of making this very mistake (Thompson 1966: 106).

Guevara qualified these arguments. Although he certainly wrote that insurgents can spontaneously 'create' the political circumstances necessary for an insurrection to take shape, he later declared that guerrilla warfare, like all forms of warfare, is a physical struggle to annihilate one's opponents, and that this struggle, like all physical activities, must conform to what he described as 'scientific laws' (Guevara 1961: 16, 19). In later chapters, Guevara proposed a template for applying such laws to overthrow governments. The Latin American's model closely resembles Mao Zedong's older and more widely studied template for waging guerrilla warfare.

Mao presented a three-phase programme for overthrowing a state. Each step in his model emphasized the role of physical force (Kane 2001: 84). In the opening period of an insurgency, Mao warned, the insurgents must recognize that they are materially weak. During this phase, the revolutionaries' main goal must be survival. To avoid destruction by superior government forces, they must flee, scatter and hide. For this reason, Mao described the first stage of a guerrilla campaign as 'withdrawal'.

During this phase, the insurgents must remain cohesive enough to reconstitute themselves for later operations. Mao advised guerrillas to resolve these conflicting challenges by migrating into remote parts of the countryside. In these regions, he hoped, the terrain would make it difficult for government forces to find and destroy them. This would give them at least a rudimentary opportunity to train, equip and organize themselves for future battles. This would also give the insurgents chances to accumulate recruits, *matériel*, covert sympathizers and other forms of support.

Even during the perilous opening period of an insurgency, the guerrillas must strike at their enemies when they can, both to destroy government assets and to convince potential supporters to take them seriously. If insurgents survive for long enough and use their time productively enough, they will eventually grow strong enough to carry out more ambitious offensive operations. At this point, they may begin the second phase of a Maoist insurgency. Mao referred to this stage as 'equilibrium'.

During the 'equilibrium' phase, insurgents will still have to retreat from large military units. Nevertheless, when they encounter smaller ones, they will be free to hold their ground and even to seize more of it. Both sides will achieve triumphs during this phase and both will suffer defeats, but if the insurgents can use their newly acquired offensive capabilities to secure greater access to resources and other forms of support, they will continue to grow stronger. Eventually, the guerrillas will be able to advance to the phase which Mao called 'general counter-offensive', in which they defeat government forces in pitched battle and go on to establish control over the entire country.

Not only does Mao's model require insurgent bands to evolve into large, heavily equipped military units, it requires insurgent commanders to use both types of forces intelligently. Mao admired Sun Tzu and, like the earlier writer, he emphasized the use of consciously planned actions to manipulate one's strategic circumstances. Where Sun Tzu focused on producing opportunities for oneself, Mao focuses on creating impossible situations for one's enemies. Rebels reach the second phase of a Maoist insurgency when they compel government forces to yield some of their territory in order to hold onto the rest. The third phase begins when the government's sacrifices become unsustainable.

The more skilfully insurgents time, direct and execute their operations, the more easily they will put their government enemies into such positions. Mao compares insurgent strategy to *wei chi*, a board game in which opponents take turns placing counters on a grid. Victory goes to players who position their pieces most effectively. Mao also notes that the art of positioning military forces in real life is as much a matter of logistical preparation as cleverness (Mao 1958: 168). (Sun Tzu, readers may recall, would probably have agreed.)

Just as Mao's approach emphasizes logistics, it also emphasizes tactical and operational skill. Like Clausewitz, twentieth-century insurgency theorists observe that guerrilla forces have distinctive capabilities. Mao's model requires them to exploit these capabilities energetically. Counter-insurgency theorists have explored corresponding steps which state armed forces may take to thwart the seeming advantages of irregular opponents. Frank Kitson, for instance, details measures which state forces may take to neutralize enemy guerrillas in his classic *Low Intensity Operations* (Kitson 1971: *passim*).

To use or counter the special capabilities of guerrilla forces effectively, one must understand precisely what these forces are. Previous chapters have noted that the strategic thinkers of earlier centuries found it necessary to ground their general theories in specific discussions of practice. Twentieth-century writers on insurgency and counter-insurgency have done the same. Guevara, for instance, opens his work on guerrilla warfare with romantic reflections on the 'essence' of his subject (Guevara 1961: 15). This abstract beginning leads on to discussions of such concrete matters as methods for overturning enemy tanks and recipes for tastier field rations (Guevara 1961: 66, 53).

Although Kitson passes over what he perceives as mere technicalities, he also finds that many technical issues have broader implications. Strategic theorists may not, in his view, need to know what types of radio are best suited for counter-insurgency operations, but they do need to pay detailed attention to helicopter tactics so that they do not let the ease of shuttling forces about by air distract them from their fundamental task of tracking down a hidden enemy upon the ground (Kitson 1971: 136, 137–8). Other seemingly tactical issues may affect the way strategists who wish to be prepared for counter-insurgency operations choose to develop their forces over the long term. Kitson notes, for instance, that British defence planners have traditionally provided infantry formations with light, mobile weapons so that they could use those units as a strategic reserve (Kitson 1971: 137). Such weapons are also essential in anti-guerrilla campaigns. If Britain's political leaders should ever choose to re-equip their army for some other role, Kitson suggests, British strategists should lobby to retain stockpiles of the lighter weapons for counter-insurgencies (Kitson 1971: 137).

As Mao, Guevara, Kitson, Thompson and others review the methods of conducting insurgencies and counter-insurgencies, they identify recurring themes. Insurgents obtain their characteristic tactical capabilities from their ability to range undetected through contested areas. This allows them to strike their enemies at critical points, and it also allows them to obtain support from the exposed civilian population. In some circumstances, civilians may volunteer their help freely while in others the guerrillas may demand it at gunpoint but, as long as the irregular fighters retain their ability to move and hide, the outcome will be much the same.

The insurgents' ability to fight in this way magnifies their psychological power as well as their material freedom of action. Successful insurgents can seem almost uncanny in their ability to vanish from stronger foes only to reappear and perform spectacular acts where their foes have not expected it. This allows them to captivate the attention of sympathizers and opponents alike: to inspire, to terrify, to bluff, to paralyse and to goad. This, in turn, simplifies the process by which insurgents use the means of physical combat to bring others into line with their broader political ends. Clausewitz admired the unique psychological capabilities of irregular popular forces, and twentieth-century writers from Mao and Guevara to Thompson have expanded on this theme.

Accordingly, the problems of creating, deploying and supporting irregular forces are largely problems of maximizing their ability to move and hide. The problems of defeating such forces are largely problems of restricting and exposing them. Throughout this process, both sides must pay attention to the psychological consequences of their actions, both within the combat zone itself, and perhaps within outside countries that happen to be playing a role in the fighting.

Movement, concealment, interdiction, intelligence and psychological effects are basic to every form of combat. In insurgencies, however, they commonly overshadow other normally fundamental considerations. Thompson, for instance, goes so far as to say that counter-insurgency is a form of warfare in which merely killing one's enemies is a 'waste of effort' (Thompson 1966: 116). This is undoubtedly an overstatement. Nevertheless, Thompson's claim helps illuminate the factors which determine victory and defeat in irregular campaigns.

An earlier paragraph noted that insurgents do not normally win conflicts simply by making themselves popular. Neither do they win through brute force. Instead, Mao suggests, the 'life of an army' is initiative (Mao 1958: 168). The concept of initiative may mean different things at different times, but it will always mean taking some sort of action of one's own choosing.

To act, Mao writes, is to 'change the position between the enemy and [oneself]' (Mao 1958: 178). To be idle is to accept the changes one's enemies have made. Thompson suggests that understanding this principle is as essential to suppressing guerrilla warfare as it is to waging it. In Thompson's view, insurgents inevitably grow more powerful and more confident for as long as they continue to attack (Thompson 1966: 115–16). If government forces can compel the insurgents to suspend their offensive operations, he adds, their movement is equally certain to fade away (Thompson 1966: 116).

A strategic *scotoma*?

If the great strategic challenge of insurgency is that irregular forces practically never begin a campaign militarily strong or politically well established enough to accomplish their ultimate goals, the great strategic potential of insurgency lies in the fact that irregular forces can practically always manufacture the opportunity to do something. For Clausewitz, this made such forces a uniquely valuable weapon in a nation's arsenal. Mao added that if irregular forces apply their potential in a coordinated way, they can take political affairs into their own hands and overthrow the very nation-states which Clausewitz expected to animate them. Guevara, Thompson and Kitson are but a few of the authors who have developed these ideas further – often after applying them in practice.

Accordingly, one may sum up the evolution of contemporary insurgency theory as a two-step process. Clausewitz recognized insurgency as a distinct and effective approach to warfare. Later writers presented literally revolutionary methods of using it, along with techniques for countering its uses. In other words, twentieth-century insurgency theorists broadened our understanding of this topic. Nevertheless, Lenin, Mao, Guevara, Thompson, Kitson and the others who wrote in their tradition would be among the first to point out that the full range of political and military issues which arise from the phenomenon of insurgency is actually far broader.

Just as Clausewitz based his writings on the national resistance movements which emerged in certain parts of Europe during the Napoleonic Wars, twentieth-century theories of insurgency and counter-insurgency emphasize specific types of campaigns which unfolded in a particular political and geographical context. The fact that Lenin, Mao and Guevara were Marxist revolutionaries writing for other Marxist revolutionaries provided them with clear answers to vital and complicated questions. Lenin, Mao and Guevara knew, for instance what goals their intended readers were fighting for. As Marxists, they hoped to replace what they perceived as unjust and self-destructive forms of society with a fairer and more sustainable socialist system.

Not only did having such an objective help these thinkers to focus their efforts, it told them where to look for support. Marx argued that primitive forms of society such as capitalism and feudalism pit their members against one another in permanent class struggle. Marxism also implies that such societies are bad for practically all of the people who live under them. Therefore, Marxists could assume that the masses would be unhappy and potentially at odds with the relatively comfortable minority, everywhere and always. Lenin extended this principle to world politics, noting that nations may temporarily pacify their own populations using wealth extracted from weaker nations, but adding that this practice must eventually lead to catastrophic war, as the strongest countries fight to control the finite resources of the earth.

More idealistic revolutionaries might hope to convince the oppressed majority to join their side. Lenin and Mao recognized that they were unlikely to convert entire populations to communism simply by preaching Marxist theory. Nevertheless, these thinkers could expect to exploit the universal conflict and misery. Mao could, for instance, expect to find partners for temporary united fronts, such as the one he formed with the Chinese nationalist leader Chiang Kai-Shek (Jiang Jieshe) against Japan. Lenin could hope to manipulate liberal reformers into serving the communist movement as 'useful idiots'.

Marx expected the most receptive audience for his revolutionary message to be urban factory workers. Mao found that, in twentieth-century China, he was able to recruit even greater numbers of supporters from the rural peasantry. This was fortunate for him since it helped him marry the political concepts of Marxism and Leninism with the tactical capabilities of irregular troops. The vast, rugged Chinese countryside offered ideal terrain for the first two phases of a Maoist insurgency, and, if Mao had been forced to operate under different geographical conditions, he might well have had to come up with different methods for reaching the third.

Marxist political thought and twentieth-century geography also provided guiding principles for counter-insurgency theory. Indeed, Thompson entitled his most famous work *Defeating Communist Insurgency*. Although Thompson and other twentieth-century counter-insurgency theorists presumably believed that the Marxists were wrong to condemn their societies as wicked and doomed, they understood that the genuine injustices within those societies provided their enemies with raw material for constructing subversive movements. Therefore, they could prescribe policies to neutralize their opponents' political programmes with some confidence that the issues they were addressing would prove relevant. In a similar vein, they could focus their tactical advice on the challenges of waging war in the rural, tropical, economically underdeveloped parts of the world where actual insurgencies were taking place. Thompson subtitled his book *Experiences from Malaya and Vietnam*.

One may certainly use insurgency and counter-insurgency methods in other political and geographical settings. Nationalists, separatists, environmentalists, religious reformers and, indeed, liberal democrats may organize revolutionary cells as easily as Marxists. Snipers are as lethal in American suburbs as in Asian forests. Although the techniques of capturing international terrorists at airport security checkpoints and ambushing guerrillas on jungle paths may differ, the principle that one defeats insurgents by finding them and interfering with their movements remains the same. Nevertheless, twentieth-century insurgency and counter-insurgency theory was not simply about tactics, it was about applying tactics systematically over time to achieve narrowly defined political results. The more one's circumstances differ from those which twentieth-century theorists envisioned, the more one must modify their systems.

Even Marxists encounter this fact. Vietnamese communists, for instance, found it necessary to rework Mao's three-step programme into a new strategy reflecting their own particular circumstances (Kane 2001: 85–9). The left-wing militant Carlos Marighella explored ways in which city-based revolutionaries might support a more traditional rural insurgency in his 'Minimanual of the Urban Guerrilla' (Marighella 1971: *passim*). State security forces have found copies of Marighella's work with a wide variety of militant groups. Many of these groups have had no comrades in the countryside to support them and only the most fanciful hope of reaching the later phases of a Maoist revolution.

Few twenty-first-century insurgents seem likely to succeed with a Maoist strategy. Moreover, few of them seem to care. Al-Qaeda, for instance, began as a distinct organization in which leaders set goals and dispatched followers to achieve them, but it has developed into a far looser collection of people united only by the fact that they respond to the rhetoric of militant Islam. Cellular phones, the internet and other forms of communications technology help these people encourage one another, exchange information and occasionally pool resources to carry out terrorist attacks. Relatively large numbers of al-Qaeda's affiliates operate in relatively well-defined paramilitary units in areas where local conditions happen to favour such activity, such as the north-western regions of Pakistan, but the movement as a whole is dispersed and diverse.

Colonel Thomas Hammes suggests that networks of this nature have improved upon twentieth-century concepts of irregular operations and, indeed, upon all earlier approaches to waging war. Since Hammes identifies three earlier eras in the evolution of military activity, he refers to networked insurgencies as fourth-generation warfare, or 4GW. Decentralized networks can certainly be challenging opponents. One reason is that these networks distribute information broadly and rapidly, permitting members to act on it faster than those bound by the procedures of hierarchical institutions (Hammes 2004: 196–7).

Another reason is that 4GW allows insurgents to exploit technology, infrastructure and institutions paid for by the very societies they hope to overthrow (Hammes 2004: 2–3). Moreover, the diverse people and groups which make up a 4GW network can strike at their enemies in an equally diverse range of ways. This forces their opponents to balance the demands of one set of operations against the demands of another. Furthermore, since the various components of a 4GW network are at least partially autonomous, their opponents will seldom be able to cripple the entire movement with a single blow.

Hammes acknowledges that 4GW cannot physically destroy opposing military forces (Hammes 2004: 211). It is, he implies, best suited for the first two phases of a Maoist insurgency. Mao would be entitled to respond that he had made similar points in his own writings, and that, although he appreciated the uses of networks, he had been more deeply concerned with the problem of overcoming their limitations. As previously noted, twentieth-century insurgency theorists assumed that communists would need help from a hodge-podge of other political actors in order to establish a viable revolutionary movement.

A hodge-podge, however, suffers from a strategic blind spot. Even if its members share an overall vision of what they might like to accomplish, and even if they are capable of acting effectively in the short term, they have no mechanism for coordinating a sustained programme of activities to realize their final goal. Islamic militants using 4GW methods of organization proved capable of executing a tactically well-choreographed attack on the Madrid train system in 2004, and the operation may well have affected a Spanish election, but the al-Qaeda network had little hope of following up on this success to achieve more lasting influence within the Spanish political system or to advance other deliberately selected goals in other parts of the world. Few members of al-Qaeda's global network of sympathizers were in a position to do so, and few had compelling reasons to try. To a guerrilla fighting to establish an Islamic state on an island in the Philippines – or even to a morally indignant young Muslim living in Yorkshire – Spain is a long way away.

Members of an informal network may cheer each other's successes and even reach out to one another for support but, ultimately, they fight separate battles alone. They may achieve common goals through fortunate circumstances and shared enthusiasm, but none of them are in a position to improve their collective chances through planning. Moreover, even if the network overwhelms its enemies, none of its members are in a strong position to ensure that the final outcome is actually the one which they envisioned. These are even greater strategic handicaps than the inability to fight in large-scale military campaigns.

Lenin's Bolsheviks overcame these problems by taking over Russia's dissident network from within. This process continued long after the revolution, as the intelligence services of the Soviet Union infiltrated organizations of exiled Russians throughout the world. Mao also stressed that a centrally organized Communist Party must establish control over the broader movement which brings it to power, including its own military forces. Such control, he famously observed, can only come from the barrel of a gun. When twentieth-century theorists referred to the political aspects of insurgency, this process of transforming loose networks into more centralized – and strategically useful – organizations was largely what they had in mind.

The same principles apply in reverse. Since insurgents subsist on division, corruption and lawlessness, the main political challenges of counter-insurgency are those of organizing the states, state agencies, non-governmental organizations and social groups which might wish to resist armed uprising into a coalition capable of cooperating to enforce collectively endorsed policies within the area of common concern. These challenges include problems of diplomacy – for the member states of NATO to wage an effective counter-insurgency campaign in early twenty-first-century Afghanistan, they not only needed to agree on a plan among themselves, they needed to secure some level of support from such parties as India, Pakistan and the government of Afghanistan itself. These challenges also include the basic problems of establishing an effective political system and forming effective military forces. The government of early twenty-first-century Afghanistan, for instance, is newly founded, and, if it is to suppress its nation's insurgent groups without foreign help, it will have to create an army capable of doing so. One notes that although pre-modern strategic thinkers said relatively little about insurgency as such, they wrote a great deal about creating armies.

Conclusion

Just as Vegetius and Machiavelli knew that there are many ways of waging war but guided their readers towards approaches featuring large forces and systematic preparation, twentieth-century insurgency theorists understood that irregular warfare has the potential to be almost infinitely malleable but advised their readers to give it definition. Wet clay is valuable as a raw material, but one cannot normally use it until one moulds it into shape and bakes it in a kiln. Lao Tzu, whose ideas may well have influenced Sun Tzu, made a similar point about uncarved blocks of wood (Lao 1972: 15).

The clay of early twenty-first-century insurgency continues to ooze. Nevertheless, contemporary insurgents remain capable of seizing the initiative at the highest levels of global affairs. A single terrorist operation – al-Qaeda's 2001 attack on New York City and Washington, DC – caused one interstate war, indirectly encouraged another, invigorated affiliated insurgent groups throughout the world, influenced domestic politics in virtually every significant country and overshadowed international relations for over a decade. In the aftermath, the world's most powerful states are in the dangerous position of being enmeshed in military campaigns at a time when their financial position seems tenuous and influential fractions of their populations are weary of war. For a strategist, this raises the question of who might next use irregular warfare in a more directed way. For a strategic thinker, this raises the more comfortably abstract question of whether one can best understand these issues by returning to Mao, Lenin and earlier authors, or whether the time has come for a third generation of insurgency theory.

Further reading

Kiras, James D. (2006) *Special Operations and Strategy: From World War II to the War on Terrorism*. London: Routledge.

Kitson, Frank (1971) *Low Intensity Operations: Subversion, Insurgency, Peace-Keeping*. Faber & Faber: London.

Lenin, Vladimir (1973) *What is to be Done?* anonymous trans. Peking: People's Publishing House.

Mao Tse-Tung (1958) *Selected Works of Mao Tse-Tung, Volume Two*. London: Lawrence & Wishart.

Marighella, Carlos (1971) 'Minimanual of the Urban Guerrilla' (anonymous trans.), appendix to Robert Moss, *Urban Guerrilla Warfare, Adelphi Paper No. 79*. London: International Institute for Strategic Studies, pp. 20–42.

CONCLUSION: STRATEGY IN THE TWENTY-FIRST CENTURY

Strategy is a brutally practical subject. Therefore, as one deepens one's understanding of strategy, one continually returns to the question of how ideas in this field inform practice. Clausewitz explores this issue in depth, and most of the thinkers discussed in this volume address it in one way or another. Nevertheless, all of us must determine for ourselves how the classic works on strategy apply to the specific challenges of our time. This concluding chapter offers twenty-first-century readers a place to begin.

The next section reviews strategic goals which the British and American governments identified as particularly pressing in 2010. A third section reviews what the various works considered in this volume had to say about such matters, noting points where classic thinkers seem to agree and also points where they seem to diverge. As one retraces these debates, one may assess the degree to which twenty-first-century governments and classic thinkers share similar priorities and one may also ask who has come closest to identifying the issues which will actually define strategy in our time. A conclusion offers final reflections on how classic strategic thought supports the process of thinking strategically. Although the classic works of strategy offer no guaranteed formula for success, they clarify the issues we must consider and encourage us in the exercise of considering.

World domination (but cheap): American and British national goals circa 2010

For those who are neither contemplating a war of conquest nor are aware of a dangerous rival who is, the first problem of strategic planning is that of specifying one's objectives. Those who emphasize immediate crises and ongoing policy debates must contend with the fact that these issues are ever-changing and innumerable. Those who aim only to achieve broad goals, such as 'security', risk framing their intentions in such general terms that they have no clear way to choose between the competing demands on their resources and attention. Therefore, even when strategists might like to focus on practice, they cannot escape discussing the esoteric relationship between case and category.

Moreover, planning not only concerns political issues, it is itself a political process. This truth applies within all human organizations, and it is particularly obvious in the governments of democratic states where leaders who wish to remain in office must proclaim goals which will help them maintain a viable constituency. Although strategy may require difficult choices, strategists may not wish to highlight the difficulties. Strategists may also need to frame issues in a way which suits a particular political party's ideological perspective and to respond to public concerns which may not be strictly relevant to the topic ostensibly under discussion.

Perhaps for these reasons, public statements on national strategy tend to be wordy. American President Barack Obama's National Security Strategy (NSS) of 2010 fills 52 pages with carefully qualified discussions of values, interests, enduring interests, security priorities and qualities to be found in 'The World We Seek' (Anonymous 2010: 35–9, 17–47, 7, 4–6, 9–14). Britain's 2010 Strategic Defence and Security Review (SDSR) also criss-crosses such terrain repeatedly and delicately throughout its 76 pages. Thus, it would be misleading to present a less nuanced summary of American or British objectives as definitive. One can, however, note themes which the British and American documents identify as important. These themes include:

Worldwide influence: Page 1 of America's 2010 NSS accepts the challenge of reordering the world (Anonymous 2010: 1). Later sections suggest that the United States hopes to transform the global political system into a just society in which all members cooperate to overcome economic, environmental and security problems (Anonymous 2010: 12). Meanwhile, the British SDSR aims to protect Britain's inhabitants, financial system and mode of living from any significant threat (HM Government 2010: 9). To this end, the SDSR commits the British government to the goal of shaping events on every part of Planet Earth (HM Government 2010: 9). The famously idealistic Obama White House may have expressed its aspirations in loftier terms than those favoured by the Conservative-led coalition which commissioned the British review but both have proclaimed the same unbounded ambition.

Limited liability: The NSS and SDSR propose to accomplish these grand goals using only the most modest of means. Both documents note that, as of 2010, their respective countries are suffering from severe financial difficulties (Anonymous 2010: 2; HM Government 2010: 3). Both also identify prosperity as crucial to strategic success. Accordingly, both reason that their countries should control expenditures tightly over upcoming decades in order to restore their ability to achieve national goals over the longer term.

Although the NSS and SDSR stress fiscal prudence, Barack Obama and the leaders of Britain's coalition government were probably also concerned with what is known as political capital. In 2010, both had recently taken office. Both had replaced long-serving governments led by opposing political parties which had pursued exceptionally muscular foreign policies. These policies had included waging war in Afghanistan and Iraq, and those wars had become increasingly unpopular. Obama and the coalition leaders probably favoured a less aggressive approach to international affairs for reasons of principle, and they also had compelling reasons to assume that their supporters expected it of them.

The NSS and the SDSR also define national security broadly. The SDSR, for instance, addresses the problems of planning for natural disasters and introducing more sustainable energy policies (HM Government 2010: 49–52). America's 2010 NSS takes on issues ranging from climate change to public health (Anonymous 2010: 47–9). These issues are crucial to the well-being of British and American citizens. Moreover, they have implications for Britain and America's continuing ability to resist violent attack. Nevertheless, for those whose primary responsibility is to maintain the military capabilities and direct political power which American and British planners also hope to enjoy, the benefits of investing in broader security issues may not emerge for generations, whereas the costs are immediate.

Legacy wars: Whatever Obama and his supporters might have wished, the United States still had troops in Iraq in 2010. Meanwhile, the war in Afghanistan remained fierce. Both the United States and the United Kingdom continue to fight in Afghanistan at the time of this writing. The NSS affirms that the United States is committed to establishing stable governments in both countries and to preventing international terrorist organizations from finding refuge in either (Anonymous 2010: 8). Britain's SDSR focuses more exclusively on Afghanistan but expresses a similar intent.

Global counterterrorism: American President George W. Bush famously called for war on terrorism. Whether one applauds G. W. Bush's resolve or shudders at his brashness, something like a war dominated American and British foreign policy throughout the first decade of the twenty-first century. American policy makers briefly referred to this campaign as the Long War, and, although they later abandoned this term, it also expresses certain truths about the undertaking.

The authors of the NSS and SDSR chose their words more discreetly but they reiterated that America and Britain place the highest priority on suppressing disruptive non-state actors. These documents also note that this struggle goes far beyond combating the latest incarnations of al-Qaeda. Criminal organizations, for instance, seem to challenge the United States and Britain in roughly the same fashion as terrorist networks. Both the NSS and the SDSR take up this point (Anonymous 2010: 33; HM Government 2010: 52–3). The SDSR includes a speculative aside which suggests that the overall 'character of conflict' is changing, and that complex disputes involving non-state actors are gaining in significance (HM Government 2010: 16). Accordingly, authors argue, Britain must configure its forces to maximize their ability to prevail in struggles of this sort.

Competence in new strategic environments: The NSS and SDSR emphasize that the American and British security establishment must foster a robust capability to act in so-called cyberspace (Anonymous 2010: 27–8; HM Government 2010: 47–8). The SDSR links this to its previously mentioned predictions about the evolving character of conflict (HM Government 2010: 16). Both the NSS and SDSR also express the desire to operate in outer space, although the two documents' discussions of this topic are briefer (Anonymous 2010: 31; HM Government 2010: 65).

Maintenance of nuclear stability: America's NSS devotes an entire section to the importance of preventing new powers from acquiring weapons of mass destruction (WMD) and, where possible, convincing those who have such weapons to relinquish them (Anonymous 2010: 23–4). The authors note that America itself is reducing its nuclear stockpile, although they add that America continues to maintain an effective deterrent (Anonymous 2010: 4). Later sections of the NSS occasionally suggest that America intends to deter various undesirable developments in world politics, although it does not always specify that the United States plans to do so through nuclear means. The SDSR expresses the same intentions but seems to reverse their order of priority, devoting a complete chapter to nuclear deterrence while offering a briefer discussion of Britain's commitment to countering WMD proliferation (HM Government 2010: 37–9, 55).

Shared efforts, shared burdens: Not only do the NSS and SDSR express the hope that the United States and Britain will be able to rely on cooperation from allies to accomplish their national goals, they emphasize that these countries must make supporting friendly international actors a central goal in its own right.

Finding focus: how theory informs practice

Even when one allows for the pressures which prevent the authors of public documents on national strategy from being overly explicit, the NSS and the SDSR feature a confusing mix of imperatives. Those with an eye on defence budgeting may find the goal of global leadership and the goal of saving money to be contradictory. There is also a certain tension, morally at least, between urging others to renounce WMD while maintaining one's own nuclear stockpile as a putative deterrent. Wisely or unwisely, the Obama administration has been exceptionally willing to acknowledge this apparent hypocrisy. As previously noted, the 2010 NSS suggests a willingness to reduce or perhaps even eliminate the US arsenal, but it remains vague on fundamental questions. Although equivocation is preferable to foolishness, it is a poor guide for future action on the world's most critical strategic issue.

Important as Afghanistan, counterterrorism, cyberspace and domestic security undoubtedly are, critical readers may want more information about how these issues relate to one another, and, perhaps, which have priority. Cooperation is unquestionably desirable, but the same critics may wish to scrutinize the terms of their partnerships. For two or more actors to cooperate effectively on matters of strategy, they must either perceive strategic issues in similar ways or have an efficient mechanism for resolving discrepancies. To their credit, the NSS and SDSR both address this matter, but the international community's ongoing (as of 2012) difficulty in formulating a broadly acceptable response to the conflict in Syria suggests that it will remain a challenge (Anonymous 2010: 40–50; HM Government 2010: 58–64).

Such paradoxes and ambiguities would have been familiar to most strategic thinkers throughout history and certainly to the ones discussed in this volume. Many of these thinkers propose principles we might follow as we organize our own thoughts on these matters and as we decide how to translate our conclusions into action. Even where the thinkers disagree, or where they fail to address the exact situations which have emerged in our time, they suggest perspectives which can help us survey our own circumstances more comprehensively. To illustrate how this process might work, the following paragraphs note a few examples of how classic writings on strategic theory might inform our attempts to mould the aspirations of the NSS and SDSR into a coherent plan of action.

Practically all of the thinkers discussed in this volume would have accepted the imperative to enhance one's control over one's political environment as the fundamental problem of strategy. Most confronted the fact that one must pursue this goal in the context of one's material capacity to do so, which typically, although not invariably, corresponds to one's finances. Moreover, virtually all found that economics is only one of the factors complicating strategy. The full title of the SDSR begins with the phrase 'Securing Britain in an Age of Uncertainty', and Clausewitz would add only that, for strategists, there can never be an age of any other kind.

Machiavelli urged readers to assert control aggressively, using large but simply equipped forces levied from the entire population. Clausewitz, Mahan and Douhet also invite us to contemplate the uses of brute force and bold action. Other thinkers, meanwhile, come at the problem of mastering one's destiny in an unpredictable environment from other directions. Sun Tzu, Corbett and Liddell Hart, for instance, would have us consider our situation at a greater level of specificity so that we can craft a plan which makes the best possible use of our circumstances. Other thinkers identify particular instruments of strategy such as ships, aircraft, nuclear weapons and networked irregular forces as uniquely valuable.

Just as these thinkers have different attitudes towards the problem of mastering one's situation, they have different attitudes towards financial matters. Again, Machiavelli is the most brazen, declaring that money is overrated. Sun Tzu takes almost the opposite approach, going so far as to itemize the expenses involved in maintaining chariots. Mahan is, perhaps, closer to Sun Tzu on this issue. His widely read chapter on the elements of sea power reflects extensively on the macroeconomic conditions which make it possible for a society to maintain a strong navy. Douhet offers similar, if briefer, reflections on the economics of air forces.

The classic works on strategy also address many of the NSS and SDSR's more specialized concerns. Chapters 7 and 8 attest to the fact that there are substantial bodies of work on both nuclear weapons and irregular warfare. Thucydides and Machiavelli devote considerable attention to both alliances and domestic security. Sun Tzu, Clausewitz, Corbett and others address these issues as well, and, although their writings on these topics may be briefer, many of their points are important nevertheless. If, for instance, we accept Sun Tzu's claim that the second-best way to undo one's enemies is to strike at them through their allies, we may wish to think carefully about how our own opponents might target our own networks of partners.

Even where the classic works on strategy fail to address contemporary concerns directly, they often take up analogous issues. Since the technology which provides access to outer space and brings cyberspace into existence is relatively new, it is no slight to the strategic thinkers who are in the process of exploring these topics to note that the theoretical literature in these fields is in its infancy as well. Nevertheless, if operations in space and cyberspace are distinct from other forms of strategic activity, many of the same questions which arise when one considers air, land and maritime warfare are likely to arise when one considers the newer environments. The importance of amassing overwhelming combat power, for instance, would appear to be as relevant – or irrelevant – to new environments as older ones.

The importance of striking an effective balance between offensive and defensive operations would appear pertinent as well. Virtually all the thinkers discussed in this volume consider these concepts in one way or another. Meanwhile, the literature discussed in chapter 5 alerts us to the fact that concepts such as combat power, offensive operations and defensive operations may take on different meanings in different environments. Mahan, for instance, suggests that the best way to realize maritime power in the late nineteenth century was to overmatch one's opponents in a clash of battleships, while Douhet suggests that the best way to realize air power in the early twentieth was to bypass enemy forces and devastate their homeland with heavy bombers. To the extent that anti-satellite weapons serve similar purposes to Mahan's battle fleet and so-called 'malware' designed to attack an enemy's national infrastructure replicates functions of Douhet's bombers, the debates over maritime and aerial warfare may inform our consideration of conflict in newer strategic environments.

The greatest challenge facing contemporary strategists is likely to be that of integrating responses to the diverse issues which confront them into a coherent policy which addresses their societies' highest concerns. This, too, is a theme throughout the classic works on strategy. Thucydides took pains to present grand concepts in the context of specific – and often obscure – historical events. Vegetius discusses seemingly technical issues of tactics and military administration in order to suggest broader points about Rome's government and Rome's people. Machiavelli, Fuller and Hart explicitly trace the connections between great matters and those which might seem to be small. Although these thinkers' approaches differ, all remind us that the way in which we handle the details of strategy may ultimately determine what our society is to become.

Conclusion: thoughts on thought

As the previous section indicates, the strategic thinkers discussed in this volume recognized the basic challenges which contemporary strategists would face. The ongoing (as of 2013) 'Great Recession' and the current war in Afghanistan are artefacts of the early twenty-first century, but the inherent difficulty of mobilizing material and psychic resources for sustained purposeful action appears to be eternal. Irregular warfare, alliance politics and the intimate relationship between strategy and society appear eternal as well. There are even classical precedents for many questions concerning emerging technology. For those who hope to apply the classic works on strategy today, the challenge lies not in finding relevant material but in choosing among contending approaches.

The theoretical choices are seldom as stark as they initially appear. Most of the classic writers on strategy were wise enough to acknowledge that their advice is more valid in some contexts than in others. Machiavelli, for instance, preferred the direct approach but he also warned readers to apply it prudently. Although Corbett favoured cruiser operations, he saw uses for the heavy firepower of battleships. Even where theorists initially seem to contradict one another, the most significant differences between their positions often turn out to be matters of emphasis.

Decisions of high policy, by contrast, are often very stark indeed. Practising strategists must determine exactly what sort of environment they are operating in, with little room for equivocation. Until they have achieved this intellectual feat, they will be unable to tell which approach to strategy is most relevant to their concerns. Thus, practitioners who wish to succeed cannot passively consume strategic thought. They must, themselves, do the thinking.

Here, the classic works on strategy cannot offer practitioners recipes to follow. The classics do, however, offer models to emulate. One may follow the well-known thinkers' processes of reasoning as an exercise to develop one's own. One may explore the reasons why highly regarded theorists took the positions they did and ask oneself whether similar factors may be at work in one's own world. Whether or not one chooses to adopt Machiavelli's disdain for money, to pick but one example, one does well to ask whether contemporary western society's obsession with this resource is strategically narrow-sighted and to be aware of the circumstances under which it might become so.

Most of the theorists discussed in this volume addressed the challenge of becoming an effective thinker in one way or another. Thucydides, for instance, provides contrasting historical examples. *On War* explicitly dissects the problem in conceptual terms. Sun Tzu implies a philosophical approach to this subject, while Machiavelli subtly conditions readers to adopt the Promethean new philosophy he disingenuously attributed to Roman antiquity. All offer inspiration. Clausewitz identified boldness as a creative force in warfare, but the spark which ignites the steady flame of a sound idea amidst the seething mists of ongoing conflict surely comes prior even to that.

Further reading

Anonymous (2010) *National Security Strategy*. Washington, DC: The White House.

Gray, Colin (2005) *Another Bloody Century: Future Warfare*. London: Weidenfeld & Nicolson.

HM Government (2010) *Securing Britain in an Age of Uncertainty: The Strategic Defence and Security Review*. London: The Stationery Office.

Kane, Thomas M. (2002) *Chinese Grand Strategy and Maritime Power*. London: Frank Cass.

Walton, C. Dale (2007) *Geopolitics and the Great Powers in the Twenty-First Century: Multipolarity and the Revolution in Strategic Perspective*. London: Routledge.

REFERENCES

Anonymous (1999) *Kosovo Chronology Timeline of Events 1989–1999 relating to the Crisis in Kosovo*. Washington: US Department of State, available online at www.state.gov/www/regions/eur/fs_kosovo_timeline.html, accessed 15 May 2013.

Anonymous (2000) *The International Institute for Strategic Studies Strategic Survey 1999/2000*. Oxford: Oxford University Press.

Anonymous (2006) *FM 3-24 Counterinsurgency*. Washington, DC: Department of the Army.

Anonymous (2010) *National Security Strategy*. Washington, DC: The White House.

Aron, Raymond (1985) *Clausewitz: Philosopher of War*, trans. Christine Booker and Norman Stone. Englewood Cliffs, NJ: Prentice-Hall.

Bassford, Christopher (1994) 'John Keegan and the Grand Tradition of Bashing Clausewitz: A Polemic'. *War in History* 1(3) (Nov.): 319–36.

Baylis, John and Garnett, John (1991) 'Introduction', in John Baylis and John Garnett (eds), *Makers of Nuclear Strategy*. London: Pinter.

Blackett, P. M. S. (1948) *Military and Political Consequences of Atomic Energy*. London: Turnstile Press.

Booth, Kenneth (1991) 'Bernard Brodie', in John Baylis and John Garnett (eds), *Makers of Nuclear Strategy*. London: Pinter.

Brodie, Bernard (1946) *The Absolute Weapon: Atomic Power and World Order*. Manchester, NH: Ayer Co.

Brodie, Bernard (1976) 'A Guide to the Reading of *On War*', in Carl von Clausewitz, *On War*, trans. Michael Howard and Peter Paret. Princeton, NJ: Princeton University Press.

Cable, James (1971) *Gunboat Diplomacy: Political Applications of Limited Naval Force*. London: Chatto and Windus.

Cassidy, Ben (2003) 'Machiavelli and the Ideology of the Offensive: Gunpowder Weapons in *The Art of War*'. *The Journal of Military History* 67(2) (Apr.): 381–404.

Clausewitz, Carl von (1976) *On War*, trans. Michael Howard and Peter Paret. Princeton, NJ: Princeton University Press.

Cobain, Iain and Evans, Michael (2001) 'Waves of B-52s hit Taleban's Hilltop Line'. *The Times*, No. 67286 (Nov. 2), p. 8.

Contamine, Philippe (1984) *War in the Middle Ages*, trans. Michael Jones. Oxford: Basil Blackwell.

Corbett, Julian S. (1911) *Some Principles of Maritime Strategy*, available online at www.gutenberg.org/files/15076/15076-h/15076-h.htm, accessed 15 May 2013.

Dorjahn, Alfred P. and Born, Lester K. (1934) 'Vegetius on the Decay of the Roman Army'. *The Classical Journal* 30(3) (Dec.): 148–58.

Douhet, Giulio (1983) *The Command of the Air*, trans. Dino Ferrari. Washington, DC: Office of Air Force History.

Earle, Edward Mead (1943) 'Introduction', in Edward Mead Earle (ed.), *Makers of Modern Strategy: Military Thought from Machiavelli to Hitler*. Princeton, NJ: Princeton University Press, pp. i–xi.

Echevarria, Antulio J. (1995–6) 'War, Politics and RMA – The Legacy of Clausewitz', *Joint Forces Quarterly*, No. 10 (Winter): 76–80.

English, J. (1996) 'The Operational Art: Developments in the Theories of War', in B. J. C. McKercher and M. Hennessy (eds), *The Operational Art: Developments in the Theories of War*. Westport, CT: Greenwood.

Ferris, John Robert (2005) *Intelligence and Strategy: Selected Essays*. Abingdon: Routledge.

Freedman, Lawrence (1981) *The Evolution of Nuclear Strategy*. Basingstoke: Macmillan.

Fuller, J. F. C. (1942) *Machine Warfare: An Enquiry into the Influences of Mechanics on the Art of War*. London: Hutchinson & Co.

Gat, Azar (1989) *The Origins of Military Thought from the Enlightenment to Clausewitz*. Oxford: Clarendon Press.

Gilbert, Felix (1971) 'Machiavelli: The Renaissance of the Art of War', in Edward Mead Earle (ed.), *Makers of Modern Strategy: Military Thought from Machiavelli to Hitler*. Princeton, NJ: Princeton University Press, pp. 3–25.

Goldstein, Joshua S. (1996) *International Relations*, 2nd edn. New York: HarperCollins.

Gordon, John IV and Pirnie, Bruce R. (2005) '"Everybody Wanted Tanks": Heavy Forces in Operation Iraqi Freedom'. *Joint Forces Quarterly*, No. 39: 84–91.

Gorka, Sebastian L. and Kilcullen, David (2011) 'An Actor-centric Theory of War'. *Joint Forces Quarterly*, No. 60 (First Quarter): 14–25.

Gray, Colin S. (1999a) *Modern Strategy*. Oxford: Oxford University Press.

Gray, Colin S. (1999b) *The Second Nuclear Age*. Boulder, CO: Lynne Rienner.

Gray, Colin S. (2010) *The Strategy Bridge: Theory for Practice*. Oxford: Oxford University Press.

Guevara, Che (1961) *Guerrilla Warfare*. London: Monthly Review Press.

Hammes, Thomas X. (2004) *The Sling and the Stone: On War in the 21st Century*. St Paul, MN: Zenith.

Handel, Michael I. (1989) *War, Strategy and Intelligence*. London: Frank Cass.

Handel, Michael I. (1996) *Masters of War: Classical Strategic Thought*. London: Frank Cass.

Handel, Michael (1998) *Who is Afraid of Carl Von Clausewitz? A Guide to the Perplexed*. Newport, RI: US Navy War College.

Handel, Michael (2005) *Masters of War: Classical Strategic Thought*. London: Routledge.

Hart, B. H. Liddell (1930) *History of the First World War*. London: Pan.

Hart, B. H. Liddell (1960) *Deterrent or Defence: A Fresh Look at the West's Military Position*. London: Steven and Sons Ltd.

Hart, B. H. Liddell (1991) *Strategy*. London: Faber & Faber.

Hébert, John R. (2003) 'The Map That Named America: Library Acquires 1507 Map of the World', *Library of Congress Information Bulletin* (Sept.), available online at www.loc.gov/loc/lcib/0309/maps.html, accessed 15 May 2013.

Heuser, Beatrice (2010a) *The Strategy Makers: Thoughts on War and Society from Machiavelli to Clausewitz*. Denver, CO: Praeger.

Heuser, Beatrice (2010b) *The Evolution of Strategy: Thinking War from Antiquity to the Present*. Cambridge: Cambridge University Press.

HM Government (2010) *Securing Britain in an Age of Uncertainty: The Strategic Defence and Security Review*. London: The Stationery Office.

Howard, Michael (1983) *Clausewitz*. Oxford: Oxford University Press.

Jervis, Robert (1982–3) 'Deterrence and Perception'. *International Security* 7(3) (Winter): 3–30.

Jomini, Antoine Henri (2005) *The Art of War*. New Delhi: Natraj Publishers.

Kagan, Donald (1965) *The Great Dialogue: History of Political Thought from Homer to Polybius*. New York: The Free Press.

Kagan, Donald (1994) 'Athenian Strategy in the Peloponnesian War', in Williamson Murray, MacGregor Knox and Alvin Bernstein (eds), *The Making of Strategy: Rulers, States and War*. Cambridge: Cambridge University Press, pp. 24–55.

Kagan, Donald (1995) *On the Origins of War*. London: Pimlico.

Kahn, Herman and Mann, Irwin (1957) *Game Theory*. Santa Monica, CA: RAND.

Kaldor, Mary (2010) 'Reconceptualising War'. *Open Democracy: Free Thinking for the World*, available online at www.opendemocracy.net/print/50438, accessed 15 May 2013.

Kane, Thomas M. (2001) *Military Logistics and Strategic Performance*. London: Frank Cass.

Kane, Thomas (2002) *Chinese Grand Strategy and Maritime Power*. London: Frank Cass.

Kane, Thomas (2007) *Ancient China on Postmodern War: Enduring Ideas from the Chinese Strategic Tradition*. London: Routledge.

Kitson, Frank (1971) *Low Intensity Operations: Subversion, Insurgency, Peace-Keeping*. Faber & Faber: London.

Klein, Naomi (2008) *The Shock Doctrine: The Rise of Disaster Capitalism*. London: Penguin.

Kohn, Richard H. and Harahan, Joseph P. (1983) 'Introduction', in *The Command of the Air*, trans. Dino Ferrari. Washington, DC: Office of Air Force History, pp. vii–x.

Krepinevich, Andrew (2002) *The Military-Technical Revolution: A Preliminary Assessment*. Washington, DC: Center for Strategic and Budgetary Assessments.

Lao Tsu (Lao Tzu/Laozi) (1972) *Tao Te Ching*, trans. Gia-Fu Feng and Jane English. New York: Vintage Books.

Lenin, Vladimir (1973) *What is to be Done?* (anonymous trans.). Peking: People's Publishing House.

Lukes, Timothy J. (2001) 'Lionizing Machiavelli'. *American Political Science Review* 95(3) (Sept.): 561–75.

Luttwak, Edward (1987) *Strategy: The Logic of War and Peace*. Cambridge, MA: Harvard University Press.

Maao, Ole Jorgen (2008) 'Leadership in Air Operations – in Search of Air Power Leadership'. *Air Power Review* 11(3) (Winter): 34–53.

Machiavelli, Niccolò (1950) *The Prince and the Discourses*, trans. Luigi Ricci, E. R. P. Vincent and Christian E. Detmold. New York: The Modern Library.

Machiavelli, Niccolò (1965) *The Art of War*, trans. Ellis Farneworth. New York: Bobs-Merrill.

Mahan, Alfred Thayer (1890) *The Influence of Sea Power upon History, 1660–1783*. Cambridge, MA: John Wilson and Son.

Manthorpe, William H. J. (1996) 'The Emerging Joint System of Systems: A Systems Engineering Challenge and Opportunity for APL', *APL Technical Digest* 17(3): 305–13.

Mao Tse-Tung (1958) *Selected Works of Mao Tse-Tung, Vol. Two*. London: Lawrence & Wishart.

Marighella, Carlos (1971) 'Minimanual of the Urban Guerrilla' (anonymous trans.), appendix to Robert Moss, *Urban Guerrilla Warfare, Adelphi Paper No. 79*. London: International Institute for Strategic Studies, pp. 20–42.

Mearsheimer, John J. (1988) *Liddell Hart and the Weight of History*. Ithaca, NY: Cornell University Press.

Meilinger, Philip S. (2007) 'Busting the Icon: Restoring Balance to the Influence of Clausewitz'. *Strategic Studies Quarterly* 1(1) (Fall): 116–45.

Menand, Louis (2005) 'Fat Man: Herman Kahn and the nuclear age'. *The New Yorker* (June 27), available online at www.newyorker.com/archive/2005/06/27/050627crbo_books?printable-true&currentPage=all, accessed 15 May 2013.

Mikheyev, Dmitry (1987) *The Soviet Perspective on the Strategic Defense Initiative*. Oxford: Pergamon-Brasseys.

Nye, Joseph (2004) *Soft Power: The Means to Success in World Politics*. New York: PublicAffairs.

Owens, William A. (1996) 'The Emerging U.S. System-of-Systems'. *Strategic Forum*, No. 63 (Feb.), available online at www.dtic.mil/cgi-bin/GetTRDoc? AD=ADA394313, accessed 15 May 2013.

Parel, Anthony J. (1992) *The Machiavellian Cosmos*. New Haven, CT: Yale University Press.

Paret, Peter (1976) *Clausewitz and the State*. Oxford: Oxford University Press.

Parkinson, Roger (1970) *Clausewitz: A Biography*. London: Wayland.

Pierce, Terry C. (1996) 'Voodoo Logistics Sink Triphibious Warfare'. *Proceedings of the US Naval Institute* 122(9) (September): 74–7.

Priest, Dana (1999) 'Kosovo Land Threat May Have Won War', *Washington Post* (Sept. 19), p. A1, available online at www.washingtonpost.com/wp-srv/national/daily/sept99/airwar19.htm, accessed 15 May 2013.

Rapoport, David C. (1968) 'The Corrupt State: The Case of Rome Reconsidered'. *Political Studies* 16(3) (Oct.): 411–32.

Robertson, Scot (2008) 'What Direction? The Future of Aerospace Power and the Canadian Air Force – Part 2'. *Canadian Military Journal* 9(1): 30–8, available online at www.journal.forces.gc.ca/vo9/no1/06-robertson-eng.asp, accessed 15 May 2013.

Sawyer, Ralph (trans.) (1993) *The Seven Military Classics of Ancient China*. Oxford: Westview Press.

Schelling, Thomas C. (1984) *Choice and Consequence*. Cambridge, MA: Harvard University Press.

Schuurman, Bart (2010) 'Clausewitz and the "New Wars" Scholars'. *Parameters* 40(1) (Spring): 89–100.

Shrader, Charles R. (1981) 'The Influence of Vegetius' *De re militari*'. *Military Affairs* 45(4) (Dec.): 167–72.

Skinner, Quentin (1981) *Machiavelli*. Oxford: Oxford University Press.

Snyder, Jack (1977) *The Soviet Strategic Culture: Implications for Limited Nuclear Operations*. Santa Monica, CA: RAND.

Strauss, Leo (1958) *Thoughts on Machiavelli*. Chicago: University of Chicago Press.

Sumida, Jon Tetsuro (1997) *Inventing Grand Strategy and Teaching Command: The Classic Works of Alfred Thayer Mahan Reconsidered*. Washington, DC: Woodrow Wilson Center Press.

Sun Tzu (1988) *The Art of War*, trans. Thomas Cleary. Boston, MA: Shambhala Publications.

Szuma Chien (1979) *Selections from the Records of the Historian*, trans. Yang Hsien-yi and Gladys Yang. Peking: Foreign Languages Press.

Tao Hanzhang (1987) *Sun Tzu's Art of War: The Modern Chinese Interpretation*, trans. Yuan Shibing. New York: Sterling.

Taylor, F. L. (1921) *The Art of War in Italy 1494–1529*. Westport, CT: Greenwood Press.

Taylor, Maxwell (1960) *The Uncertain Trumpet*. New York: Harper.

Thompson, Robert (1966) *Defeating Communist Insurgency: Experiences from Malaya and Vietnam*. London: Chatto and Windus.

Thucydides (1997) *The History of the Peloponnesian War*, trans. Richard Crawley. Ware: Wordsworth Classics.

Toffler, Alvin and Toffler, Heidi (1993) *War and Anti-War: Survival at the Dawn of the 21st Century*. London: Little Brown and Company.

Ullman, Harlan K. et al. (1996) *Shock and Awe: Achieving Rapid Dominance*. Washington, DC: National Defense University.

Van Creveld, Martin (1977) *Supplying War*. Cambridge: Cambridge University Press.

Van Creveld, Martin (1991) *Technology and War from 2000 BC to the Present*. New York: The Free Press.

Van Evera, Stephen (1984) 'The Cult of the Offensive and the Origins of the First World War'. *International Security* 9(1) (Summer): 58–107.

Vegetius, Renatus Flavius (1993) *Vegetius: Epitome of Military Science*, trans. and annotations N. P. Milner. Liverpool: Liverpool University Press.

Vego, Milan (1990) *RECCE-Strike Complexes in Soviet Theory and Practice*. Fort Leavenworth: Soviet Army Studies Office.

Villacres, Edward J. and Bassford, Christopher (1995) 'Reclaiming the Clausewitzian Trinity'. *Parameters* 25(3) (Autumn): pp. 9–19, p. 11.

Viroli, Maurizio (2005) *Machiavelli*. Oxford: Oxford University Press.

Waltz, Kenneth N. (2000) 'Structural Realism after the Cold War'. *International Security*, 25(1): 5–41.

Watts, Barry D. (1984) *The Foundations of US Air Doctrine: The Problem of Friction in War*. Maxwell Air Force Base: Air University Press.

Watts, Barry D. (1996) *Clausewitzian Friction and Future War*. Washington, DC: Institute for National Strategic Studies.

Watts, Barry D. (2005) untitled. *Joint Forces Quarterly*, No. 38 (Third Quarter): 109–10.

Welch, David A. (2003) 'Why International Relations Theorists should Stop Reading Thucydides'. *Review of International Studies* 29(3): 301–19.

Wood, Neal (1965) 'Introduction', in Niccolò Machiavelli, *The Art of War*, trans. Ellis Farneworth. New York: Bobs-Merrill, pp. ix–lxxxvii.

Zhuge Liang and Liu Ji (1989) *Mastering the Art of War*, trans. Thomas Cleary. Boston, MA: Shambhala.

INDEX